D1580012

Market-Place Trade —

Periodic Markets, Hawkers, and Traders in Africa, Asia, and Latin America

Robert H.T. Smith, Editor

Centre for Transportation Studies
University of British Columbia
Vancouver, Canada

Cataloguing in Publication Data:
Market-place trade
  Bibliography: p.
  ISBN 0-919804-05-5
    1. Markets — Africa — Addresses, essays,
lectures. 2. Markets — Asia — Addresses,
essays, lectures. 3. Markets — Latin America —
Addresses, essays, lectures. I. Smith, Robert
H.T. 1935-   II. University of British
Columbia. Centre for Transportation Studies.
HF5470.M37   381   C77-002212-X

THE CENTRE FOR TRANSPORTATION STUDIES is funded by Transport Canada through the Research and Development Centre. Its purpose is to improve the quality of transportation education through a variety of education endeavours.

The grant makes possible many of the Centre's activities. It underwrites seminars, symposia, and other gatherings of interest to academicians, to government officials, and to the business community. It enables the University to bring distinguished visitors to the campus, thus enriching the classroom experience. By providing for fellowships, assistantships, and other financial aids, the Centre makes it possible for good students to learn about transportation and to prepare themselves for useful careers in this field.

Central to the Centre's activities is its program of research. Faculty members associated with the Centre have undertaken a substantial number of research projects dealing with many facets of transportation. Some of these projects are funded by the business community. Others are supported by the provincial government, by the Canadian Ministry of Transport, and by other organizations. Some research is supported entirely by funds from the Transport Canada grant.

The research reported in this book deals with market-place trade in many parts of the world. Since trade and transportation are so intimately intertwined we believe that the subjects treated in this book will be of interest to large numbers of people.

Centre Advisory Council

J.H. Morgan
Transport Canada, Research and Development Centre

J.R. McCaig
Trimac Limited

Paul E. Martin
Canada Steamship Lines (1975) Ltd.

C.F. Armstrong
CN Rail

Ian A. Gray
CP Air

D.H.W. Kirkwood
Transport Canada

G.F. Farry
Greater Vancouver Regional District

F.J.N. Spoke
Port of Vancouver

John Gratwick
Canadian National Railways

Ian S. Ross
Swan Wooster Engineering Co. Ltd.

T. Barrie Lindsay
Johnston Terminals Ltd.

Peter Akroyd
Transport Canada

Roy Illing
B.C. Ministry of Energy, Transport and Communications

Foreword

Scholarly work on the economies and societies of 'third world' countries has long relied heavily upon contrasts as an aid to understanding, if not explanation. Such terms as "developed/under-developed", "production for use/production for exchange" and "traditional/modern" have been much used in the recent literature, generating a great deal of controversy. The modernization school has come under increasingly vigorous attack, and there has been a resurgence of interest in the so-called traditional (or non-modern, non-western) activities of developing countries. This book is an important contribution to the development and understanding of this trend. The essays within are concerned largely with the geographical aspects of a pervasive, traditional activity, namely market-place trade.

Geographers and anthropologists in particular have long had an interest in market-place trade. An incomplete theoretical basis has been provided by central place theory, but now this foundation is being broadened. Detailed problem-oriented field studies offer great promise for our theoretical and practical understanding of these traditional activities. The collection of essays presented here will not only serve to further our comprehension in this way, but also point the way for future studies of this type.

When considering market-place trade, we must recognize the close complementarity of transportation. Thus, if it is important that traditional activities such as market-place trade be incorporated into development initiatives, it is equally important that both sides of the transport coin — movement *and* exchange, as well as their interrelationship — be recognized clearly. In this context, it is indeed gratifying that these studies of market-place exchange are being published by the Centre for Transportation Studies. I fully expect that the book will be received with much interest by scholars interested in transportation or in market-place trade.

Walther Manshard,
Vice-Rector for Programme
(Natural Resources)
The United Nations University and
Secretary General and Treasurer
International Geographical Union

Tokyo, Japan
November 18, 1977

Contents

Contributors

Dr. I.A. Adalemo is a Senior Lecturer in Geography at the University of Lagos, Nigeria.

Ms. J.B. Burrough is a freelance Editor in Sydney, Australia.

Dr. R.J. Bromley is a Lecturer in Social Administration at the University of Wales, Swansea.

Mr. G.A. Gezann is an Urban Analyst with the Northern Ohio Research Corporation, Cleveland, Ohio, U.S.A. (formerly a Teaching Fellow in Geography at Kent State University).

Professor Dr. E. Gormsen is a Professor in the Department of Geography at Mainz University, Mainz, West Germany.

Dr. W. Penn Handwerker is an Assistant Professor in the Department of Sociology, Anthropology, and Social Welfare at Humboldt State University, Arcata, California, U.S.A.

Ms. S. F. Ho teaches secondary school geography in Hong Kong.

Dr. Diana Howlett is a Research Fellow in the Department of Human Geography, A.N.U., Canberra, Australia.

Dr. R.T. Jackson is a Senior Lecturer in Geography at the University of Papua New Guinea, Port Moresby.

Dr. C.C. Kissling is a Fellow in the Department of Human Geography, A.N.U., Canberra, Australia.

Dr. T.G. McGee is a Senior Fellow in the Department of Human Geography, A.N.U., Canberra, Australia.

Dr. M.L. McNulty is an Associate Professor in the Department of Geography at the State University of Iowa, Iowa City, U.S.A.

Dr. J. Pyle is Chairman of the Department of Geography at Mankato State College, Mankato, Minnesota, U.S.A.

Dr. P.O. Sada is a Senior Lecturer in Geography at the University of Lagos, Nigeria.

Dr. R.H.T. Smith is a Professor of Geography at the University of British Columbia, Vancouver, Canada (formerly Professor of Geography at Monash University, Melbourne, Australia).

Dr. R. Symanski is an Assistant Professor of Geography and Latin American Studies at the University of Texas, Austin, Texas, U.S.A.

Mr. J.K. Thorpe is a Research Officer in the Department of the Environment, Manchester, England (formerly a Research Student in Geography at the University of Durham).

Dr. R.G. Ward is Professor of Human Geography, A.N.U., Canberra, Australia.

Mr. H.C. Weinand is a Research Fellow in the Department of Human Geography, A.N.U., Canberra, Australia.

Dr. L.J. Wood is a Lecturer in Geography at the University of Tasmania, Hobart, Australia.

Dr. Yue-man Yeung is a Senior Program Officer in the International Development Research Centre, Asia Regional Office, Singapore (formerly a Lecturer in Geography at the University of Singapore).

Preface

The internal exchange of goods and services is one of those commonplace activities taken for granted in many countries of the world to-day. Of course, the number of people involved and the technology employed varies, but these variations are at least partly predictable from certain characteristics of the economy. This collection of essays is less concerned with employment in and the technology of internal exchange, and more with such less familiar marketing institutions as periodic marketing and periodic market-places. The essays focus on both urban and rural situations in Africa, Asia and Latin America, and are organised around three themes: origins, development and change; urban market-place systems and mobile vendors; and rural periodic market systems. The introductory essay reviews the theoretical literature on periodic market-places and periodic marketing.

As is usual in a collection of essays, acknowledgement is due to many people. The contributors have been especially helpful; indeed, the lengthy gestation period is due more to editorial delays than to tardiness on the part of contributors. The staff of the Technical Services Section of the Department of Geography at Monash University (Hervé Alleaume, John Missen and Gary Swinton) deserve special thanks for their ability to deliver quality work at the appointed time. The person with the longest acquaintance with this project other than myself is my secretary, Ms. J. Roder, whose willingness to type innumerable drafts and yet retain an attitude of cheerful equanimity was most essential to the successful completion of the book.

Robert H. T. Smith
Melbourne
July, 1975

1 Periodic market-places, periodic marketing and travelling traders
Robert H.T. Smith

Periodic market-places continue to claim the attention of a substantial number of scholars, many of whom draw their conceptual sustenance from central place theory (Christaller, 1966). This dependence on a corpus of theoretical propositions has not always characterised studies of periodic markets. Thus, in many ethnographies and travel accounts, periodic market-places are regarded as curious socio-cultural artifacts, worthy of description and catalogue but of little else. Several quite influential studies published in the 1960s contained strong expressions of doubt about the relevance of central place theory for an understanding of periodic markets (Hill, 1966, 298; Hodder, 1961, 150-1; 1965a, 53), but the burden of opinion favoured a central place interpretation, however modified (Stine, 1962; Skinner, 1964, 65; Alao, 1968).

A review of the periodic market-place literature can be structured either regionally (Bromley, 1971; Bromley and Symanski, 1974) or thematically. The regional framework is less appropriate for the present purpose than the thematic. To the general themes of size, location, periodicity and development identified by Symanski and Bromley (1974, 383) can be added several others: functions, hierarchies (Bromley, 1971), synchronisation in space and time (Riddell, 1974), origins (Hodder, 1965; Good, 1973; Riddell, 1974), and so on. This essay will not proceed with an exhaustive review of the literature under these and other headings. Rather, an introduction of this kind is better devoted to a small number of key issues, to set the scene for most of the essays that follow. It will commence with a few matters of definition, which will be followed by a detailed and deliberately expository review of the research devoted to an understanding of periodic markets and periodic marketing. Itinerant traders, the key participants in the market-place, and market rings (cycles or circuits) will then be discussed. The essay will conclude with some comments on traditional institutions and informal sector activity in development.

* I gratefully acknowledge the support of the Canada Council and of the School of Graduate Studies and Research, Queen's University, for the analysis reported in the third section of the essay. Valuable assistance with calculations, computer programming, etc. was provided by Glenn Johnson and John Scott at Queen's. The essay incorporates part of a paper presented at the 70th Annual Meeting of the Association of American Geographers, Seattle, 1974.

Definitions and Characteristics

The definition of a market-place used by Hill (1966, 295) is a useful starting point: 'an authorised concourse of buyers and sellers of commodities, meeting at a place more or less strictly limited or defined, at an appointed time'. Thus, a market meeting usually has the sanction of authority, and it occurs regularly at a given location on a set temporal schedule. Buyers and sellers of services should also be included, and the temporal schedule can be daily or periodic (or episodic, or recurrent); if periodic, market meetings are separated by market-less days (or by a level of activity substantially less than on the main market day) (Symanski, 1973, 262-6). Diurnal variations also occur (Hodder, 1961, 149). The term 'market-place' is used deliberately; several markets exist which have no relevant spatial coordinates (e.g. a capital market, a labour market, etc.). Market-places may or may not be enclosed (Garst, 1974, 62-5), there may or may not be permanent and semi-permanent stalls (Alao, 1968, 2), they may have a rural or an urban location, and there is no real size criterion except that at least one potential buyer and one potential seller must be present.[1]

The matter of participants in the market-place requires some clarification. Even though the definition of a market-place refers to 'buyers' and 'sellers', the question of their identity remains. If the discussion is restricted to what C.A. Smith (1974, 168) refers to as 'simple agrarian marketing systems', there are two groups of people to be found buying and/or selling in the market-place: farmers and non-farmers. Examples of the latter are craft producers, service providers and traders. These terms have a compelling intuitive appeal, and they are complicated by the degree to which they are a part- or full-time occupation, by the commodity (or service) specialisation, by the scale at which the participant works, by the location of the participant's home base (urban or rural), and so on. Adoption of the part-time/full-time distinction and exclusion of those people in the market-place who are there to neither buy nor sell provides a useful typology (Table 1.1).

The full-time/part-time distinction as applied to farmers is intended to distinguish between those who derive their support primarily from farming, and those who have a regular additional non-farming source of income. Thus, case I is akin to the purchase of a convenience good at a corner store (often necessarily preceded by case II to obtain cash); case III describes the horizontal exchange so typical of rural market systems in many parts of Africa, Asia, and Latin America. The same set of statements could apply to a part-time farmer, but cases IV, V and VI are more likely to involve trading activity, that is deliberate purchase (or production) of a commodity for resale (after storage, processing or transport). In West Africa at least, part-time farmers are the rule: 'in many of the so-called agricultural households the head of the household trades part-time even during the normally short farming season . . . ' (Bauer and Yamey, 1951, 745). While part of this type of market-place trade would be horizontal, a sizeable proportion would also be vertical trade; further, local or imported manufactured goods might also be involved. The non-farming category (cases VII, VIII and IX) is meant to accommodate those predominantly village or urban based people who are involved in market-place trade. (A distinction could be made between non-farmer participants who spend all of their time in market-place trade, and those who occupy only part of their time in this way.) There are numerous types of such market-place participants; for example, Ilori (1968, 150) identifies five categories of middlemen involved in distributive trades in western Nigeria, and similar examples could be quoted for other areas (Wood, and Symanski, this volume; Farruk, 1970, 53-6). It is amongst the ranks of the non-farmer market-place participants that the large-scale traders are found. The kind and number of non-farmer market-place participants will vary in different periodic market systems (as is shown in the five essays on rural periodic market systems below), if only because the length of the marketing chain (Bromley, 1971, 179) is itself variable. However, all market-place participants can be accommodated by the typology presented in Table 1.1.

Table 1.1: A typology of market-place participants

Participants	Reason for presence in the market-place		
	To buy	To sell	To buy and sell
Full-time farmer	I	II	III
Part-time farmer	IV	V	VI
Non-farmer	VII	VIII	IX

These definitional comments would be incomplete without some reference to market-place functions. The discussion of Table 1.1 implies that a substantial number of participants are present in the market-place to obtain cash through the sale of goods and services or to obtain or order goods and services. Of course, other purposes can be served by a visit to the market-place, and some people are present in the market-place neither to offer goods and services for sale nor to purchase goods and services. Berg observes that the *plaza* (market-place) in Oaxaca, Mexico has three functions in addition to its obvious economic role: social, political and religious (Berg, 1968, 36-7). The Bohannans make a similar claim for Tiv markets: 'on the one hand, Tiv market-places are institutions within which goods and money are exchanged on a free market . . . on the other hand, there are political, religious, and recreational aspects of the market places' (Bohannan and Bohannan, 1968, 188). Burrough in this volume argues that for the average Sabahan, the weekly *tamu* is an important social event. And Agrawal (1970) demonstrates the interdependence of religious and economic networks as expressed in fairs in a district of India. Examples such as these could be multiplied many times over, and no good purpose is served by attempting to document an enormous number of cases. The fact that market-places have economic and non-economic functions is accepted without dispute, as is the fact that the degree to which each is present varies. It is appropriate in the present context to consider briefly the economic functions of periodic market-places.

'Market sites mesh supply and demand in both their spatial and temporal variation. In so doing, the rural markets of Nigeria's Lagos and Western states perform three economic functions simultaneously: *local exchange, internal trade, and central place functions*' (Eighmy, 1972, 299; emphasis added). Thus does Eighmy identify the different economic functions of periodic market-places in southwestern Nigeria. *Local exchange* 'mediates family surpluses and deficits' (Eighmy, 1972, 299); it is based on a small-scale division of labour, requires no more than a subsistence economy, and the services available at the market-place are simple. *Internal trade* implies specific complementarity between areas of supply and demand; market-places facilitate bulking and consignment of local surpluses, and this involves participants who play no role in local exchange (Table 1.1). 'As internal trade begins to dominate local exchange at a market site, the services performed by the market become more complex' (Eighmy, 1972, 300). The *central place functions* of market-places involve low order manufactured goods, exotic foodstuffs and certain services; and these are paid for with the cash proceeds of internal trade (and, occasionally, of export crops). The assertion that 'the main function of most periodic market-places seems to be to supply urban-oriented middlemen with rural goods produced in small individual lots, rather than to supply peasants with retail goods' (C.A. Smith, 1974, 184) implies that internal trade functions dominate both local exchange and central place functions, and is far too strong.[2] These three economic functions are present to varying degrees in all market-places and, with Table 1.1, provide a further basis of classification.

The Theory of Periodic Markets and Periodic Marketing

Contributions to the theory of periodic markets initially emphasised a central place theory approach, but recent work has been cast in a broader context. Stine contributed the first attempt at a theory of periodic markets: 'the basic problem [of the paper] is concerned with the travelling merchant and the associated periodic market' (Stine, 1962, 68). In fact, Stine was concerned primarily with mobile firms (itinerant or travelling traders), and only secondarily with market-places that met periodically. Indeed, Stine seems to argue that periodic markets resulted from the agglomeration of several mobile firms: 'such spatial behaviour of the individual producers gives rise, in the aggregate, to the "fair" or periodic market. *Two or more merchants meeting at the same location at the same time are apt to sell more than if the time of their visits were [sic] not coordinated'* (Stine, 1962, 70; emphasis added). Consumers also adopt periodic marketing behaviour: 'the consumer, by submitting to the discipline of time is able to free himself from the discipline of space' (Stine, 1962, 70). The mobility of firms can be understood in terms of the relationship between Christaller's concepts of the minimum and maximum range of a good; 'the farthest distance the dispersed population is willing to go in order to buy a good offered at a place' (Christaller, 1966, 22) is the maximum range. The minimum range of a good is 'the minimum amount of consumption of this central good needed to pay for the production or offering of the central good' (Christaller, 1966, 54). If the maximum range is greater than or equal to the minimum range, the firm will be fixed in location. However, where the minimum range exceeds the maximum range, the firm would be obliged to adopt a mobile strategy. Both ranges are related closely to demand characteristics. As C.A. Smith (1974, 182) observes, 'the mobile firm obviously would be greatly convenienced by periodic markets, especially if they occurred on different days of the week,' because then the mobile firm could 'jump' from market-place to market-place in order to transact a threshold amount of business in a given period of time (the market week?). The length of each jump is related to the maximum range, while the number of jumps is a function of the minimum range. Both of these notions imply that there are given sites widely recognised as market-places and that their meetings are so sequenced in time and space that it is possible for a mobile trader to do sufficient business in a given period of time to remain viable.

It is not surprising, therefore, that Stine did not consider the question of the trajectory of mobile firm movements through this given set of sites (market-places).

Stine provided an explanation for mobile firms, but he did not satisfactorily explain how and why mobile traders chose particular sites for their periodic agglomerations, nor did he explain why two or more traders would sell more at a given location when their periodic visits were coordinated than if they acted simply as independent peddlers (Plattner, 1973a). He also suggested that there is a high-to-low mobility continuum for firms which is related directly to the degree of commercialisation and to the adequacy of transport. Two comments should be made: firstly, mobile marketing is not necessarily associated with a low score on the commercialisation-transport scale (Benedict, 1972, 81-93); and secondly, mobile traders can operate successfully without market-places (Plattner, 1973a and 1973b).

In his monumental discussion of marketing and trade structure in rural China, Skinner (I, 1964; II, III, 1965) did not attempt to provide an explanation for periodic markets and periodic marketing; however, some of his arguments and findings are relevant in the present context. Skinner's interpretation of the marketing system is couched in an explicitly spatial, central place framework, and in his discussion of standard, intermediate and central market towns he draws freely on the notions of hierarchies of central places, central functions and service areas. In contrast to Stine, Skinner's concern with the periodicity of market-place meetings cannot be described as secondary, and he suggests that the periodicity feature of traditional rural markets may be understood from several points of view. Firstly, for the mobile firm, 'the total amount of demand encompassed by the marketing area of any single rural market is insufficient to provide a profit level which enables the entrepreneur to survive . . . when a group of related markets operates on coordinated periodic (as opposed to daily) schedules, he can arrange to be in each town in the circuit on its market day' (Skinner, I, 1964, 10). Secondly, for the consumer, 'the periodicity of markets amounts to a device for reducing the distance he must travel to obtain the required goods and services' (Skinner, I, 1964, 10). Skinner observes that periodic rather than daily market meetings permit a dense distribution of market towns which in turn serves the convenience of the spatially disadvantaged villagers. And he relates periodicity of market meetings in traditional agrarian societies to the rudimentary state of transport that normally prevails.

Skinner's analysis is comparable to Stine's in that it emphasises mobile firms and consumer convenience, but it differs in two important respects. Firstly, Skinner does not claim directly that two or more mobile firms are likely to sell more at a periodic market-place than if their visits were uncoordinated, and thus (inadvertently?) avoids the problem of agglomeration. Perhaps more importantly, Skinner draws attention to the significance of the diffuseness of economic roles in traditional China: 'a firm which is at once producer and trader finds periodicity advantageous even when only one market is exploited' (Skinner, I, 1964, 10). The implications of diffuse economic roles for periodic marketing were noted by Bromley (1971, 129) and, more fully, by Hay (1971, 393-401) whose explanation of periodic marketing does not appeal to the concept of range. There is, of course, far more in Skinner's essays, but these are his major contributions to the discussion of periodic markets and periodic marketing.[3]

During the 1960s, several other authors followed Stine's elaboration, and Berry's discussion of periodic markets in peasant societies (Berry, 1967, 93-9) draws heavily on both Stine (1962) and Skinner (I, 1964; II, III, 1965). However, Berry does comment on one aspect of periodic markets largely ignored by Stine and Skinner when he observes that 'if the details of periodicity, commodities traded, and forms of social integration vary culturally, so do the locations of periodic markets. *All locate to serve buyers and sellers efficiently . . .* ' (Berry, 1967, 98; emphasis added). Stine was concerned with mobile trader behaviour, and an agglomeration of two or more such traders seemed to constitute a periodic market. Although this point is not pursued further, Berry seems to suggest that the identification of a site as a periodic market-place results from a deliberate decision, quite different from that of several mobile traders agreeing to meet simultaneously in a given place. Thus, Berry implicitly moves beyond an explanation for periodic marketing.

Alao's (1968) review of Stine's theory was prompted at least partly by dissatisfaction with Hodder's interpretation of periodic markets in Yorubaland (Hodder, 1961, 1965a).[4] Alao recognises that Stine's theory fails to explain the location of markets in space and he is quite emphatic about the link between Stine's elaboration and Christallerian central place theory. Alao also refers to some additional matters, one of which is the need for 'a theoretical rationale for the *diagonal* shifting of periodic markets' (Alao, 1968, 16; emphasis added) which he implies is the standard pattern. However, the pattern of market shift is itself variable, sometimes diagonal and sometimes circumferential.

Ukwu's analysis of the marketing landscape in Iboland, southern Nigeria, makes reference to neither Stine nor Skinner, but his interpretation of periodic markets is very much in the Stine tradition (Ukwu, 1969, 152-72). Thus, Ukwu asserts that 'periodicity of markets and itinerancy of traders sustain each other. Together they make possible the passive role of the market-place in the exchange process and inhibit the crystallisation of central-place type institutions about the market place' (Ukwu, 1969, 156). Ukwu identified the possibility of substituting temporal for spatial competition between market-places (Wood, 1974b, 23-34), and this relationship has since been subjected to some scrutiny. Proximity in space does seem to imply separation in time, which is to be expected if the market-place threshold (minimum range) is to be achieved (Fagerlund and Smith, 1970; Smith, 1971c, 1971b; Good, 1972; Yeung, 1974). In addition to considerations of price and economic distance weighed by the consumer contemplating a market visit, Ukwu added the cost of waiting until a meeting occurred at the nearby market-place. However, apart from his observation that market-place periodicity and trader itinerancy are mutually self-sustaining, Ukwu does not comment on the reasons why there are particular sites at which itinerant traders agglomerate regularly. Eighmy asserts that economies arising from the spatial agglomeration of mobile firms give rise to periodic market sites (Eighmy, 1972, 301-2), which is presumably what Stine meant by his observation on the volume of sales to be made by two or more merchants meeting simultaneously at the same location (Stine, 1962, 70).

Almost a decade after Stine's essay was published, there was an explanation for periodic marketing by mobile traders but none for periodic markets. The early 1970s saw several departures from the essentially central-place-theory-bound approach to an explanation of periodic markets and periodic marketing. In an important paper, Hay (1971) demonstrated that periodic marketing could be explained without recourse to the concepts of market areas and the range of a good, and that Stine had in fact identified a special case of mobile marketing. Hay based his explanation on trader costs; for the selling trader, if the demand curve is at no point higher than the average cost curve, there is no viable scale of spatially-fixed trading activity. The same situation will obtain for the buying trader when average total outlays exceed the expected retail price at all scales of operation. The trader's decision to adopt periodic marketing can have one of three intentions: to achieve viability (i.e. to lower the average cost or average total outlay curves); to earn excess profits (essentially the same objective as viability); or to meet competition by lowering retail prices (selling trader) or by raising producer prices (buying trader). The critical variable is overhead costs; they can be spread over several market-places or over several commodities (Bromley, 1971, 129; 1973, 20, 21), but only in the former case will periodic marketing result. However, periodic marketing will also come about when a trader adopts *part-time marketing* (Skinner, 1964, 10; Good, 1972, 210). Clearly, Hay's analysis questions Ukwu's proposition that 'periodicity of markets and itinerancy of traders sustain each other' (Ukwu, 1969, 156); when the minimum range exceeds the maximum range, the trader can do one of three things: offer a 'generalised bundle' (C.A. Smith, 1974, 183) of goods in one market-place; trade part-time in one market-place; or become itinerant and regularly visit several market-places. Hay's concluding comments are significant: 'the existence of periodic marketing is a necessary, but not sufficient, precondition for the existence of *periodic markets* . . . it is one step further still to *periodic market systems*, which imply the existence of complementary periodicities among markets in close geographical proximity' (Hay, 1971, 401). Thus, Hay was aware of the problem of agglomeration of sellers (or periodic markets) and did not, like Stine, ignore it (Webber and Symanski, 1973, 215).

The question of agglomeration of sellers is one of several considered by Webber and Symanski (1973, 213-27); the others are the periodicity of 'peasant markets' and the mobility of sellers. They attempt to model the various conditions of periodic marketing in a formal, economic way; a number of assumptions is adopted, including economically rational behaviour on the part of both sellers and consumers in an isotropic linear region. Further, 'questions of time are largely ignored so that spatial organisation may be specified more completely' (Webber and Symanski, 1973, 216). Four problems are posed for analysis: what are the location patterns in a single good system? what are the conditions under which firms will be mobile and full-time rather than fixed and part-time? in a small market region, when is a firm mobile rather than immobile? and when do vendors agglomerate? Webber and Symanski suggest that vendors will be part-time or mobile depending on 'the density of profit per unit length of the market, vendor transport costs, and vendor overheads' (1973, 225). They also conclude that 'since mobile firms may be more profitable than immobile ones, and agglomerated vendors may be more profitable than isolated ones, the first firms in the region may be agglomerated mobile sellers' (Webber and Symanski, 1973, 225). The two conditions on which the existence of periodic markets in less developed economies depend are specified as, firstly, a low density of demand which enables vendors to concentrate sales into short periods (periodicity depends only on this factor); and secondly, vendor mobility is more likely in less developed economies because the ratio of the costs of moving a vendor and his goods to the cost of vendor overheads is lower than in a developed economy.

There are two further issues in the theoretical literature: first, mobile traders are not necessarily associated with periodic market-places; and secondly, can the number of vendors of the same good present in a periodic market-place be specified? Plattner's explanation for periodic trade without periodic market-places is based on a developmental model of regional exchange systems (Plattner, 1973a, 10-17). The first uncentralised stage, involving 'multiple communities in dyadic, or reciprocal exchange' (Plattner, 1973a, 11), is followed by the development of a central place surrounded by rural farm villages; 'intercommunity exchange (between farming villages) occurs within the town and also *in the far hinterlands* through the services of travelling specialists based in the centre, since the costs of transportation for farmers is too high and the demand density in the far areas too low to support fixed supply firms or even periodic market-places' (Plattner, 1973a, 11-12; emphasis added). Thirdly, some of the rural farm villages become periodic markets 'as a consequence of increases in demand intensity and decreases in the costs of transportation for farmers, relative to the opportunity costs of farm-work not done while they are traveling' (Plattner, 1973a, 12). Population density, commercialisation and transport costs are components of *economic demand per unit area*, which declines with increasing distance from the central place (thus, the minimum range increases, while the maximum range falls). Peddlers are viable in a middle zone of the city's hinterland, because the potential 'daily income' in this area is above this threshold income level (Plattner emphasises *peddler income* whereas Hay's analysis is concerned with *trader costs*). In this middle, interstitial zone, peddlers have an increasing monopoly on supply and this can have the effect of decreasing the minimum range and increasing the maximum range. The peddlers' periodicity of supply increases sales per day by concentrating a long 'time-span of demand into a short time-span of actual purchases' (Plattner, 1973a, 21). This periodicity of supply is inconvenient for the consumer and hence the peddlers' possession of a relative monopoly in sales is almost mandatory: 'consumers wait for him to arrive because he is the only one who will arrive' (Plattner, 1973a, 21). Plattner's explanation of periodic traders without periodic market-places depends on the familiar relationship between the minimum and maximum range of a good, and on an economic demand density which steadily declines with increasing distance from a central place. Itinerant peddlers are seen as an additional stage in the development from 'multiple communities in dyadic, or reciprocal exchange' to an integrated network of central places which may have supported periodic markets in the post-peddler phase.

Regardless of which of the Stine or Hay-Webber-Symanski arguments is followed, it is clear that a trader will not frequent a periodic market-place every day of the market week (that is, on both the recognised market and non-market days). Hay draws attention to a curious paradox: 'now if either of the arguments is correct it would be expected that only one (*or at least a smaller number of traders than days in the cycle* [market week]) would be present at a particular location . . . It is however difficult to conceive of demand which would be sufficient to support 20 or 30 traders one day in six but incapable of supporting a single permanent trader' (Hay, 1974; emphasis added). Hay presented an alternative economic rationale for part-time marketing: a producer-retailer (farmer) can sell to a trader at the farm-gate, or he can sell in a periodic market-place. The farm-gate price will be the market price less the intermediary's margin and transport costs. The trader must achieve transport scale economies if he is to secure farmgate sales. Where transport is rudimentary this will be difficult, hence many producer-retailers will choose to market their goods personally; thus, 'many producer-retailers may appear as part-time marketers in local markets regardless of the spatial demand conditions' (Hay, 1974).[5] Hay explains the adoption of a periodic schedule by an interregional trader ('the outsider who comes as a buying trader of surplus production') as follows: where the surplus is insufficient to support permanent activity the trader's movements are synchronised with 'the endogenously established periodicity of market meetings';[6] in circumstances of sufficient trade for permanent activity, 'the buying trader may find that the offering of produce is so concentrated in time by the established part-time periodic marketing habit' that permanent occupation is unjustified.

Other matters considered by Hay include trader time as an element of trader costs. Hay argues that the view of trader time costs as a variable cost (Webber and Symanski, 1973) leads to several difficulties, especially as related to turnover and hours of operation, and also to the number of markets visited by a mobile trader. However, if trader time costs are regarded as overheads, and if a degree of collusion amongst traders is accepted, periodic marketing is a viable proposition; 'once again the pre-existence of periodic market habits in the culture would reinforce the economic rationale for such behavior' (Hay, 1974). The number of market-places visited then becomes a function of the relationship between the decline in time cost overheads at each market-place as one more market-place is added to the itinerary, and the concomitant rise in intermarket variable movement costs. Hay also suggests that overhead costs may be geographically fixed (rent on market stalls) and geographically divisible (a regional trading licence fee). Periodic marketing in less developed countries is characterised by many more geographically divisible than geographically fixed overheads. Hay concludes by again pointing out that an explanation of periodic marketing does not constitute an explanation of periodic markets or of 'interdependent synchronised market rings' (Hay, 1974).

Periodic marketing occurs when traders operate part-time or become mobile, both of which are strategies to achieve viability. Individual mobile trader profitability is likely to be higher when the trader is part of an agglomeration than when he works in isolation; there will therefore be an incentive for agglomerative behaviour, which *may* give rise to periodic markets.[7] The presence of numerous producer-retailers (farmers) in a market-place may result from the inability of traders (who purchase at the farm-gate) to achieve scale economies in transport. Adoption of the existing periodicity of market meetings will allow an interregional buying trader to be viable where the surplus is inadequate for permanent activity (the same applies for a selling trader). Even where it is, the part-time periodic marketing habit may be so ingrained that the interregional buying trader persists with periodic marketing. A trader's optimum itinerary will involve n market-places; the reduction in overhead costs resulting from inclusion of the nth market-place in his itinerary is equal to the increased costs of movement occasioned by visiting this additional site. Overheads for traders engaged in periodic marketing are primarily geographically divisible rather than geographically fixed. Theoretical discussions of periodic markets and periodic marketing must still take the *location* of market-places and the *periodicity* of meetings at the sites largely for granted. Perhaps insights into questions of location can be found partly in the origin literature and also partly in the geometries of central place theory. Market periodicity could well be related to rural supply density, and periodic market-places may disappear when the rural scale of production is enlarged, rather than when demand for consumer goods increases (C.A. Smith, 1974, 184).

Itinerant Traders and Market Rings

The itinerant (or mobile, or travelling, or ambulant) trader or vendor is a central figure in the attempts at an explanation of periodic markets and periodic marketing, and this essay would be incomplete without some discussion of this important market participant. The trader who visits several market-places can make daily trips from a home base (as, for example, do most traders in north-eastern Ghana (McKim, 1972, 342) and in the vicinity of Lucknow and Allahabad in northeastern India (Singh, 1965, 14-15)), or he can move from market-place to market-place (for example, the inter-market itinerant traders of the Oaxaco Valley, Mexico and of Guatemala (Waterbury, 1968, 10-11, 45; and Church, 1970, 76-7, respectively), the mobile cloth dealers of Garhakota near Allahabad (Tamaskar, 1968, 46-7), and itinerant traders in Szechwan (Skinner, 1964, 25, 27-8)). The mobile vendors so central to Stine's theory and its derivatives seem to have been of this latter kind, and the ensuing discussion will be limited to them.

The mobile vendor's itinerary is selected with the periodicity of a given set of market-places in mind (C.A. Smith, 1974, 182). Thus, if there are, say, nine market-places within working distance [8] of the vendor's home base (which is itself a market-place), and if there is a market at each of the ten sites every sixth day (i.e. there is a five-day market week) such that on any day of the five-day market week there are meetings at two market-places, the mobile vendor has a wide choice of itineraries (Good, 1975, 58). Clearly, many of the issues raised in the previous section enter into the choice of a precise itinerary. It is also possible that the mobile trader selects a particular itinerary at least partly because he perceives it as corresponding to some integration which already exists amongst the market-places. This seems to be one implication of 'market rings' (or cycles or circuits) which are defined as 'being composed of a complete and integrated sequence of markets taking place over four-day or multiples of four-day periods' (Hodder, 1961, 152). These terms were given wide currency by Hodder's writings on Yorubaland in the 1960s (Poleman, (1961, 162) used the term 'market circle' when discussing the movement of foodstuff in Ghana). On the question of integration of market rings, Hodder observed that very few were self-contained, and that 'adjacent market rings often impinge on one another, resulting in a loose chain-mail pattern of rings' (Hodder, 1965a, 56). There was not, however, 'a complete system of interlocking cycles' (Hodder, 1965a, 56; 1967, 173; 1969, 66-7). Alao defined a market ring quite precisely as a 'group of markets serving a specified area and unified by a known order of market shifts . . . ' (Alao, 1968, 3).[9] Numerous authors imply the existence of totally integrated market-place systems (e.g. Berg, 1968, 18-19; Yang, 1944, 25-26; Barth, 1967, 154-5), but recently the notion of market rings was subjected to close and critical scrutiny by Symanski and Webber, who observed that 'neither sellers nor consumers have uniform activity patterns, not all periodic markets meet just once during a market week, not all markets are of equal size, and not all goods are ubiquitous in a group of markets' (Symanski and Webber, 1974, 203; see also C.A. Smith, 1974, 185).

The itineraries of mobile vendors (which may vary only little over long periods) should be distinguished clearly from market cycles. Market cycles are of special relevance for the local predominantly agrarian population (consumers), because they identify the periodic markets available locally to consumers (Bromley, 1973, 16; van Apeldoorn, 1971, 55-7). The trader's itinerary may include some of the local market-places, but it may well extend to more distant markets; thus, the total distance travelled by each of twelve Ugandan traders ranged from 240 km (150 miles) to 1,800 km (1,100 miles) in a twenty-eight day period, and the number of market-places visited varied from ten to twenty-four (Good, 1975, 60). The travelling trader itinerary represents a sequential path through a series of nodes. The length of any particular path will fall somewhere on a continuum between the shortest (a circumferential, travelling salesman route (Harvey, Hocking and Brown, 1974, 33-52)) and the longest routes (a diagonal, inter-secting route pattern) through these nodes. The travelling trader cannot vary the periodicity of a market-place and to this extent his movement costs are fixed once his itinerary is chosen (Good, 1975, 63-4). Only by substituting one or more alternative market-places in his original itinerary can he vary his movement costs. It has been argued that travelling traders would, *ceterus paribus,* prefer circumferential routes because trader movement costs (which weigh heavily in the travelling trader's locational calculus) would then be minimised (Smith and Hay, 1970; Hay, 1974). However, the itinerary is not selected with only movement costs in mind; presumably the traders assess the likelihood of there being a sizeable gathering of buyers and/or sellers at particular market-places (Good, 1975, 70). Consumer convenience in the matter of periodic market-place meetings calls for an intersecting or diagonal pattern of market shift. If there is a sufficient number of market-places with different meeting schedules within the travelling trader's working distance, he could conceivably obtain a nearly circumferential pattern and, if there was a sufficient number of travelling traders with different itineraries, the convenience of consumers could also be served. However, if this is not the case for whatever reason, the travelling trader will have to settle for a less than optimal route.

A test of these hypotheses can be conducted on maps showing the location and days of meeting of market-places in an area. The scheduling by spatially adjacent market-places of meetings close together in time is consistent with travelling trader circumferential routes. The reverse situation ('proximity in space implies separation in time' (Fagerlund and Smith, 1970, 343)) suggests diagonal patterns of market shift which work to the advantage of the consumer. Average location spacing values can be calculated for market-places with different temporal spacing characteristics (the latter chosen to represent the two sets of conditions), but results of initial tests have been inconclusive (Smith, 1971a, 183-9; Hill and Smith, 1972, 349-53; Thorpe, in this volume). Part of this unsatisfactory result may be due to the fact that the calculations were carried out on networks of market-places which did not bear any relationship to market cycles as perceived by either traders or consumers. More seriously, they ignore hierarchical, functional and size stratification of market-places (C.A. Smith, 1974, 185; Gormsen, in this volume). Further, lack of deliberate competition between any pair of spatially proximate market-places can arise from agreements between local elders (Hay, 1974) and, as Wood suggests elsewhere in this volume, it is probably unwise to push the examination of spatio-temporal synchronisation beyond same day and adjacent day market-places (see also Yeung, 1974, 150).

A much more satisfactory approach to this problem is to place a travelling trader's route on the continuum from the shortest to the longest path through the nodes identified in his itinerary. The procedure varies the day of meeting of a market-place analytically; it has no relevance for the actual trader, but it does provide a normative frame of reference in which to evaluate his itinerary. If the size (in terms of number of market-places) of a trader's itinerary is determined by the length of the market week (n), there are $[(n-1)!]/2$ different routes through that network. There is no optimal route through a three-node itinerary; the number of possible routes through market-place networks with up to eight nodes is given in Table 1.2. The following examples drawn from published trader itineraries illustrate the variation in the degree to which traders achieve optimal routes. Fogg recorded the weekly 'round' of markets followed by craftsmen and traders in the former Spanish zone of Morocco north of Rabat (Fogg, 1938, 439). Traders effectively had a choice of itineraries depending on which of two Tuesday markets they visited (Fig. 1.1a and 1.1b). If they proceeded south after the Monday market, only 8 per cent of all routes through the seven points were longer than the actual route. However, by visiting the northeastern Tuesday market considerable savings in distance travelled resulted, and 18 per cent of all possible paths through the seven nodes were longer than the actual route. The route followed by a Dagomba weaver based in Bimbilla in northeastern Ghana (McKim, 1972, 342) is shorter than 72 per cent of the other possible routes through this essentially linear network (Fig. 1.1c), suggesting that he has selected a route approaching trader optimality.[10]

Table 1.2: Number of routes through market-place networks [a]

Number of market-places (n)	Number of routes
4	3
5	12
6	60
7	360
8	2,520

[a] Calculated from $\frac{(n-1)!}{2}$

Travelling traders by definition have itineraries, which may or may not lend cohesion to the set of market-places visited. The existence of tight market rings or cycles is much more doubtful, although there seems to be some evidence for the proposition that an agrarian population recognises a local, basic cycle of market-places. If travelling traders had to concern themselves only with movement costs, circumferential itineraries would prevail. While accurate information on these itineraries is scarce, preliminary analyses suggest that there is enormous variation in the degree to which travelling traders achieve this assumed objective.

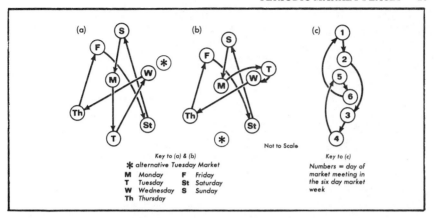

Figure 1.1   Travelling trader itineraries in former Spanish Morocco (a and b; Fogg, 1938, 439) and northeastern Ghana (c; McKim, 1972, 342)

Conclusion

Considerable progress has been made in identifying the reasons for the existence of periodic markets and periodic marketing, although blank spots in understanding and grey areas of interpretation persist. It could well be that there are alternative explanations for some aspects of these economic phenomena (Bromley, Symanski and Good, 1975). The same situation does not characterise knowledge of the role, if any, of these institutions in promoting economic development, a process which is itself complex and incompletely understood (Brookfield, 1975). Periodic markets, the practice of periodic marketing and itinerant traders are best regarded as traditional institutions in the sense that they were characteristic of many of the indigenous societies of Africa, Asia and Latin America prior to the colonial period. There are three relevant comments to be made in this context. Firstly, it is of crucial importance that extravagant claims for the potential contribution of periodic markets and marketing to development be avoided, if only because there is enough anti-traditional sentiment abroad without fueling the fire (McGee, 1975); for example, 'primitive markets of Latin America are essentially indigenous institutions in which customs and traditions have been handed down from generation to generation . . . developed economies of today no longer depend upon this type of marketing mechanism' (Olivieri-Rodriguez, 1961, 49, 54). This prejudice has not been confined to the Western 'modernisation' school, the disastrous attempt to dispense with the traditional institution of peasant marketing in China in the late 1950s being a case in point (Skinner, 1965, 371). Eighmy's reference to periodic markets ('these durable and flexible institutions'; 1972, 313) as potential diffusion centres for modern innovations is perfectly reasonable; unfortunately, the hypothesis remains untested, and there is precious little documentation of this role. In a similar vein, Good's (1975, 49-50) virtual aside on the performance of market-places as development nodes (which is reminiscent of Johnson, 1970) is entirely plausible, but again many of the associated hypotheses need to be tested. These remarks are not meant to be critical of the work of these two authors; rather, it is intended that they draw attention to the relative lack of concern with explicit and precise policy implications and prescriptions in research on periodic markets.

This is a pity, especially in relation to the second comment: 'informal sector' activities (those which, amongst other things, use traditional forms of economic and social organisation) have been given greater attention in several recent development plans (e.g. Overseas Development Group, 1973). Viewed in a broader context these activities could well be significant components of the 'organisational systems that bind together people and economic activities' (Logan, 1972, 244). Indigenous internal trading institutions (often involving periodic markets) are informal sector activities *par excellence* and, while excessive enthusiasm for the capacity of these activities to provide employment is imprudent (Conroy, 1974), there is a pressing need for carefully designed research which evaluates the potential of these institutions. And this raises the third and final matter, which also provides an appropriate note on which to conclude: the essay by Ward *et al.* in this volume incorporates one such policy-oriented investigation, and it will be interesting indeed to monitor the success of the *maket raun* in Papua New Guinea as a catalyst for rural development.

[1] Several of these features characterise aggregations of hawkers in urban areas, but as McGee and Ho show elsewhere in this volume, the Hong Kong authorities are reluctant to sanction hawker activities. Where the interests of authority are served by periodic markets and mobile vendors in urban areas, attitudes can be much more permissive, as the essays by Pyle on Mexico City and Yeung on Singapore demonstrate.

[2] For example, comparison of the periodic market-place networks in Kenya and Tanzania described in this volume by Wood and Gezann, respectively, demonstrates the varying presence of these three economic functions. In Kenyan rural markets, the local (horizontal) exchange function predominates; in contrast, the internal trade and central place functions are of considerable importance in Tanzania. Further, itinerant traders seem to be more significant in Tanzania than in Kenya.

[3] Of particular importance is his discussion of the standard marketing community as the unit of social organisation (especially for changes which occurred after 1949) and the cyclical theory of marketing intensification.

[4] Hodder rejected a central place theory interpretation, although he did not cite Stine's paper. Alao might also have mentioned Hill's assertion that 'the "central-place theory" developed by Christaller and others has no application in such regions as Yorubaland and Iboland, *at any rate as far as periodic markets are concerned* . . . ' (Hill, 1966, 298; emphasis added).

[5] However, a distinction should surely be made between the (full-time) buying trader and the (part-time) producer-retailer. The ratio of the number of the latter to the former is surely important to this argument, as is the turnover of the two groups of market-place participants. Further, the producer-retailers would seem to be involved primarily in horizontal exchange, while the intermediaries by definition are engaged in vertical trade.

[6] Good is quite emphatic on this point: 'Market calendars are social and cultural in origin' (Good, 1975, 51). See also Bromley, Symanski and Good, 1975.

[7] However, itinerant peddlers can operate successfully in the hinterland of a central place when economic demand per unit area permits threshold daily sales on each trip.

[8] 'Working distance' means the area within which the trader operates; it will vary with the scale, commodity specialisation, etc. of traders. Good uses the term 'practical radius of operation' (Good, 1975, 64).

[9] There is some real scepticism about the existence of market rings as Hodder described them. Thus, Marshall argued 'that rural market rings are relative entities rather than absolute ones . . . ' (Marshall, 1964, 111), while according to Ukwu, 'the concept of the marketing ring must be applied with caution, since it suggests an institutionalised order and a uniformity that may not exist' (Ukwu, 1969, 159). Both Ukwu (1969) and Eighmy (1972) suggest that the ring is meaningful only for the people in the local area.

[10] Similar analysis of three 'basic cycles' in the Northern and Upper Regions of Ghana which might be thought to be 'consumer itineraries' yielded conflicting results. These cycles were identified by informants in administrative centres in response to being asked whether days were counted by names of the markets and whether appointments were made a 'A- market day', 'B- market day', etc. The informants then gave 'a sequence of markets that constitutes a "market cycle" from their (the centres') points of view' (van Apeldoorn, 1971, 55). For Tamale, 7 per cent of the routes were longer; for Wa, 18 per cent; and for Lawra, 77 per cent (van Apeldoorn, 1971, 52-4). The Tamale market cycle tends towards consumer convenience, while the Lawra cycle approaches trader convenience.

PART ONE
Market-place and market-place trade origins, development and change

A familiar theme in the literature on markets and internal exchange concerns origins, development and change. Frequently, the period spanned by the retrospective review witnessed an event or series of events which had far-reaching implications for the functioning of market-places and for internal exchange generally. Such events include conquest by an alien group and consequent alterations in local administrative and organisational arrangements; introduction and adoption of innovations (such as new crops, a new technique of production, etc.); a technological breakthrough (particularly in transport); and so on. As a result, market-places swell or shrink in size, the number and variety of goods and services present in them change, the hinterlands and distribution areas expand or perhaps contract, and changes occur in the groups of people for whom the market-place and internal exchange generally is important.

The five essays in this section are concerned with very different facets of origin, development and change. Bromley examines the growth of market centres in highland Ecuador since 1800, and evaluates the relevance of notions of traditional and modern change. Traditional change results in an increase in the total number of market centres, especially in the number of lower order market centres; it takes place under conditions of population growth without transport improvements. Modern change occurs under conditions of population growth, but it is associated with transport improvements and general socio-economic modernisation; the total number of market centres decreases, and the relative importance of the upper layers of the hierarchy increases compared with the lower levels. Reference is made to the detailed evolutionary models of Eighmy (1972) and Skinner (1964, 1965), and to Good's (1970) diffusion interpretation of Ugandan market centre growth. Bromley's essay proceeds in an explicitly spatial framework: a brief description of the regional setting precedes a discussion of the historical reconstruction of market foundations since the sixteenth century. This is followed by an analysis of change in the size of market centres in the decade to 1971, which reveals the differential spatial incidence of traditional and modern change. Bromley's essay concludes with the presentation of a six-stage graphical model of central place development in a typical Andean basin; the model incorporates elements of diffusion processes and takes into account the gradually emerging predominance of modern change

The west coast clustering of *tamus* (periodic markets) in Sabah has persisted for several centuries, and in the second essay Burrough argues that proximity to international trading routes (Chinese, Hindu, and Moslem traders all visited this part of Sabah, the Chinese as early as the ninth century) was the catalyst leading to the evolution of *tamus* in this area. By the eighteenth century, a rudimentary network of internal trade routes had evolved; this facilitated the collection of local goods from the predominantly Kadazan population for exchange with the alien traders. The settlement of sea-faring Moslem people (especially Bajaus) in coastal estuaries further encouraged trade, and in this zone of culture contact between Moslem and pagan (Kadazan) people, large coastal *tamus* developed (local trade was also stimulated by the ecological contrasts between the narrow coastal plain and the nearby mountains). *Tamus* were neutral ground on which the customary confrontations between the piratical Bajaus and head-hunting Kadazans were suspended, and when agents of the British North Borneo Company arrived in the late nineteenth century, *tamus* were well established.

The European administrators (Chartered Company and later, Colonial officers) used the system of *tamus* to promote peaceful trading. They also re-sited several *tamus*, attempted to standardise days of meeting, established *tamus* in areas where they were previously unknown (these efforts were not very successful), and augmented the social component of *tamus*. Perhaps most importantly, they rationalised the network of *tamus* in relation to the location of administrative centres and to improved communications generally.

Recent expansion of the road network has led to the establishment of more *tamus*, but attempts to develop *tamus* on the east coast have failed. The State Government has actively encouraged *tamu besars* (yearly fairs), which have an impact far beyond the economic sphere. The results of vendor surveys in two *tamus* illustrate the characteristics of contemporary *tamus:* female vendors predominate; there is marked ethnic specialisation according to goods sold; full-time traders are few, and most transactions involve producer-consumer exchange; hinterlands are quite restricted; and the *tamus* have an important social function. Indeed, for the majority of Sabahans, ' . . . the *tamu* is a splendid opportunity to exchange news and gossip.'

The nineteenth-century market-place and internal exchange systems of Ethiopia and Madagascar are the subject of Jackson's essay. He notes the similarities between these two countries on the basis of topography (each being dominated by central mountain ranges), and the presence of a dominant and powerful aristocracy. Jackson's purpose is to show how strong marketing systems with similar functions developed in each country under vastly different political conditions. The essay is less concerned with the precise details of market-place location than it is with the presence of the market tradition and internal trade generally, especially in rural areas. In Ethiopia (as elsewhere in Africa), markets pre-dated the arrival of Europeans and there is evidence to suggest that local and regional market-places were organised temporally and spatially in such a way as to suit the convenience of the large trading caravans. The coastline was controlled largely by Arabs, hence most of the caravans pushing to the interior comprised Moslem traders; the local barons levied tolls on certain routes, but trade was indisputably in the hands of this alien Moslem group. The fact that the northern Danakil depression (rich in salt, which was the primary currency of the time) was also held by Arabs reinforced their control of trade in much of central and northern Ethiopia. The extent of Arab trade and, by implication, the prosperity of systems of market-places, was largely a function of the perishability of salt, and many of the peripheral areas of Ethiopia were not brought into the internal exchange economy until after the construction of roads and semi-fortificated garrison towns by Menelik late in the nineteenth century.

The development of market-places and internal trade in Madagascar from late in the eighteenth century to the early part of the nineteenth century followed a very different course. The King Andrianampoinimerina saw in market-places a magnificent opportunity to extend his power in Imerina, the highland plateau area of Madagascar. For the duration of his reign from 1787 to 1810, each market-place was invested as one of his royal enclosures. Thus, rivals and alien traders were neutralised, and local people were encouraged (indeed, coerced) to participate actively in market-place trade. Jackson documents the incredibly pervasive role played by Andrianampoinimerina in the organisation of market-place trade; this ranged from selection of the location of market-places and days of meeting, to specifying the layout of the market-place, and to introducing measures and balances and controlling interest rates. Trade outside the market-place rarely occurred, there were few if any alien traders, and only limited quantities of foreign goods. They were, in fact, markets without traders, and in contrast to Ethiopia, the prosperity of the system stemmed from Andrianampoinimerina's benevolent dictatorship set in the context of the natural complementarities of the area.

As transport improves and socio-economic modernisation proceeds, changes in the spatial patterns of market-places occur. In Bromley's essay, these changes were examined over several centuries, and also during a recent decade. Thorpe's essay on periodic markets in the Caspian lowlands of Iran is partly similar in that the spatial patterns of market-places are analysed at two points in time, 1915 and 1973. It is not Thorpe's objective to present a model of market-place development; rather, he uses the Caspian littoral as a laboratory in which to test several hypotheses that have been advanced recently about market-place location and function. Implicit in his discussion is the impact of improving transport networks and rising per capita income on predominantly rural periodic market-places.

As the plain of Gilan is primarily a Moslem area, Thorpe examines several hypotheses concerning the frequency of market meetings on particular days of the week. As in Moslem Hausaland in northern Nigeria (Hill and Smith, 1972), Friday might be expected to have an above-average number of market meetings, but this was not the case. Indeed, in the sixty-year period since 1915, the identity of Friday as a religious, rest day seems to have intensified. The number of market meetings per week and the number of market-places both declined during this period (in almost identical relative proportions), and Thorpe suggests at several points that this is a reflection of the improvement of roads, and of the growing importance of Rasht as a regional centre. Thorpe also examines the frequency of market meetings in the context of several other hypotheses (Symanski, 1973).

A substantial section of Thorpe's essay examines the question of synchronisation of periodic market-places. As with numerous studies elsewhere, there is more convincing evidence for periodic market meetings being sequenced in space and time for the convenience of consumers than for travelling traders. Indeed, the importance of travelling traders seems to have declined over the sixty-year period, again due partly to improving road and access conditions. Finally, the pattern of market-places at both time periods is examined for evidence of the presence of space competitive processes. Even though the number of market-places declined from 1915 to 1973, the similarity to a uniform distribution persisted, suggesting that the markets are indeed space competitive. The essay complements Bromley's discussion of highland Ecuador, and in the process presents some welcome analysis of market-places in the Middle East.

The first four essays in this section have a more or less distinct historical flavour, but in the chapter by Ward *et al.* the focus shifts to market origins in the present. The emphasis is on periodic market-places as policy instruments, and Ward *et al.* argue that 'planners have tended to overlook the advantages provided by periodicity of service'. They suggest that 'periodic markets should not be viewed as relict features in a modern commercial structure, but in appropriate circumstances can be encouraged by government as a dynamic means of promoting rural development'. Papua New Guinea provides the setting for the essay; for reasons related both to the forbidding physical geography of the country and to the particular pattern of colonial development, there are few urban centres, the gap between the traditional and modern sectors being extraordinarily wide. There is a real need to promote rural growth centres, but it is questionable whether investment in the existing urban structure would achieve this. Ward *et al.* propose that the establishment of the *maket raun*, in which higher order services are provided regularly in a familiar setting on a mobile basis, offers the most suitable alternative. While the emphasis would be on the fostering of commercial activity by the provision of goods and services normally unavailable in rural areas, certain government and related services could be provided as well. The question of site location and periodicity is crucial, and Ward *et al.* note that the system should be viable and, perhaps more important, must be accepted by rural inhabitants. It is proposed that a fortnightly cycle be adopted; allowing for week-ends and one maintenance day per week, eight sites could be included in a cycle. A location-allocation model was employed to select sites, but the final choice depended on local conditions and preferences of the rural inhabitants. Similarly, while several scheduling options are available, the final choice took into account local conditions and preference. Ward *et al.* discuss likely benefits of the system, and provide some specific evidence of savings to rural dwellers in travel costs. The proposal was accepted by the Papua New Guinea government, and pilot projects in two locations were to commence in 1975.

The five essays in this section share the common theme of origin, development and change, even though the regional settings are diverse in the extreme. In only one essay (Ward *et al.*) is a concern for policy explicit, while the other four place deliberate emphasis on conceptual understanding. The approach of each essay varies considerably, but as a group they provide a comprehensive perspective on the central theme of the section.

2 Traditional and modern change in the growth of systems of market centres in highland Ecuador
R.J. Bromley

In highland Ecuador, as in most populated areas of Latin America, a substantial proportion of present day wholesale and retail trading takes place in open market-places and public market buildings. Periodic and daily market gatherings were an integral part of commerce during the Spanish colonial period from 1534 to 1822, and there is evidence that market-place trading was widespread in pre-colonial times (Hartmann, 1968). Thus, as a trading institution in highland Ecuador, markets possess elements of long-term continuity spreading over more than four centuries, and they can be treated as one of the most basic central place institutions throughout the history of the region. Over this period, however, and especially during the last century, there have been marked changes in the distribution and nature of market-place trading associated with the world-wide processes variously described as 'development', 'modernization', and 'westernization'. This combination of institutional continuity and socio-economic change provides a suitable basis for a study and projection of the development of markets and central places. The purpose of this paper is to examine the growth of systems of market centres in highland Ecuador within a conceptual framework emphasizing processes and patterns of change.

Today, periodic markets are found in all the larger nucleated settlements with over 250 houses, and many of these settlements also have daily markets. A substantial number of the smaller nucleated settlements with 15 to 250 houses also have periodic markets, and a few have small daily markets. Both in terms of functions and population, the central places with markets *(market centres)* vary in importance. These variations generally correspond approximately to a simple rank-size or primate rank-size distribution, and the central places can be classified in hierarchical schemes based upon the fact that there are relatively few large market centres and many smaller ones.

* The author gratefully acknowledges financial support for fieldwork in 1970-71 from the Frederick Soddy Trust and other bodies. Historical population data were provided by Mrs R.D.F. Bromley, and most of the historical source material on markets was initially located by her or by Mr Robson Tyrer in the course of their own investigations.

Processes and Patterns of Change in Central Place Systems

Functionally inter-related groups of periodic and daily markets or of market centres can be described as *market systems,* these systems being tied together by the movements of commodities, traders and consumers. Individual market centres may be part of one or more market systems, and small systems can be considered as sub-systems within larger systems. Market systems alter considerably as demographic, environmental, economic, social and technological changes take place. The total volume of commercial activity in a given region may increase, decrease or remain stable, and the spatial distribution of commerce may become more dispersed, more concentrated or remain the same. In highland Ecuador, as in most of the rest of the world, the long-term trend has been one of population growth and increasing per capita consumption. As a result, commercial activity has increased in volume and central place systems have grown in size and functional complexity.

Berry (1967, 114-15), following terminology applied to Chinese market systems by Skinner (1965, 195-228), has divided the growth of central place systems into two basic categories, *traditional change* and *modern change.* Traditional change is likely to occur under conditions of population growth without transport improvements or more general socio-economic modernization. It takes place by the addition of new, lower order market centres, the reduction of the market areas served by most of the older centres, and a general *downward shift* in the relative importance of the layers of the hierarchy. Thus there is an increase in the importance of the lower layers relative to the higher ones, and Lösch's k increases, for example from $k=3$ to $k=4$ (Lösch, 1967, 130-3; Berry, 1967, 65-8). Modern change normally occurs because of transport improvements and general socio-economic modernization, and it is usually also associated with population growth. It takes place by a decrease in the total number of centres, an increase in the size of the market areas of the larger centres, and a general *upward shift* in the relative importance of the layers of the hierarchy. In other words, there is an increase in the importance of the upper layers relative to the lower ones, and Lösch's k decreases. Traditional change occurs through the proliferation of small market centres, whilst modern change occurs through the concentration of commercial activity into fewer, larger centres. Berry's dichotomy between traditional and modern change can be improved by the addition of a third and intermediate category of *allometric growth,* where all parts of the central place system grow at the same rate, and eventually, new lower order centres are founded at the bottom of the hierarchy. If central place systems are represented as hierarchical pyramids (Fig. 2.1), then there are three basic pyramidal forms: a low, broad pyramid resulting from traditional change; a regular pyramid resulting from allometric growth; and a high, narrow pyramid resulting from modern change. The pyramid resulting from modern change may well be narrower at the base than higher up.

Since Christaller's (1966, 84-132) seminal study of the development of central place systems in southern Germany, a number of descriptive studies have been made of the development of systems of periodic and daily markets, for example the works of Dickinson (1934, 176-82), Hodder and Ukwu (1969, 24-49 and 126-51), and Gormsen (1971). Good (1970, 209-25) has introduced a useful element of theory, interpreting the growth of Ugandan market systems in

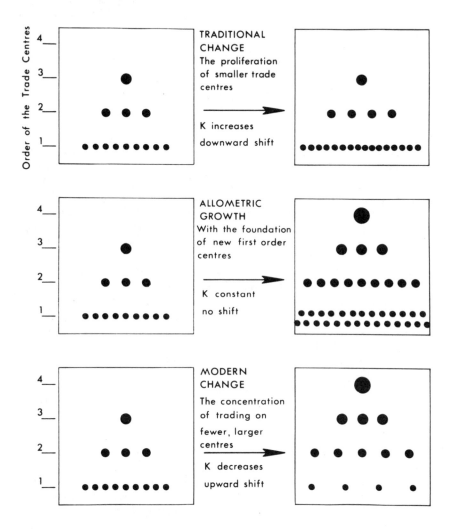

terms of diffusion process following the typical S-shaped cumulative growth curve. Using Hägerstrand's basic terminology, he suggests that there are four major stages in the process: a primary stage when the number of market centres increases relatively slowly; a diffusion stage when the number of centres increases rapidly; a condensing stage when the rate of increase in the number of market centres gradually declines; and a saturation stage when no further market centres are founded.

Figure 2.1   Alternative growth patterns in hierarchical central place systems

Skinner (1965, 195-203) and Eighmy (1972, 304-13) have gone considerably further by proposing detailed evolutionary models for the development of local systems of market centres in China and West Africa, respectively. Eighmy has used diffusion principles to stimulate the sequential location of markets on a rectangular grid of potential market sites. His model assumes that the potential market sites nearest to an existing market site are more likely to have a market founded than potential sites located further away. This principle is directly opposed to Skinner's model of the development of market systems. Skinner assumes that the first development stage is the foundation of widely spaced markets whose market areas cover most of the zone under study. In the later development stages, further markets are founded in between the existing markets. Thus, while Eighmy proposed outward diffusion of market foundations, Skinner suggests progressive infilling of new markets in the spaces between existing market centres. Eighmy's model involves a process of spatial trend diffusion, while Skinner's model involves a process of spatial inversion diffusion (Cox, 1972, 89).

The Regional Context

Highland Ecuador is defined here as the area of the country more than 1,500 metres (5,000 feet) above sea level. The region covers about 77,000 square kilometres (30,000 square miles) and forms a continuous belt 40-120 km (25-75 miles) wide stretching about 620 km (390 miles) from the Colombian frontier in the north to the Peruvian frontier in the south (Fig. 2.2). Altitudes range from 1,500 metres (5,000 feet) to over 6,000 metres (20,000 feet), and substantial uninhabited areas are found above the altitudinal limit of agriculture at about 3,500 metres (11,500 feet). Settlement is concentrated at altitudes between 2,000 and 3,000 metres (6,500 and 10,000 feet) in various basins and valleys which are separated by uninhabited and sparsely populated mountain areas. Communications have traditionally been relatively good on the main north-south route linking the major Andean basins and valleys but, until recently, links with the adjacent lowlands to the west and east have been very inadequate. In 1972, the population of the region was estimated to be three million, the average population density being about 40 persons per square kilometre (100 per square mile; Bromley, 1974a). In the same year, about 33 per cent of the population were estimated to be living in urban centres with over 5,000 inhabitants, the main cities and towns being Quito (population c. 580,000), Cuenca (c. 81,000), Ambato (c. 81,000), and Riobamba (c. 54,000).[1]

The data presented on contemporary market centres in highland Ecuador were collected in 1970 and 1971 as part of a broader study of the organization of periodic and daily markets. Several social survey methods were used, including formal and informal interviews, participant observation, systematic observation, and counts of traders, pedestrians, and vehicles. Livestock trading is not considered here, and attention is focused upon market-place trade in foodstuffs, consumer durables and services. Markets are defined as agglomerations of traders on public land (streets, open spaces and municipal market buildings) having more than ten trading units[2] and occurring regularly on one or more days each week. Market centres are discrete, nucleated settlements with one or more markets on one or more days each week.

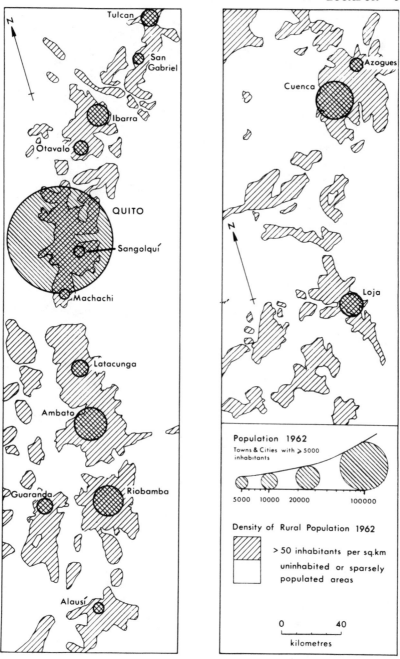

Figure 2.2   Rural and urban population distribution in highland Ecuador in 1962 (the map of the southern highlands is on the right)

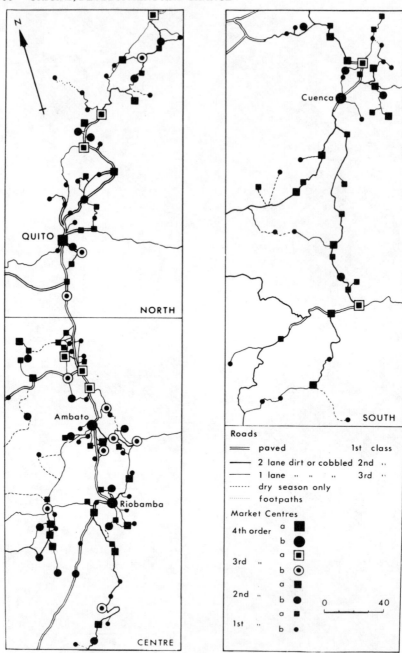

Figure 2.3   The distribution and sizes of market centres in highland Ecuador in 1971 (a and b as in Table 2.1)

In 1971, there were 164 market centres in highland Ecuador (Fig. 2.3). The centres can be ranked on the basis of average total weekly trading activity; not surprisingly, a primate rank-size distribution emerges, ranging from Quito with over 80,000 trading units per week to the smallest market centres with 11 to 20 trading units per week. Because of this size distribution and the great variation in the size of the market centres, they were classified according to size on a logarithmic scale (Table 2.1). The average first order market centre is one tenth the size of the average second order market centre, one hundredth the size of the average third order market centre, and one thousandth the size of the average fourth order market centre.

Table 2.1: Classification system for market centres (total number of trading units per week in markets)

Order		Number of trading units (logarithmic)	Class limits in trading units	
1	1b	$10^{1.01}$ to $10^{1.50}$	11 to	31
	1a	$10^{1.51}$ to $10^{2.00}$	32 to	100
2	2b	$10^{2.01}$ to $10^{2.50}$	101 to	316
	2a	$10^{2.51}$ to $10^{3.00}$	317 to	1,000
3	3b	$10^{3.01}$ to $10^{3.50}$	1,001 to	3,162
	3a	$10^{3.51}$ to $10^{4.00}$	3,163 to	10,000
4	4b	$10^{4.01}$ to $10^{4.50}$	10,001 to	31,623
	4a	$10^{4.51}$ to $10^{5.00}$	31,624 to	100,000

The Historical Reconstruction of Market Foundations

The Spanish conquest in the sixteenth century led to a major redistribution of population and a reorientation of commercial relationships in Ecuador. Settlement patterns and central place systems were rapidly-altered, with many new settlements being founded by the Spaniards, and most of the indigenous central places gradually fell into disuse. The Spaniards encouraged the diffusion of Spanish and Quechua as the main languages and rapidly imposed Roman Catholicism as the sole official religion. The Christian calendar and the seven-day week replaced earlier calendars, and monetized exchange gradually replaced barter for major transactions. New crops and varieties of livestock were introduced to Ecuador and inevitably new diseases took their toll. As the Spaniards generally took up residence in the newly founded nucleated settlements, it was particularly important to establish these settlements as centres of government, evangelization, and commerce. The townsfolk relied upon the rural Indian population for much of their food supply, fuel and fodder, and many attempts were made to persuade or coerce the Indians to visit the towns and villages to attend mass and to bring in products for urban consumption (Kaplan, 1964, 63-4). Thus the sixteenth century was a period of disruption and drastic reorganization of commerce and central place systems.

In contrast to the sixteenth century, and in spite of notable demographic and economic changes, the seventeenth and eighteenth centuries were periods of relative stability and continuity of commerce and central place systems. Although a few settlements were relocated due to the effects of earthquakes and volcanic eruptions, their names were usually retained, and most of their central functions were generally transferred to the new sites.[3] During the nineteenth and twentieth centuries, marked socio-economic changes have occurred following Eucador's political independence and the population growth, urbanization and transport improvements associated with development. In general, however, the locations of major central places have not changed and the nineteenth and twentieth centuries can be characterized as periods of growth and continuity of commerce and central place systems.

The foundation of markets can be either organized or spontaneous and both types of foundation have been important in the development of the present-day pattern of market centres in highland Ecuador. Organized foundations occur when a person or group of persons, or an organization or governing body, designates a site and frequency of meeting for a market and announces the date on which the market will begin to meet (e.g. La Paz, Carchi, whose market was founded in 1970 on the initiative of the local priest and the parish council). Spontaneous foundations occur when individual traders begin to trade regularly in a particular place and, because their business is relatively successful, they attract other traders to the same location (e.g. Urcuquí and Pablo Arenas in Imbabura Province, which both spontaneously developed Sunday markets in the 1960s). For most of the market centres in highland Ecuador, it is impossible to date the foundation of their markets with precision. Historical documentation of markets and marketing is very poor, and few documents of any sort survive from the sixteenth and seventeenth centuries. Spontaneous market foundations are often never recorded, and in general, small, newly-founded markets receive much less attention in the available documents than larger, longer-established markets. Oral history enables approximate dating of market foundations after 1900, but estimated dates are rarely dependable and a considerable amount of cross checking is essential. It is particularly difficult to judge whether a market was regular, and whether the volume of trading activity exceeded the minimum of ten trading units, or their historical equivalent. Some markets have grown rapidly since their foundation, others have developed slowly, still others have died out altogether (e.g. Asunción and Quisacoto in Bolívar Province), while a few have been founded and re-founded several times (e.g. Pindilig and Taday in Cañar Province, which both founded short lived Sunday markets in the 1940s and then, after a marketless period, established Friday markets in the early 1960s).

A preliminary attempt to reconstruct the pattern of market foundations in highland Ecuador is presented in Figure 2.4. Most of the data are taken from documentary sources in municipal and national archives,[4] together with oral histories collected in most of the market centres of the highlands. A limited amount of local historical information was obtained from published sources such as the works of Seeman (1853, 144-217), and Penaherrera, Costales and Jordan (1961, 407-19). In Figure 2.4 and Table 2.2, the foundation of each market in existence in 1971 has been allocated to a specific historical period. The time

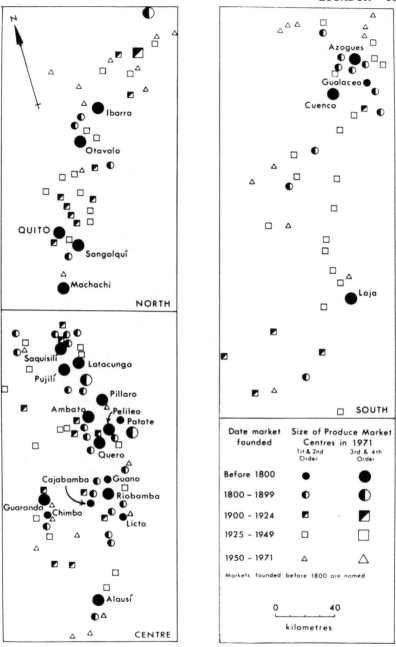

Figure 2.4   Dates of market foundation for highland Ecuadorian market centres in existence in 1971

Table 2.2: Market centres in 1971: size and period of foundation

Date of foundation	Size of market centre in 1971 (order[a])					Cumulative total over time periods	Average growth in number of market centres (% per annum)
	1	2	3[b]	4[b]	Total		
before 1800	0	6	14	4	24	24	—
1800–1899	17	18	3	0	38	62	0.95
1900–1924	18	7	1	0	26	88	1.41
1925–1949	33	11	0	0	44	132	1.64
1950–1971	27	5	0	0	32	164	0.99
Total	95	47	18	4	164	164	—

[a]Figure 2.3 and Table 2.1

[b]Aggregating 3rd and 4th orders to produce a 3 x 5 table (excluding the totals) yields a chi-square value of 109.9 which, with 8 degrees of freedom, is statistically significant at the 0.001 level.

periods vary in length according to the general accuracy of the source data, so that the risk of allocation to the wrong period is avoided, or at least minimized.

The data in Table 2.2 show that the markets founded in earlier time periods tend to be larger than those founded in later time periods, thus demonstrating an approximate preservation of rank-size relationships in the expanding market systems. Not surprisingly, however, there are some notable exceptions to the general rule that the earlier a market is founded, the larger it eventually becomes. These exceptions are of four types: 1. Pre-historic markets which died out soon after the Spanish conquest. 2. Markets founded since the Spanish conquest which have died out and have subsequently not been refounded. 3. Markets founded in the colonial period which have failed to grow beyond second order. Notable examples are Guano and Patate, both of which have declined considerably in recent years due to the improvement of communications and their relative proximity to larger centres. 4. Markets founded in the twentieth century which have grown to considerable importance. Perhaps the best example of this is San Gabriel, in Carchi Province, which did not establish a market until the first decade of the twentieth century, but which has now developed into a third order market centre. The preservation of rank-size relationships in the market systems is not greatly affected by the extinction of small, newly-founded markets. These short-lived markets were founded in small settlements at the bottom of the settlement hierarchy, and the resulting market centres occupy the bottom strata of the hierarchy of market centres. Foundations and extinctions at the base of the hierarchy of market centres leave the medium-sized and larger market centres more or less unaffected. There is no recorded case of a large, important market centre disappearing from existence since the mid-eighteenth century.

The growth in the number of market centres in highland Ecuador since the late eighteenth century is shown in Figure 2.5 together with demographic estimates and censuses for the region.[5] Although both sets of data inevitably contain minor inconsistencies and errors, they both clearly show a pattern of slow growth in the eighteenth and nineteenth centuries and faster growth since the

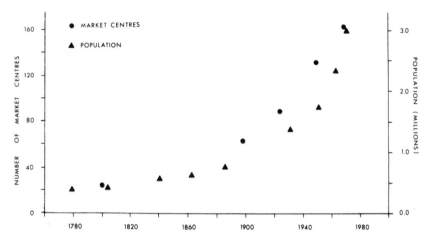

Figure 2.5   Growth in market centres and population in highland Ecuador, 1780–1971

beginning of the twentieth century. It is likely that similar growth patterns would obtain for urbanization, expansion of the transport network, increasing personal mobility, and average per capita consumption of energy and of industrial goods. Whilst the fastest growth in the number of market centres occurred between 1900 and 1949 and growth rates have declined considerably since then (Table 2.2), population has grown faster since 1949 than ever before. Like population growth, urbanization rates have probably been greater since 1949 than in preceding periods. The decline in the growth rate of the number of market centres in highland Ecuador over the last twenty years suggests that modern change is gradually replacing traditional change in the growth of the central place system. Concerning the S-shaped diffusion curve postulated by Good (1970, 209-25), the diffusion of market centres in highland Ecuador passed from the primary stage to the diffusion stage around 1900 and passed from the diffusion stage to the condensing stage in the 1960s.

Recent Changes in the Size of Market Centres

From the results of detailed local interviews and extensive cross checking,[6] each market centre has been allocated to one of three basic categories of change for the decade 1961-1971: 1. Larger in 1971 than in 1961 (positive change); all markets founded after 1961 and still in existence in 1971 automatically fall into this category. 2. Approximately the same size in 1971 as in 1961 (no change). 3. Smaller in 1971 than in 1961 (negative change). These categories of change are based upon estimates of the average number of stalls and traders in the produce markets of each market centre in each of the two years in question. The spatial pattern of change for 1961-1971 is shown in Figure 2.6, and the relationship between present size and recent development is shown in Table 2.3. These data suggest that while most of the larger market centres are increasing in size, the smaller market centres are very variable: some are increasing, some are decreasing, and some are remaining stable. The spatial distribution of change shows that most of the smaller market centres which are increasing in size are located at considerable distances from larger market centres. Thus, the average

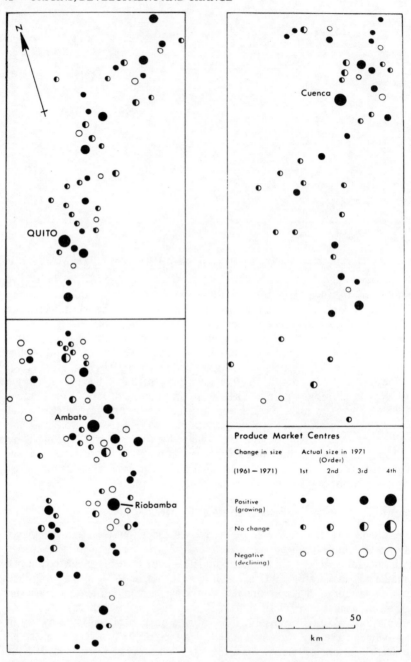

Figure 2.6   Change in the level of market activity in highland Ecuadorian market centres, 1961–71

Table 2.3: Changes in the size of market centres 1961 to 1971 in relation to the number of market centres in each order of magnitude in 1971

Change in size 1961–71	Size of market centre in 1971 (order[a])				Total
	1	2	3[b]	4[b]	
Positive	22	24	15	4	65
No change	50	13	2	0	65
Negative	23	10	1	0	34
Total	95	47	18	4	164

[a]Figure 2.3 and Table 2.1

[b]Aggregating 3rd and 4th orders to produce a 3 x 3 table (excluding the totals) yields a chi-square value of 34.5 which, with 4 degrees of freedom, is statistically significant at the 0.001 level.

declining first and second order market centre is located 16 km (10 miles) by road from the nearest higher order centre, whilst for the average growing first and second order market centre, the corresponding distance is more than double at 33 km (21 miles).[7] Of the growing first and second order market centres, 47.8 per cent lie over 30 km (19 miles), and only 19.6 per cent lie under 15 km (9 miles), by road from higher order centres. In contrast, only 15.2 per cent of the declining first and second order market centres lie over 30 km (19 miles), and 66.7 per cent lie under 15 km (9 miles), by road from higher order centres.

In the more densely populated areas of the highlands within 10 to 25 km (6 to 16 miles) of the larger urban centres (the *core areas*), a process of modern change is occurring in the central place systems as communications are improved, consumer demand increases, and trade becomes more concentrated in the larger, higher order market centres. Thus, within 15 km (9 miles) of the large and rapidly growing market centres of Ambato and Riobamba, for example, most smaller market centres are declining as local consumers switch their custom to the larger centres. In the less densely populated and less accessible areas further away from the larger urban centres (*peripheral areas*), however, many smaller market centres are growing and new markets are still being founded. In northeastern and northwestern Cañar Province, for example, seven market centres have been founded since 1950, and most of these new first and second order market centres are still increasing in size. Thus, the less densely populated and more remote areas of the Andean highlands are still experiencing traditional change with the proliferation of new market centres as the local population increases and becomes more integrated into the commercial economy.

Prior to 1920, traditional change was clearly dominant over modern change in the expansion of the systems of market centres in highland Ecuador. Since then, however, modern change has gradually replaced traditional change as the dominant process except in the areas which are most remote from the influence of major urban centres. In spatial terms, it is clear that the process of modern change first developed around the larger urban centres, and that it is gradually diffusing from these more urbanized core areas towards the less urbanized and more remote peripheral areas.

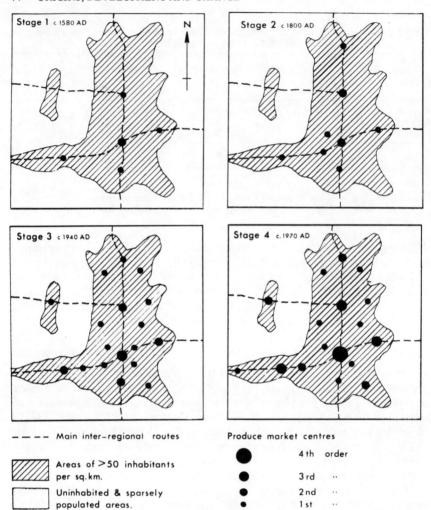

Figure 2.7   A four-stage model of the development of a central place system in a hypothetical Andean basin between 1580 and 1970

Conclusions and Speculations

The process of change in the spatial pattern of market centres from mid-colonial times to the present can be summarized initially as a four-stage model showing the process of development of a system of market centres in a hypothetical Andean basin (Fig. 2.7). The basin drains westward through a narrow valley to the coastal lowlands, and is surrounded on all other sides by sparsely populated areas above the altitudinal limits of cultivation. From the late sixteenth century until the mid-nineteenth century, the population increases relatively slowly with no marked trend towards urbanization. From the mid-nineteenth century onwards, the rate of population growth gradually increases and accelerating trends of urbanization and transport improvement continue to the present. Most of the earlier market centres to be founded remain the main market centres throughout the four stages, so that rank-size relationships are maintained. The four-stage model takes account of the assymetrical shape of most Andean basins and of the relations between central place development and interregional transport routes.

In highland Ecuador, the gradual proliferation of new market centres corresponds to a process of spatial inversion diffusion, with new centres being founded between the existing market centres. At the reduced scale of individual basins and provinces, the process of spatial inversion diffusion of market foundations is also evident, particularly between stages two and three of the four-stage developmental model. However, at this scale, spatial trend diffusion of new market foundations out from the densely populated core areas to the less densely populated peripheral areas is also evident. If seen in isolation from spatial inversion diffusion, the process of spatial trend diffusion takes the form of a diffusion wave of new market foundations gradually spreading outwards from the core areas. Stage four of the four-stage developmental model shows the first evidence of a second diffusion wave spreading outwards from the core areas towards the peripheral areas. This second wave involves the decline and extinction of some of the smaller market centres in close spatial proximity to larger, expanding centres. As modern change becomes more accentuated in the growth of central place systems, this process is likely to continue and to extend to greater distances from the main urban centres. At present, however, the wave of market foundations affecting the peripheral areas is stronger than the wave of market declines and extinctions affecting parts of the core areas, and the spatial and temporal separation of the two waves is clearly evident. Eighmy's spatial trend model of the diffusion of market foundations and Skinner's spatial inversion model have both proved to be relevant (if somewhat inadequate) in the Andean context. Instead, a model is required which combines both types of diffusion and also takes into account the gradual replacement of traditional change and allometric growth by modern change.

In Figure 2.8, a highly simplified six-stage developmental model is presented. Each stage takes the form of a cross-section of a hypothetical, symmetrical Andean basin showing the central places that would lie on, or near, the line of the section at different periods between A.D. 1550 and 2000. This six-stage model deliberately ignores the assymetry, varying resources, and varying sizes of real Andean basins. Real world deviations from the model can be explained by these variations together with such peculiar and often unique local circumstances as the effects of natural disasters; the location and re-location of interregional trade routes; changing evaluations of natural and human resources; the commercial and political rivalry of some pairs of neighbouring settlements; and the recent development of commuter villages around Quito. In stages one to three of the six-stage model, traditional change is the dominant process of growth in the market system of the basin. In stages four and five, traditional change is gradually replaced by modern change until, in stage six, modern change is dominant. Within the basin, market foundations in stages two and five take place by outward spatial trend diffusion from the centre of the basin towards the periphery. The market foundations in stages three and four take place by a combination of spatial inversion diffusion and spatial trend diffusion. In stages four to six, modern change, involving the gradual decline and extinction of small market centres, gradually diffuses outwards towards the edge of the basin.

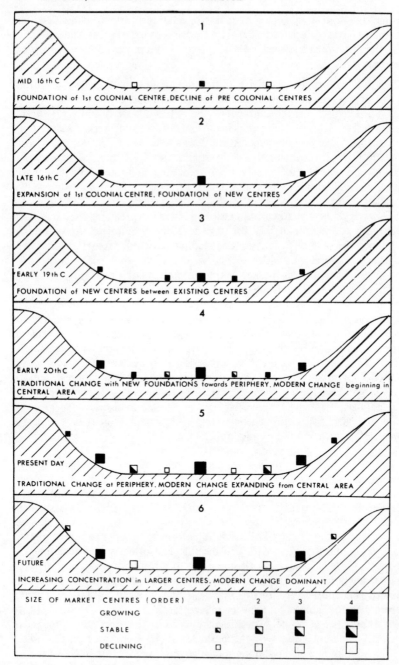

Figure 2.8   A six-stage cross-sectional model of the development of central places in a hypothetical Andean basin

Using this diffusion process interpretation, it is possible to assess the likelihood of new market foundations in different localities and to assess the likelihood of growth, stability, or decline of each of the existing market centres in highland Ecuador. Over the next two decades, growth is likely to continue in the larger market centres, and particularly in Quito, Cuenca, and Ambato (the three largest urban centres in the highlands). Growth in market activity is also likely to occur in many of the smaller market centres in peripheral parts of the Andean basins, and new market foundations are to be expected in these areas. Decline and extinction of markets is likely to continue in the small market centres close to larger, growing centres, although a few exceptional cases of growth may occur when small settlements develop into expanding residential satellites of the major towns.

[1] The population data given here and in Fig. 2.2 are based upon adjusted data from D.G.E.C. (1964; 1968a; and 1968b).

[2] A full definition of the trading unit is given in Bromley (1974b). Trading activity is initially measured by counting stalls at peak trading hours. The term stall is used to refer to all independent retailing, wholesaling and service establishments on public land, whether fixed or mobile in location. Stalls are classified into two groups, large and small, based on an estimate of their daily turnover. Each large stall is considered to be equivalent to four trading units, and each small stall to one trading unit. The total trading activity in each market on each day of the week is measured in terms of the total of trading units. The weekly total of trading activity is the sum of the seven daily totals, e.g. one small stall working on all seven days of the week is equivalent to a weekly total of seven trading units.

[3] The most important town to be moved, and also the town to be moved furthest, was Riobamba. The town was largely destroyed by an earthquake in 1797 and was subsequently moved from its old site (present day Cajabamba) to a new site 13 km (8 miles) to the northeast.

[4] The documentary sources used are listed in Bromley (1975).

[5] The basic population sources are: ANH/Q (1780), AHN/B (1814, vol. 123, 220), Alomia L. (1910, 131), A.N.E. (1863, 142), M.I.R.E. (1886, 22), M.G.P.S. (1933, 211), D.G.E.C. (1960, 7-10; 1964; 1968a; and, 1968b). The source data have been corrected to conform with the definition of highland Ecuador used here.

[6] In 1971, the author visited almost all of the market centres and interviewed several local dignitaries and traders in each one. The people interviewed were asked to compare the area occupied by the market(s) in the market centre in 1971 with the area that the market(s) had occupied in 1961. They were also asked to compare the total volume of market trading in an average week in 1971 with the equivalent volume for an average week in 1961. As well as making these comparisons for their own market centre, the informants were asked to make similar comparisons for neighbouring market centres, so as to obtain a larger sample of opinion and complete coverage of market centres.

[7] The standard deviation of the road distances from declining first and second order centres to the nearest higher order centres is 12.8 km (8 miles); for growing first and second order centres, it is 22.1 km (14 miles).

3 The *tamus* of Sabah
Joy Boenisch Burrough

In Sabah,[1] a periodic market is called a *tamu*. This word is derived from the
Malay *bertamu* ('to pay a visit'), which in Sabah has the connotation 'meeting'.
There are over 90 official *tamus*[2] in Sabah today (Fig. 3.1). A *tamu* is quite
different from a *pasar*[3] (cf. bazaar) or town market, which is a daily, day-long
market with permanent stalls and professional vendors. *Pasars* are found in
market buildings in each small town in Sabah and were introduced as a concomitant of urbanisation; they are very similar to the small urban markets found
in all tropical countries. *Tamus* are early morning markets and are more than
mere trading sessions; they are also important social events. The *tamus* in Sabah
pre-dated the arrival of European entrepreneurs and they were not a formal
feature of kampong (village) layout. In the following outline of the origins of
Sabah *tamus*, the functions and characteristics of these periodic markets will
emerge. This will provide a basis for discussion of the characteristics of contemporary *tamus*, supported by data collected from vendor surveys at the two
largest *tamus* held in Sabah today.

The Evolution of Tamus

To understand how *tamus* evolved, it is essential to know the main features of
Sabah's physical and cultural geography. The west coast of Sabah consists of a
coastal plain rarely exceeding eight km (13 miles) in width, paralleled by the
Crocker range of mountains whose summits range from 900 metres to the 4,102
metres (2,950 to 13,450 feet) of mighty Kinabalu (the highest peak in southeast
Asia). Further inland, though there are a few broad fault-controlled valleys, the
terrain remains mountainous. However, the eastern coast is dominated by the
extensive floodplains of several major rivers.

The western coastal plain and the Crocker mountains were traditionally the
domain of the Kadazan[4] people, who grew hill rice, tobacco and tapioca (the
tobacco and tapioca were probably introduced from the Philippines). In certain
inland valleys and on irrigable sites along the coast, these people also cultivated

---

*   I gratefully acknowledge comments on earlier drafts from Dr J. Angel
(Department of History, Sydney University), Dr P.A. Burrough (School
of Geography, University of New South Wales), and Dr D.J. Prentice
(English-Malay Dictionary Project, Australian National Univeristy).

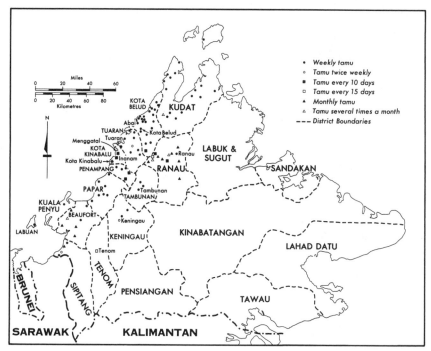

Figure 3.1   The distribution of *tamus* in Sabah

wet rice. In the rugged terrain of southern Sabah, Murut[5] tribes hunted, and grew hill rice. Eastwards, along the banks of the large east coast rivers lived other groups of shifting cultivators who eked out a precarious existence under the threat of frequent and devasting floods. Of all these indigenous groups of pagan people, the Kadazans were undoubtedly the most stable and well-organised.

With only a few exceptions, contemporary *tamus* in Sabah are found in those areas where Kadazans live. Very few *tamus* are held in Murut country; the isolation and self-sufficiency of Murut groups and the prevalence of bitter head-hunting feuds undoubtedly discouraged the development of Murut inter-tribal trade. The *tamus* held in Murut territory today (for example, those at Keningau and Tenom) were initiated in this century. There were at least two Murut *tamus* which pre-dated the Chartered Company (Woolley, 1962, 2), where Muruts obtained goods from the coast, but these no longer survive. No *tamu* ever developed on the east coast of Sabah. Thus, it seems very probable that *tamus* originated on the west coast of Sabah; not only are most contemporary *tamus* found in this area, but also conditions on the east coast and in the interior of the country were not so conducive for the development of periodic markets. Four factors were of vital importance in fostering *tamus* on the west coast: an interface between two contrasting environments (the coastal plain and the mountains); a well-organised, stable indigenous population; important off-shore international trade routes; later, a zone of culture contact between a maritime people and the indigenous farming people.

The catalyst which triggered off a west coast trading network was probably the existence of international trading routes off the west coast of Borneo. In Sabah, overland trade routes of the magnitude of those found in West Africa (where established trade routes were instrumental in the development of Yoruba periodic markets (Hodder, 1965b)) have never existed, but there is a long history of external off-shore trading. Traders from China were certainly visiting Brunei in the ninth century A.D. and in 977 Brunei sent its first mission to the Imperial court (Chau, 1966). There is evidence to suggest that the Chinese established trading contacts with west coast Sabah as early as the eleventh century. The Sabah Museum has excavated Sung (960-1279 A.D.) pottery from a site near a long-standing *tamu* ground at Abai, on the coast near Kota Belud (Whelan, 1970, 12). Glazed Chinese jars of the T'ang or Five Dynasties period (seventh to tenth centuries A.D.) have for long been greatly prized by the Kadazans. Chinese jars several centuries old can be found in Kadazan (and Murut) *kampongs* today, together with Chinese gongs and beads (Harrisson and Harrisson, 1971). It is therefore reasonable to infer that the Kadazans bartered jungle produce to obtain these goods.

Moslem and Hindu traders also called in at ports in western Borneo, notably Brunei and Bandjermasin in present-day Kalimantan. The important trade route from Malacca to the Philippines skirted the west coast of Borneo. Traders from Java were particularly active from the twelfth century onwards, shipping goods from Brunei.

After the Portuguese conquered Malacca in 1511, Brunei prospered and its rise to importance had repercussions further north in Sabah; as the Sultan's power increased, so he was able to extend his control northwards. Many of the lowland river valleys of western Sabah came under his sway and he appointed *pengirans* (overlords) to collect taxes from the local populace. These taxes in kind may have been handed over to the *pengirans* at formal sessions; if this was so, this could have been another stage in the institutionalising of a trading network.

In order to collect goods to trade with visiting Chinese, Hindu, or Moslem traders, or to meet the *pengirans'* tax demands, a rudimentary network of internal trade routes must have evolved among the indigenous west coast peoples. It is in this context that the physical geography of the west coast is important; the interface between coastal plain and mountain environments would have stimulated and sustained exchange of goods between lowland and highland tribes. Such exchange would most probably have evolved between lowland and highland Kadazans (socially the best-organised indigenous peoples).

By the seventeenth or eighteenth centuries then, there would have been a system of west coast trade routes linking highland and lowland, with some links with off-shore international trade. At about this time, three important events occurred almost simultaneously: European colonists and merchants (mostly Portuguese, Spaniards and Dutchmen) disrupted traditional maritime trading patterns in southeast Asia; the Sultan of Brunei's control over his Sabah territories began to wane; and, most importantly, sea-faring Moslems from the Philippines and east Malaya migrated to northern Borneo. These Moslem peoples (Bajaus,[6] Illanuns and Suluks) settled in estuaries along the Sabah coast. Near Kota Belud many Bajaus and Illanuns subsequently moved on to the land and became rice farmers. The resulting confrontation between the aggressive, one-time piratical Bajaus and Illanuns, and the head-hunting, farming Kadazans was the final stimulus to *tamu* development. From this time, internal trade on the west coast of Sabah became more dynamic, for the Bajaus and Illanuns (the Suluks settled mostly on the east coast) slotted into the existing framework of coast-mountain trade. The result was the evolution of very large coastal *tamus* in the zone of culture contact between the Moslem and pagan (Kadazan) peoples.

It was fortuitous that the Kadazans were sufficiently well-organised not to be intimidated by the belligerent Bajaus, for though at one time they did pay a tax to the Bajaus,[7] they eventually won the Bajaus' respect, thus ensuring that the Bajaus traded with them on a reciprocal basis. In contrast, Bajaus and Suluks on the east coast exploited the disorganised and impoverished pagan tribes. Important trade items such as ivory, camphor, and birds' nests were obtained by the Sultan of Sulu's agents (many of whom were Bajaus) and shipped out, together with turtleshell, sea-slugs and pearls obtained from the coast (St. John, 1863, Vol. I, 402).

There is evidence that when the Bajaus arrived in Sabah, a marketing infrastruture already existed by means of which Kadazans exchanged produce intertribally or with alien traders. This may be inferred from the difference between coastal and inland *tamus*. Not all *tamus* were held on the coastal plain; a line of 'feeder' *tamus* evolved in the mountains further inland. Whereas the coastal *tamus* became large Kadazan/Bajau *tamus*, the inland *tamus* were exclusively Kadazan and served as collecting points at which Kadazans from remote mountain *kampongs* could barter their goods (tobacco and jungle produce) for coastal goods brought up from the lowland. All the inland *tamus* were held at multiples of five-day intervals,[8] for Kadazans traditionally reckoned in units of five days. However, several of the coastal Kadazan/Bajau *tamus* were also held at multiples of five-day intervals. This suggests that the original periodic market network was organised according to the Kadazan calendar. Many of the Bajau/Kadazan coastal *tamus* (presumably those sparked off by the Bajaus' arrival) were held at weekly intervals, for Bajaus, being Moslem, use a seven-day week.

Reciprocal trade between Kadazans and Bajaus was stimulated by the difference between the environments and cultures of these two peoples. The sea-faring Bajaus could offer fish (fresh and dried), powdered shell (an accompaniment to betel nut), woven cloth, brass and salt (sea salt and salt obtained from burning the roots of the *nipah* palm). In return, the Kadazans produced rice, fruit, baskets and hats, tobacco and jungle produce (*damar, rotan,* honey, beeswax, etc.).

The vital prerequisites for successful trading between the piratical Bajaus and headhunting Kadazans were peace and mutual trust. Though these were rarely achieved in everyday relationships between the two peoples, they were established in the sphere of trading, by designating *tamu* grounds as 'neutral areas' where all feuds and differences of opinion were suspended. In a special inaugural ceremony, tribal chiefs and headmen swore to uphold the sanctity of the *tamu* ground and the blood of a sacrificed buffalo was used to seal their oaths. In addition, a large stone was erected to serve as a permanent reminder of the neutrality of the *tamu* ground. These *batu sumpah* (oath stones) can still be seen today at certain west coast *tamu* grounds (for example, Menggatal, Tamparuli and Inanam). The concept of a 'neutral' meeting-ground was longstanding among Kadazans and Muruts, but it assumed a special significance for the Kadazan-Bajau trading encounters.

Because *tamus* were held on neutral ground, the *tamu* ground was not a formal feature of *kampong* layout. Ease of access was a critical factor in determining *tamu* sites and therefore coastal *tamus* were often held on river banks at points accessible by boat and by foot. Inland *tamus* were commonly held at the junction of several footpaths.

By the mid-nineteenth century, Sabah's *tamu* system was firmly established. The biggest *tamu* in nineteenth century Sabah was held 11 km (seven miles) from Kota Belud (where a Government Station was established) on the banks of the Tempasuk (Kadamaian) river. This *tamu* was called *Tamu Darat* ('inland *tamu'*) and was held every 20 days; a smaller *tamu*, *Tamu Sisip* ('slipped in between *tamu'*) was held every ten days on the same site. Kadazans from the Kinabalu highlands would walk for several days down the Tempasuk valley to reach *Tamu Darat*. After attending the *tamu* in 1915, one observer noted that

> . . . besides *damar*, beeswax and wild rubber, the Dusuns bring with them various articles of their own manufacture – hats of various types made of plaited and dyed rattan or bamboo, rope of twisted tree-bark and coils of rattan cane cut into strips and dyed black – as well as rice, mangoes, durians, belunos and other kinds of fruit, and, most important of all, tobacco, which is largely cultivated at Kiau, on the slopes of Mount Kinabalu, as well as at Bundutuhan and other more lowland villages (Evans, 1923, 131).

There are few contemporary descriptions of the Kadazan *tamu* held further inland. Whitehead (1893, 107) refers very briefly to the 'tamels' held 'in dried-up river-beds' in the Kinabalu foothills. Rutter described an exclusively Kadazan *tamu* held in the Kinabalu area at an altitude of some 700 metres (2,300 feet) at Gerunting, on the banks of the Koriyau river[9] as follows:

> This market, held every thirty days is one of the most interesting in the district; it is under no Government supervision and all the arrangements are made by the natives . . . No Chinese or Bajau have access to it, but Dusuns who have just returned from the coast barter again the goods they have brought back, such as salt, dried fish and matches, for tobacco and other products of the hills (Rutter, 1929, 361).

The Effects of European Administration on the Tamu System

Although the British North Borneo Company was not granted a charter until 1881, direct European administration of parts of western Sabah began in 1878. From this time the European administrators began to exercise control over the *tamus* and indeed used the *tamus* as a means of promoting peaceful trading in the territory. In 1885, Daly, a Resident of part of west coast Sabah travelled into Murut country and established a *tamu* and a police station at Tenom.

Between 1895 and 1896, several strictly controlled *tamus* were initiated on upper Kinabatangan rivers in eastern Sabah (Black, 1970, 284). Later, in 1901, experimental restrictions were placed on river traders, requiring that all trade be conducted at fortnightly *tamus* and forbidding the giving of more than Malay $10 credit. The first *tamu* held at Keningau (in interior Sabah) took place on January 8, 1898 and attracted over 1,000 people, despite floods.

As well as establishing *tamus* in areas of Sabah where these markets were not traditional, the Chartered Company administrators moved certain west coast *tamus* to sites which were easy to supervise. Evans (1923, 130) mentions that *tamus* in the Tempasuk District had been moved coastwards by an early District Officer. In 1897, the Company closed the important *tamu* held at Inanam because the rebel native leader Mat Salleh had been particularly active in that area. As a result Putatan *tamu*, some 16 km (ten miles) further south, prospered.

These efforts on behalf of the Chartered Company to create new trading patterns were not very successful. The *tamus* established in the interior and on east coast Sabah petered out as soon as the administrators turned to other business, and Chinese and Dayak[10] traders moved in. However, in the traditional *tamu* areas of Sabah, new European-initiated *tamus* met with more success. In the 1880s, the Chartered Company was intent on encouraging European trade and since European vessels required deep water for anchorage, administrative and trading centres were established nearer the coast than the indigenous trading settlements. *Tamus* established at these points often thrived. At Tuaran, the weekly *tamu* (known as *Tamu Opis* because it was held near the District Office) grew to supersede the traditional *tamu* held at Pampang. Since 1945, a weekly *tamu* held at Kota Belud, formerly the administrative centre of the Tempasuk District, has replaced *Tamu Darat*.

As well as influencing the siting of certain *tamus*, Chartered Company administrators also attempted to control the trading procedures on the *tamu* grounds. At certain large west coast *tamus*, a flagpole was erected on the *tamu* ground and trading could not take place until the flag had been unfurled (Cook, 1924, 123). Police attended these *tamus* to ensure that these regulations were enforced and to uphold law and order. All participants at the *tamu* were required to leave their weapons outside the *tamu* ground, in charge of a police officer.

The well-intentioned but rather ludicrous regulations imposed on *tamu* trading by the Chartered Company lapsed after the Japanese occupation in 1942, and the tradition of early morning trading reasserted itself. However, one more sensible procedure was retained and is still important in *tamu* today: the appointment of official *Tamu* Masters who collect fees from vendors. Every official *tamu* in Sabah today has a *Tamu* Master (usually he is a Native Chief or a headman) who is responsible for the collection of fees and who may issue regular vendors with licences. In the colonial period (1946-1963), District Councils were made responsible for all the official *tamus* and all moneys collected from the vendors were used to maintain and improve the *tamu* grounds. This practice continues today and as a result, many *tamu* grounds have been equipped with wooden stalls or cemented selling areas.

There is evidence that Chartered Company administrators attempted to standardise *tamu* days because of the difficulty of keeping track of *tamus* held at five, ten, or 20 day intervals. Many *tamus* held at these intervals were brought into line with the European calendar. Some *tamus* became weekly (usually Sunday) events instead of being held every ten days; others were held on fixed calendar dates. Thus, today in Sabah only three every-ten-day *tamus* survive (Kaung, Menggatal and Inanam), though two *tamus* in Penampang District and two in Ranau District are held on fixed calendar dates which approximate to ten day intervals. Most *tamus* held in Sabah today are held on specific dates (Table 3.1) but it is interesting to note that Sunday is the most popular *tamu* day, not Friday as might be expected on the Moslem west coast (cf. Hill and Smith, 1972, 346-48).

Tamus were important not only for their market function, but also as social events. At *tamus*, news and gossip could be disseminated; the evening before the *tamu* it was customary for those people who had travelled some distance to the *tamu* to camp with people from the same ethnic group (Evans, 1923; Glyn Jones,

Table 3.1: *Tamu* days in Sabah, 1972

District	Mon	Tues	Wed	Number of *Tamus* Thur	Fri	Sat	Sun	*Tamus* on specific dates	Every ten days	Total
Kudat	1	1	1	3	1	5	4	1	–	17
Ranau	–	–	–	–	–	–	1	12	–	13
Kota Belud	1	2	6	4	3	4	1	–	1	22
Tuaran	–	2	1	3	–	–	1	–	–	7
Kota Kinabalu	–	–	–	1	–	–	–	–	2	3
Penampang	1	–	–	–	–	1	1	2	–	5
Papar	–	–	–	2	1	1	2	–	–	6
Kuala Penyu	–	–	–	–	–	–	1	–	–	1
Beaufort	–	–	–	–	–	1	2	3	–	6
Sipitang	1	–	1	–	2	–	1	–	–	5
Tenom	–	–	–	–	–	–	–	1	–	1
Keningau	–	–	–	1	–	1	2	–	–	4
Tambunan	–	–	–	1	1	–	1	–	–	3
Labuan	–	–	–	–	–	–	1	–	–	1
Total	4	5	9	15	8	13	18	19	3	94

Source: Boenisch Burrough, 1972 and 1973.

1953, 59). On the *tamu* day itself, cock-fighting sessions often took place after trading had finished, and this is still a feature of some contemporary *tamus*. The Chartered Company and subsequently the Colonial government, augmented the social aspects of *tamus*. Horse racing and buffalo racing were introduced to certain coastal *tamus*, notably Tuaran. The multi-functional aspect of the *tamu* was expanded as the administrators took advantage of the presence of large crowds at *tamus* by sending Government dressers to administer medicines and treatment and by encouraging Native Chiefs to hold informal court on *tamu* days to settle cases of native law. In addition, the *tamu's* role as a meeting where news and ideas could be disseminated was expanded; at some of the coastal *tamus*, officers provided agricultural and veterinary information to the people.

Large, less frequently held *tamus* on the lines of agricultural fairs were also established. These attracted people from throughout a particular District and were originally intended to foster community spirit. At first, therefore, these *tamu besars* (big *tamus*) were little more than well-organised parties, with singing, dancing, blowpipe-shooting contests and *tapai* (rice wine) drinking as well as tug-of-wars, football matches, and other events reminiscent of English country fetes. Subsequently, *tamu besars* became an important means of disseminating information on the progress of the country and the facilities available to the people.

Changes in the *tamu* system which arose indirectly from the policy of Chartered Company and Colonial administrators are no less important than those which can be ascribed to direct European intervention. The most important of these changes was the rationalisation of the *tamu* network in response to improved communications. The early years of this century saw the opening up of bridle-paths linking the newly established administrative centres (Black, 1970, 369 and 372). For a time, many natives preferred their traditional routes (Evans, 1923, 132), but inevitably certain *tamus* declined as travelling became easier. In addition, the pax Compania encouraged people to venture into previously hostile territory; this heightened sense of security, coupled with the Administration's promotion of *tamus* at sites near administrative centres, also contributed to the decline of some *tamus*. Evans noted how *Tamu Sisip* was being bypassed in 1915:

> . . . it is now no uncommon thing for the people of the interior to go straight through to Tamu Timbang, which is held every Wednesday, not far from the Government station and the Chinese shops. By doing this, a man bringing in a load of jungle produce is enabled to obtain slightly higher prices and can also have a better selection of shop goods to choose from in return (Evans, 1923, 133).

A number of *tamus* that flourished in the nineteenth century are no longer held today. Other *tamus* have lost their trading function entirely and survive only as social events. Thus *Tamu Darat* (which was last held in 1945) has degenerated into a cock-fighting meeting and general get-together, as have Putatan (Penampang District) and Berunggis (Tuaran District).

Another change arising indirectly from European administration has been the replacing of bartering by cash transactions, though it is arguable that cash would have eventually entered into the *tamu* system even without the presence of a cash-oriented administration. Straits Settlements silver dollars and Chartered Company notes and coinage began to circulate at *tamus* in the early years of the twentieth century. By 1915, payment in cash was at a premium at *Tamu Darat*, although at that time bartering still predominated:

> This bartering is of course very much to the liking of the Chinese, who will not part with cash unless forced to do so, since by bartering their cotton goods, beads, gambier, kerosine and other articles, they obtain a double profit on every deal (Evans, 1923, 131).

The assimilation of aliens into the *tamu* system can also be ascribed to Chartered Company policy. The Chinese were the most important aliens to arrive in North Borneo. Before 1880, there were only a few Chinese traders living on the west and east coasts of Sabah, but after this time the number of Chinese in the Territory increased rapidly in response to the Company's policy of encouraging immigration to provide a labour force. Between 1901 and 1911 the number of Chinese in Sabah rose from 12,000 to 26,000 (Black, 1970, 369 and 372). Most of the immigrants were Hakka agriculturalists (the major Chinese group in Sabah today), though Cantonese from Hong Kong entered the country in increasing numbers from 1920-1940 (Tregonning, 1965). Many of these Chinese became petty traders and shopkeepers and by the second decade of this century, Chinese traders controlled the jungle produce trade at *Tamu Darat* and also organised the export of tobacco grown in the Kinabalu highlands to Brunei (Evans, 1923, 132). Sikhs also became specialist vendors at Sabah *tamus*. From the 1880s Sikhs were recruited to be police officers for the Chartered Company (Black, 1969, 249-350). Today, their descendants may be seen at *tamus* selling patent medicines.

Recent Changes in Tamus

The changes in the *tamu* system which were initiated by European administrators have continued, particularly since Sabah joined Malaysia. Between 1960 and 1970, there has been a dramatic improvement in the country's road network (from 1,238 to 2,890 km (770 to 1,800 miles) of road) and this has had repercussions on the spatial distribution of *tamus*. The opening up of the Kota Kinabalu (then called Jesselton) to Ranau all weather road in 1963 stimulated the establishment of at least two *tamus*, one held at Mile 11, which has been held weekly since 1960, and the other at Simpangan (Mile 24). A small *tamu* is now held approximately every ten days at Mile 28 on the Tambunan-Kota Kinabalu road (completed 1969).

As roads have been extended, travelling Chinese salesmen have penetrated into formerly remote areas. These salesmen now attend the hill *tamus* which were formerly exclusively Kadazan. In addition, small *tamu*-like markets have sprung up in areas where *tamus* are not indigenous, particularly in Murut country. Though these markets primarily involve the sale of mass-produced shop goods (sarongs, tinned foods, crockery, etc.) to people in remote areas, their existence stimulates the development of local trading, for people begin to bring with them any surplus produce (vegetables, eggs, etc.) they may have, so that they may engage in small-scale trade with people from adjacent *kampongs*.

The State Government, following Chartered Company precedent, has attempted to establish *tamus* on the east coast, but these have failed. However, in 1972 a *tamu* was successfully inaugurated on Labuan island, off the west coast. In addition, the Government has continued to promote *tamu besars*. A *tamu tahunan besar* (big yearly *tamu*) is now held annually in the administrative centre of each District. The District Officer sponsors the *tamu besar* and funds are provided by the District Council. At these *tamus* there are stalls illustrating the State's progress and policies, exhibitions of local handicrafts as well as many competitions and sports. Some measure of these *tamus'* effectiveness as sources for the dissemination of information and the consolidation of peoples' ideas can be ascertained from the fact that during the state of emergency (1969-70) which followed political troubles in Kuala Lumpur, no *tamu besars* were held in Sabah.

Finally, it is worth noting that the migration of Kadazan peoples from Tambunan District in the last 20 years has resulted in the establishment of two *tamus* in Keningau District. The Kadazans have moved to Murut country because of population pressure on agricultural land in the Tambunan area.

The Characteristics of Contemporary Tamus

In 1972, with the help of local schoolchildren, vendor surveys were conducted in the two largest *tamus* in Sabah today: Tuaran and Kota Belud (Boenisch Burrough, 1974). The surveys were, perforce, limited to certain aspects of *tamu* vending only, but as they are the only data so far available on *tamus* they provide the basis for some observations on the characteristics of contemporary *tamus*.

Tuaran and Kota Belud tamus

Tuaran and Kota Belud are coastal towns and lie north of Kota Kinabalu, Sabah's capital city (Fig. 3.1). Both *tamus* are Sunday *tamus* and were established near administrative centres by District Officers early this century. Tuaran *tamu* has replaced the *tamu* held at Pampang (six km (four miles) south of the town) which used to take place every ten days and was the most important *tamu* in the area. The town *tamu* has had several official sites, but the current *tamu* ground is on the left bank of the Tuaran river, just north of the shophouses. Because it is often muddy, this field is unpopular with vendors and therefore on most Sundays, although the *tamu* begins on the official ground at 8 a.m., unless there is some police control vendors soon move into the centre of town. By

Table 3.2: Goods sold at Tuaran *tamu*, August 27, 1972

Goods	Kadazan M[a]	Kadazan F[b]	Bajau M	Bajau F	Chinese M	Chinese F	Malay M	Malay F	Indian M	Indian F	Other M	Other F	Total M	Total F	Grand Total
							Vendors by ethnic group								
Fruit & vegetables	12	78	2	5	8	26	—	—	—	1	1	—	23	110	133
Poultry	1	2	9	1	3	—	—	—	—	—	—	—	13	3	16
Fresh fish	—	1	1	14	—	—	—	—	—	—	—	—	1	15	16
Crabs & shellfish	—	—	5	8	—	—	—	—	—	—	1	—	6	8	14
Cakes & sweets	—	—	—	5	—	4	2	—	—	—	—	—	2	9	11
Tobacco	4	5	—	—	—	—	—	—	—	—	—	—	4	5	9
Baskets & mats	—	—	3	4	—	—	—	—	—	—	—	—	3	4	7
Salt fish	1	—	—	5	—	—	—	—	—	—	—	—	1	5	6
Medicine	—	—	1	—	—	—	1	—	2	—	—	—	4	—	4
Rice	—	3	—	—	—	—	—	—	—	—	—	—	—	3	3
Miscellaneous[c]	5	1	3	1	—	—	1	—	—	—	—	—	9	2	11
Total	23	90	24	43	11	30	4	—	2	1	2	—	66	164	230
Grand total	113		67		41		4		3		2		230		

Source: Author's survey.

[a] Male
[b] Female
[c] Includes bees, coffee, eggs, rice wine, sunglasses, crockery, gongs, spices, cloth.

Table 3.3: Goods sold at Kota Belud *tamu*, September 10, 1972

Goods	Kadazan M[a]	F[b]	Bajau M	F	Chinese M	F	Illanun M	F	Pakistani M	F	Other M	F	Total M	F	Grand total
Fruit & vegetables	12	59	3	34	–	1	–	1	–	–	–	–	15	95	110
Cakes & sweetmeats	1	–	–	66	1	1	1	1	–	–	–	–	3	68	71
Tobacco	23	18	8	–	3	6	–	–	–	–	–	–	34	24	58
Fresh fish	3	2	12	26	–	–	3	6	–	–	–	–	18	34	52
Refreshments	–	1	11	24	12	4	–	–	–	–	–	–	23	29	52
Clothes, cloth	–	3	1	5	18	20	–	–	–	–	1	1	20	29	49
General goods	1	2	1	–	22	18	–	–	–	–	–	–	24	20	44
Buffalo	23	–	8	–	–	–	11	–	–	–	–	–	42	–	42
Shellfish, crabs, prawns	1	–	4	18	–	–	1	8	–	–	–	–	6	26	32
Betel nut	6	4	–	18	–	–	–	1	–	–	–	–	6	23	29
Betel leaf	6	15	–	3	–	–	–	–	–	–	–	–	6	18	24
Cigarette leaf wrapper	–	–	9	1	–	–	9	4	–	–	–	–	18	5	23
Mats, hats, baskets	2	4	3	8	–	–	–	6	–	–	–	–	5	18	23
Salt fish	–	–	4	14	–	1	1	3	–	–	–	–	5	18	23
Jewellery	–	–	–	–	1	1	–	–	10	–	2	–	13	1	14
Yeast	–	–	–	4	–	–	–	8	–	–	–	–	–	12	12
Rice	1	2	5	2	–	–	–	1	–	–	–	–	6	5	11
Lime (for betel)	–	–	–	9	–	–	–	–	–	–	–	–	–	9	9
Medicine	1	–	1	–	–	–	–	–	–	–	7	–	9	–	9
Sugar	–	–	–	5	–	–	–	–	–	–	–	–	–	5	5
Miscellaneous[c]	1	–	2	5	4	1	1	–	–	–	1	–	9	6	15
Total	81	110	72	242	61	53	27	39	10	–	11	1	262	445	707
Grand total	191		314		114		66		10		12		707		707

Source: Author's survey.

a Male

b Female

c Includes coffee, knives, flour, coral, seeds, spices, books, paraffin, mouth oil, poultry.

10 a.m. the *tamu* is in full swing on the roadsides and in the open space in front of the *pasar* building.[11]

Kota Belud is 40 km (25 miles) north of Tuaran. Though the town is much smaller than Tuaran (2,211 compared with 3,358 inhabitants (1970 census figures)), the Kota Belud *tamu* is much larger. It has superseded *Tamu Darat*, which used to be held every 20 days at a site 11 km (13 miles) upriver from Kota Belud town. Kota Belud *tamu* ground is also adjacent to this river (the Tempasuk) and it is about one km from the shophouses. The moneys levied from vendors have been used to improve the *tamu* ground; concreted selling areas have been provided and lines of wood and palm shelters have been erected. These shelters are available for hire. At Kota Belud, a buffalo mart takes place every Sunday next to the *tamu* ground. A clerk is in charge of the transactions; for every animal weighed and sold, the District Council collects Malaysian $10. Whereas Kadazans are the most important ethnic group in Tuaran District, on the lowlands around Kota Belud, Bajaus predominate.

The Tuaran vendor survey was carried out on 27 August, 1972. A nine-item questionnaire was used and the following information was recorded for each vendor interviewed: sex and ethnicity; goods sold; vendor's home *kampong* and its distance from the *tamu*; mode of transport used to reach the *tamu*; the day on which the vendor arrived at the *tamu*; how often the vendor attended the *tamu*; and the source of the goods being sold. The Kota Belud survey was conducted two weeks later (10 September, 1972). A shorter questionnaire was used in order to facilitate the interviewing of a large number of vendors. The survey aimed to record the sex and ethnicity of each vendor; goods sold; vendor's home *kampong* and its distance from the *tamu*; and how often the vendor attended the *tamu*. Of the approximately 700 vendors present at Tuaran *tamu*, 230 were interviewed (Table 3.2). At Kota Belud over 1,000 vendors attended and 707 were interviewed (Table 3.3).

The tables reveal several characteristics: firstly, a much more varied range of goods is sold at Kota Belud *tamu* than at Tuaran *tamu*, but women vendors predominate in both (72% of the Tuaran sample, 63% of the Kota Belud sample); secondly, at both *tamus*, the medicine vendors were male and at Kota Belud, men sold jewellery, buffalo, general goods and tobacco; thirdly, there is marked ethnic specialisation according to goods sold. At both *tamus* the people selling fresh and salt fish, shellfish and crabs, were Bajaus (at Kota Belud, Illanuns were also important); tobacco sellers were predominantly Kadazans. Two groups of Chinese can be recognised: the market gardeners selling fruit and vegetables at Tuaran *tamu*; and the shopkeepers selling shop goods ('general goods'), clothes and cloth, and refreshments at Kota Belud. Around Kota Belud there are no significant enclaves of market gardening Chinese as there are at Tuaran. The difference in the goods sold by Chinese at Tuaran and Kota Belud also reflects the character of the two townships: Kota Belud town is not as good a shopping centre as Tuaran and it is also further away from the cosmopolitan delights of the capital, Kota Kinabalu. Therefore there is more scope for vendors of manufactured goods at Kota Belud *tamu*. The medicine and jewellery vendors are distinctive; they are usually Indians, Malays or, in the case of jewellery vendors, Pakistanis.

At both *tamus*, and indeed at *tamus* throughout Sabah, there is a characteristic *tamu* ground spatial pattern, because not only do vendors from the same *kampong* like to sit together, but people selling the same commodity tend to congregate together. (The latter is not necessarily a consequence of the former!) The *tamu* layout is maintained week after week (Fig. 3.2 and Fig. 3.3). The medicine men are the only vendors who do not keep together. They are in competition with each other, not only in the similarity of the goods sold but also in the volume of their portable loud speaker systems, and so it is to their advantage to be some distance from any rivals.

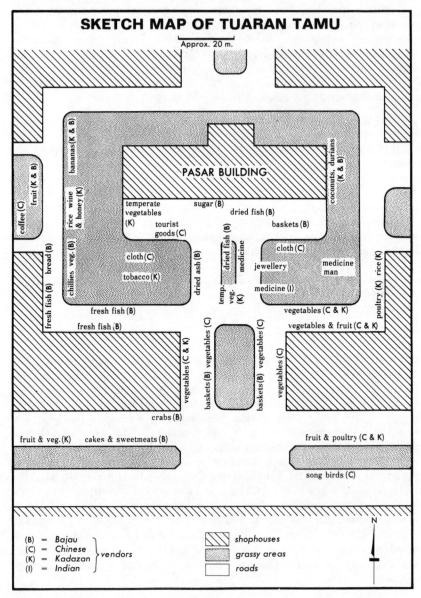

Figure 3.2   Tuaran *tamu*

A most striking feature of contemporary *tamus* is the elementary level of the trading; the vast majority of the transactions comprise direct producer-to-consumer sales. At Tuaran, vendors were asked whether they had made, grown, reared, collected, or caught what they were selling; whether they had bought their goods from other *kampong* people (i.e. whether they were middlemen); or whether they were selling manufactured goods. The results confirmed that most of the *tamu* trade was producer-to-consumer: 83% of the sample were producer-vendors and only 17% of the sample were middlemen and professional vendors. A mere 12% of the sample were true middlemen. Unfortunately, comparable data were not obtained at Kota Belud, though there was evidence of Chinese and Bajau involvement in the tobacco trade. These tobacco traders came from townships; most of the tobacco is grown in remote *kampongs* in the hills. As approximately 15% of the vendors at Kota Belud were selling manufactured goods (jewellery, general goods, clothes, and cloth), it is not unreasonable to assume that perhaps 80% of the *tamu* trade was producer-to-consumer, as at Tuaran.

Tamus have very localised hinterlands. Most of the vendors at Tuaran and Kota Belud came from within a radius of 16 km (ten miles) from the *tamu* ground. At Tuaran, 74% of the sample lived less than 16 km (ten miles) from the *tamu* ground and only 8% lived over 25 km (16 miles) away. At Kota Belud, the percentages were 82 and 14 respectively. Few female vendors travelled more than 25 km (16 miles) to the *tamu*. There is considerable dependence on modern transport, and the most popular form of transport used to reach Tuaran *tamu* was the bus service. Taxis, hire cars and landrover buses were also important.

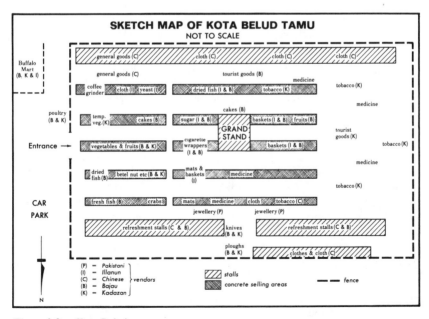

Figure 3.3   Kota Belud *tamu*

With the exception of the alien medicine sellers, *tamu* vendors do not have an aggressive sales technique, nor are they strongly profit-motivated. The *tamu* has an important social function, and to most vendors the *tamu* is more than an opportunity to sell any farm produce they may have, it is also an opportunity to meet friends and to patronise local coffee shops or refreshment stalls and even indulge in a mild spending spree. Some vendors bring very small loads of produce to sell (perhaps only a small basketful) which hardly justify attendance at the *tamu*. Peasant farmers and fishermen are reluctant to sell their produce to a middleman and thereby deny themselves an outing and higher profit, hence the small proportion of true middlemen at the *tamus*. Important exceptions to this rule are the farmers who grow temperate vegetables in the Kinabalu highlands; many sell their produce at roadside collecting points to enterprising Kadazans and Chinese who own landrovers and who take the vegetables to *tamus*, particularly to Kota Belud, Tuaran, Tamparuli and Kiuli, on the west coast and to Keningau in interior Sabah.

Further evidence that *tamu* vendors are not solely motivated by rational economic considerations can be seen in the tradition of camping on the eve of the *tamu* to exchange gossip. At Tuaran, 15 of the 230 vendors interviewed had arrived at the *tamu* ground on the day before the *tamu*. Most of these people had travelled a short distance; nine came from less than eight km (five miles) away, two came from nine to 16 km (six to ten miles) away and the remaining four travelled over 25 km (16 miles) to reach Tuaran.

Most vendors attend their local *tamu* regularly. At Tuaran, 53% of the sample attended the *tamu* every Sunday; at Kota Belud, regular weekly vendors accounted for 67% of the sample. Not surprisingly, these vendors were mostly selling non-perishable goods, or items available all-year-round. However, medicine and jewellery vendors (particularly the former) tended not to be regular weekly vendors. These alien, male, professional traders are itinerant. Unfortunately, the data on these Indian, Malay, Indonesian and Pakistani vendors are not sufficiently conclusive to be able to confirm that market rings similar to those in West Africa exist in Sabah (Bromley, 1971; Fagerlund and Smith, 1970; and Hodder, 1965a).

If there are market rings in Sabah, they must be modern phenomena, because until recently, conditions on the west coast hindered movement between *tamus*. Communications and trade networks were controlled by topography. Movement from highland to lowland following valleys was easy, but movement across the grain of this pattern was difficult. The unsophisticated methods used to carry produce to the *tamu* also restricted travel. On the coast, boats and buffaloes could be used to carry produce, but most people, especially the hill Kadazans, carried their goods in baskets strapped on their backs. To warrant carrying small loads between *tamus*, the goods must be valuable and not bulky. Of all the traditional *tamu* trade items, only tobacco meets these requirements, so it is possible that rudimentary market rings involving tobacco traders have existed in Sabah. Several informants reported that even today, Kadazan middlemen travel from *tamu* to *tamu* in the highlands, buying up stocks of tobacco.

Since the country's road network has been improved, travel has become easier. As a result middlemen now operate in the larger *tamus*, dealing in tobacco from interior and highland Sabah, or in temperate vegetables from the slopes of

Mount Kinabalu. But of all the vendors at the west coast *tamus*, the most mobile are the alien itinerant traders. Many *tamus* are very small, attracting no more than 100 people, and one might surmise that these itinerant vendors follow a random route on weekdays, visiting small *tamus*, but that they attend the large town *tamus* held at weekends. Most producer-vendors are neither very mobile nor very economically motivated, and this implies the existence of open-ended market routes, rather than finite market rings.

Conclusion

Trade has always been a fundamental part of *tamus*, but for many Sabahans the *tamu* is also a social event. Successive administrations modified *tamu* trading both directly and indirectly and, as a result, vendors have become more profit-oriented (the Chinese and itinerant aliens most of all). However, the majority of Sabahans who attend *tamus* are not highly profit-motivated; they often bring small quantities of goods to sell and are rarely interested in haggling. To them the *tamu* is a splendid opportunity to exchange news and gossip. The *tamu's* importance as a social event is borne out by the continuing practice of camping overnight before the larger *tamus*, the popularity of *tamu besars*, and by the holding of cockfights and get-togethers at *tamu* sites where trading no longer takes place. Therefore, as long as they fulfil a social need, *tamus* will be held in Sabah and will function on a separate economic plane from introduced urban markets.

[1] Sabah is the traditional name of the area of north Borneo which was administered by the British North Borneo Chartered Company from 1878 to 1941, and which was a British Colony from 1946 to 1963. In 1963, Sabah became one of the States in the newly formed Federation of Malaysia.

[2] This is an anglicized plural of the word *tamu*.

[3] See Dewey's (1962) study of the *pasar* at Modjokuto in Java.

[4] 'Kadazan' (formerly a tribal name referring only to people inhabiting the Penampang area) is now applied to all the groups of people to whom the exonym 'Dusun' ('man of the orchards') was formerly given (Apell, 1969).

[5] 'Murut' is an exonym meaning 'man of the hills', which is applied in Sabah to a group of people with very similar customs and habits. In Sarawak and Brunei 'Murut' refers to what Sabahans call 'Lun Daye'. Sarawakians call the Sabahan Muruts 'Tagals'!

[6] 'Bajau' and 'Suluk' are also exonyms. The autonyms are 'Sama' and 'Tausug', respectively.

[7] At one time the Kadazans near Tuaran paid a tax of ten *gantangs* of rice per head to the Bajaus (Black, 1970, 7-8, and 179-80).

[8] Five-day markets are traditional in other parts of southeast Asia, for example in Burma (Hall, 1968, 224) and in Java (Dewey, 1962, 63-5). Evans (1923, 130) noted that 'up country markets such as *Tamu Darat* are held once in twenty days in view of the fact that some Indonesians have a week of five days'.

[9] I have been unable to find this location.

[10] Dayaks or Ibans are a Sarawak people.

[11] This migration of vendors makes it difficult to carry out a comprehensive survey!

4 Nineteenth century market systems in Ethiopia and Madagascar
Richard T. Jackson

It is generally accepted that pre-colonial traditions of marketing in eastern Africa were restricted in areal extent and weakly developed. However, if the view of eastern Africa is extended a little beyond the boundaries of the former English colonies and protectorates, marketing systems are encountered which certainly deserve attention. Today, the markets of Addis Ababa and Tananarive are certainly amongst the largest in Africa. Moreover, their present size is only one indication of the importance of markets in the economic histories of their respective countries, the Empire of Ethiopia and the Malagasy Republic.

Apart from similarities of physical geography (both countries are dominated by central mountain areas), Ethiopia and Madagascar have similarly strong, if very different, cultural traditions. The one is dominated by Amharic and Tigrean Coptic nobles, proud and xenophobic; the other is dominated by Merina aristocrats (*andriana*) who, whilst accepting both Protestant and Catholic forms of Christianity from the third decade of the last century, continued to revere their ancestors who had settled the 'red island' from southeast Asia at least four hundred years before. Whilst the fragmented baronies of highland Ethiopia were united by religion against Islamic intruders, the warring princelings of highland Madagascar were united by their common tongue. Whilst the Malagasy economy was centred on paddy rice cultivation to a degree unique in Africa, Ethiopian diets relied on crops virtually unique in the world: *t'ef* (a grain), *noug* (an oilseed), and *enset* (a root). Despite its physical isolation, Madagascar eventually succumbed to French colonialism at more or less the same time as Ethiopia was attaining independent political unity under Menelik at the expense of Italian ambitions.

If their cultural traditions are remarkable, so too are Ethiopia's and Madagascar's marketing systems. In Ethiopia, trade flourished long before the political unification achieved by the great emperor Menelik. In Madagascar, the establishment of new, and the reorganisation of old markets played a vital political role in the unification by the great king Andrianampoinimerina of his highland kingdom, Imerina, in the last decade of the eighteenth century prior to the extension of Merina rule and influence to most of the remainder of the island in the nineteenth century. This essay shows how two strong marketing traditions with similar functions grew up in vastly different political circumstances.

Ethiopian Marketing Systems

Most European travellers to nineteenth century Ethiopia journeyed only in the northern provinces of the present Empire, for at that time the country's limits were far more restricted than today, scarcely extending south of the Awash River (Fig. 4.1). Not until the end of the century did Europeans reach Ethiopia from the south, by which time Menelik had established, more or less, the modern boundaries of the Empire. Almost all these travellers describe markets, partly because they were dependent upon them for fresh supplies, and partly because markets were such an important feature of Ethiopian life. From these accounts the characteristics of the markets are fairly clear.

Markets were the only form of retail activity and trade, and shops were unknown. According to Lefebvre (1845/9, III, 228)

> since no town has anything resembling retail trade, the inhabitants are more or less forced to go to market for all their weekly provisions . . . the market place serves as a town hall, and is the focal point of all meetings which might be described as political in nature. Proclamations sent down by the authorities are read out there; executions are carried out there; and lastly it is there that the *nagarit* is sounded to call the soldiers to arms . . .

In the 1880s, Portal (1892, 80) noted the absence of shops in towns, and forty years later Maydon (1925, 34 and 138) made similar comments of Adwa (where 'there are no shops as in most Ethiopian towns . . .') and of Gondar where he expressed disappointment at the lack of supplies. In some areas of Ethiopia today retailing establishments are often absent and even where 'small retail shops have become a standard part of the retail structure of towns' (Horvath, 1968, 47), these are still known as *arab bet* (arab house) or *suq* (market). There is little doubt, therefore, that markets monopolised trade in the nineteenth century.

The markets were not usually associated with urban centres of administration but rather were located in grassy, open spaces by the side of routeways along which passed the long distance caravans. Lefebvre's observation (1845/9, II, 198) provides the exception to prove the rule, and at Madjetie he noted that

> unlike the other places in Abyssinia this market is held in an enclosed area which is marked by palisades, with guards posted at the gate acting as police. This precaution avoids disputes and also facilitates the collection of taxes (one-eighth of the value of the goods).

Horvath (1970, 83) has also noted the traditional dissociation of markets from administrative centres. The explanation for this feature partly lies in the fragmented form of power structures in Ethiopia before the accession of Menelik and the impermanency of the princes' capitals which tended to be nomadic. The site of the market-place was, on the other hand, determined by the more or less fixed routes travelled by the caravan trains (Fig. 4.1).

The markets were organised temporally and spatially so as to minimise distances travelled to them on the one hand and, more importantly, to suit the needs of the caravans of merchants on the other (Simoons, 1960, 201). Days of operation of minor markets were determined by their relationship with the regional market which acted as caravanserais. As Portal (1892, 125) noted,

> almost the whole of Abyssinia appears to be divided into commercial districts or 'arrondissements' in different parts of which markets are held on certain fixed days of the week. No two markets within the district are held on the same day and the travelling merchant is thereby enabled to buy and sell in several different markets in the course of the week.

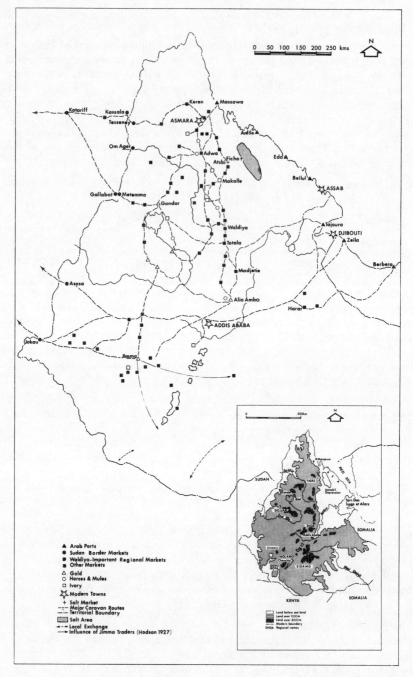

Figure 4.1   Major markets and routeways in Ethiopia in the late nineteenth century

De Young (1967a, 104) has pointed out that regional markets are generally held on Saturdays (the Coptic Christians observe a seven-day week) and are approximately 70 km (44 miles) apart. The implication that caravans travelled about 12 km (8 miles) a day is not unrealistic, indeed this probably overestimates their speed.[2]

The regional markets were large; they were stopping places for caravans and they also attracted traders from neighbouring provinces who would distribute the imported goods brought by the camel trains in their trade areas. Lefebvre (1845/9, II, 161) described the market at Waldiya in 1842 as follows:

> Oualdia market is held on Tuesdays, and as we have said traders from almost all the provinces of Abyssinia are found here. Those from Tigre (up to 150 km distant) bring salt here, which commodity serves as currency, as well as red and blue guinea cloths. In exchange they take mules, horses and silver; traders from Gojjam (up to 300 km distant) aside from a few guinea cloths, bring only beads. Those from Ouadela bring furs and skins whilst the Adales (from the Rift Valley) drive their animals up here and return with grain.

The hinterland of Waldiya might therefore be estimated as covering as much as 50,000 square kilometres (about 20,000 square miles). Tigre merchants also told Lefebvre 'with admiration of the place's women of pleasure and of their unusual abilities'.

The Role of Moslem Traders

The routeways and trade thereon, although taxed by Ethiopian princes, were under the influence of and were the prerogative of non-Christian and mainly non-Ethiopian merchants. It was usual for local barons to raise revenues not only at the markets but along the routes of trade, erecting toll gates where negotiations over the exact amount of tax to be paid might take days or weeks to complete. Such taxes were a recognised source of local revenues until well into the present century. Hodson (1927, 27) noted that there existed 'at intervals all along the main tracks customs gates' and 'that dues are levied at six to eight different customs gates between Sidamo and Addis Ababa'. These taxes were eventually abolished by the Italians in their brief but harsh period of rule and were not reinstated by Haile Sellasie on his return to power.

The routeways reflected Arab control of the coastline (Fig. 4.1), Ethiopia's present control of which only dates from the incorporation of Eritrea. The caravans set out from Arab ports and travelled westwards, especially from Massawa in the north, and from Tajoura, Zeila and Berbera in the south. From Massawa, routes fanned out south to Alio Amba the market of Ankober, capital of Shoa (Addis Ababa was not established until 1896). There they linked up with routes followed by traders from Harar. Routes also ran from Massawa to Keren and to Gondar via Adwa in the west, and from these places to the great trans-Sudanic routeways via Tesseney and Kassala, Katariff and Metemma/ Gallabat. The latter was attended in the dry season by merchants from as far afield as Arabia and was 'the market place for all commerce between Abyssinia and the Egyptian provinces' (Baker, 1867, 503). Caravans from the southern ports converged upon the Moslem city of Harar before moving westwards along the belt of Moslem settled land as far as Jumma and beyond to the Sudanic gateways of Asosa and Jokau (De Young, 1967b, 24). This latter route was less frequently used as Ethiopian Christianity reasserted itself.

Even in the heartland of nineteenth century Shoa, long distance trade was almost exclusively in Moslem hands. Whilst Harris (1844, II, 388 (a generally unreliable source)) estimated that one quarter of the people at Alio Amba were 'Hurrurhi' or Danakil, Krapf (1843, 91) was of the opinion that 'the inhabitants are nearly all Mohammedans'. Trade, therefore, if not independent of local political circumstances, continued in spite of them, because the control of it lay in Moslem hands.

Salt and Other Forms of Currency

The control of the means by which trade was made possible was also in outside hands for long periods. Caravans depended for their success to a very large degree upon the use of salt as a widely and commonly accepted currency. The chief source of salt was the northern part of the Danakil depression, an arid wasteland between the Ethiopian Highlands and the Red Sea (Fig. 4.1). It was distributed from two major markets, Ficho and Atsbi on the borders of Agame and Enderta. Control of the mines and the markets was of prime political importance, and moved back and forth between Tigre, Danakil, and Arab rulers, but chiefly lying directly or indirectly with the Arabs. From these markets, caravan trains of salt travelled to the major trading centres of all Ethiopia and may still be seen today plodding into Makalle.

According to Abir (1966, 7) salt 'facilitated inter-regional trade and was indispensable to the long range caravan trade'. Almost every European traveller notes its importance, and Johnston's (1844, 97) remarks are typical: 'everything that is exposed to sale in the market pays a kind of duty . . . either in kind or an equivalent in salt prices'. Even at the end of the century when Menelik was starting to introduce metal currency, the money most commonly accepted in Addis Ababa's *mercato* was the salt bar or *amole* (Wellby, 1901, 94). Unfortunately, the *amole* was fragile, easily shattered in rough journeys along rugged roads and liable to disintegrate in the moist climate of the highlands. Consequently, its value declined sharply inland from the salt markets. The exchange value of salt in thalers is plotted against distance from the salt mines in Fig. 4.2 (Abir, 1966; Lefebvre, 1845/9, III, 82), revealing a close but indirect relationship. The range of caravan trade was limited by the length of the journey the salt bars could survive as a viable currency. Without alternative supplies of salt or alternative forms of currency, the caravan trade could not have extended much more than 1,000 km (620 miles) from the Danakil area, even accounting for the added incentive of very high profits in such remote areas.

Other forms of currency did exist, and gold was used in several areas. More importantly, from the end of the eighteenth century the Austrian Maria Theresa thaler began to circulate. However, the position of salt as a currency does not seem to have been undermined until much later, possibly because of the scarcity of Maria Theresa thalers until the second half of the nineteenth century (Pankhurst, 1963, 8). These thalers are still accepted in remote areas, although their main use is as raw material for ornaments and as tourist souvenirs. When Menelik introduced his own currency, the thaler had wide, even exclusive acceptance in many areas.[3] The stability conferred by Menelik's conquests, and the circulation and use of metallic coinage (whose value inflated over time, not over distance) boosted the potential for long-distance market trade.

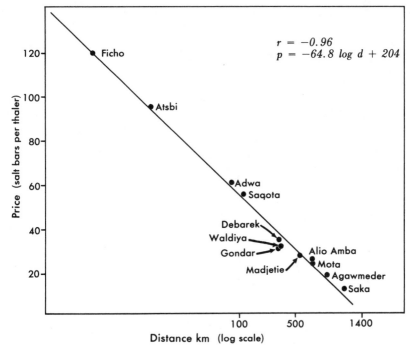

Figure 4.2   The relationship between distance from the salt mines and the value of salt (Abir, 1966 and Lefebvre, 1845-9)

The post-Menelik Expansion of Trade

Gemu Gofa province (Straube, 1963), located at the southernmost tip of the Ethiopian plateaux, was not visited by Europeans until the late nineteenth century and consequently there are few accounts of its markets. It is unlikely that the great caravan routes of the north ever extended this far south; the area is more than 1,100 km (680 miles) from Danakil and unlike the Jimma area (which is nearly as distant) it was not adjacent to other important trade routes. The problems of currency must have been very great; local salt was available from the Rift Valley lakes.[4] At the beginning of the twentieth century, currency in the markets of Wolamo (north of Gemu Gofa, Fig. 4.1), was the *dorma*, 'a thin piece of iron with one end bent measuring about two feet long and one inch broad' (Wellby, 1901, 144). About fifteen such pieces were equivalent to one thaler. The very existence of such cumbersome currency implies that actual exchanges of *dormas* for thalers occurred, and that thalers themselves were not in wide circulation. Stigand (1910, 293) also observed the use of these iron bars in Wolamo, calling them *marcho*. It would seem then that Wolamo, on the presumed limits of the area in which salt could play a useful role as a currency, had developed its own. It is also likely that if long-distance trade did exist it was with the Moslems of Jimma (Pankhurst, 1965, 37) rather than with the north, and that the greater part of trade in this area and in Gemu Gofa was fairly localised, based upon the strong ecological contrasts existing between the high, cool plateaux and the hot, dry lakeshore areas (Whitehouse, n.d., 318).

The extension of *pax Amharica* was achieved by the construction of roads and the placement at strategic points along such roads of semi-fortified garrison towns or *katama* (Déherain,. 1914, 225). This pattern of Amharic conquest undertaken by Menelik between 1895 and 1905 was not peculiar to the south, and roads and garrisons were established in almost all the conquered territories. Thus, in Gojjam (a trading partner of Shoa and Tigre long before its conquest) 'the *katama* are typical of the administrative centres (which are) combined with market places which often have urban characteristics. No peasants live in them. They represent a relatively new element in the social scene . . . '(Kuls, 1963, 70). Similarly in Gemu, the clustering of services and economic activity around *katamas* inhabited largely by Amharas contrasts sharply with pre-existing settlement patterns (Jackson, 1970, 25). Thus, a two-tiered pattern of settlement and markets may be discerned today.

Local rural markets, which are held in the open countryside away from permanent settlements, exhibit a random spatial distribution pattern. This randomness reflects the nature of the physical environment, clan boundaries, and the distribution of population. The highlands here are divided into well-marked valleys each usually inhabited by a single clan and each possessing its own market. All the specialist markets are located along routeways which might have existed before 1900 but which were certainly improved as arteries of Amharic control after the subjugation of the area. Almost all these markets are associated with *katama* built by Menelik's men at the turn of the century and still inhabited by Amharic administrators. These markets are not only spaced more regularly than the local ones but are held predominantly on Thursdays and Saturdays. Attendance at them is more a function of regional rather than local clan populations and of regional accessibility, and most attract sellers from long distances. Some combine the *katama* function with that of an ecologically favoured market, since they overlook routes down into the rift valley. All are centres of specialist traders (Jackson, 1971, 3).

The extension of trade to southern Ethiopia, as well as to other areas of Menelik's empire, was as much a function of military and political strategy as of economic development. It was achieved not by caravans paying their way in salt but by Menelik's soldiers paying, if the locals were lucky, in coin. It is this modern portion of market history in Ethiopia rather than the era of Islamic caravans, that bears most resemblance to the circumstances in which Madagascar's markets developed.

Malagasy Market Systems and the Great King Andrianampoinimerina

In many parts of East Africa the origins of periodic markets can be traced without too much difficulty. Quite a few of these systems developed under the impetus of the respective colonial administration and parallel with the competing commercial systems. Market systems in West Africa and Ethiopia are much more deeply rooted in traditional society, but details of their origins are often lost to history. In the case of Madagascar, the events related to the reorganisation of old markets and the creation of new markets at the end of the eighteenth century by Andrianampoinimerina were recorded by R.P. Callet in the 1870s from early offical records and from verbal informants. His document *Tantaran' ny Andriana* (The Chronicles of the Kings) was translated into French by Chapus and Ratsimba, and the volume relating to markets was published by the Academie Malgache in 1958. Most of the following discussion of the functions, mechanics of and reasons for establishment of markets, currency, and traders relies heavily on this valuable source, referred to as 'the chronicles' or 'TNA'.

Andrianampoinimerina (the 'most powerful of all the nobles of Imerina') came to power in 1787, and rapidly overcame his neighbouring rivals to unify Imerina, the densely populated plateau and highland area immediately surrounding the present capital, Tananarive. He quickly extended the influence of Imerina, a process continued after his death in 1810 by his son, Radama I. Simultaneously, he embarked upon a wide-ranging revolution involving the improvement of the physical environment,[5] reorganisation of government, the creation of social conditions in which the unity he had forged could endure, and the establishment of markets.

Each of the markets Andrianampoinimerina created was invested as one of his *lapa* or royal enclosures thus making each market a symbol of his presence. The markets, therefore, became a unifying symbol of Andrianampoinimerina's realm. Figuratively speaking, markets were 'not held in two places but in one alone . . . there is only one *lapa*, no more than one exists throughout the land'.[6] One of the most important sacerdotal and, incidentally, economic features of the *lapa* had been the sacrifices made there of cattle and the subsequent presentation of portions of the meat to the king *(vodihena)*. By slightly altering the rules relating to *vodihena*, Andrianampoinimerina simultaneously limited the powers of his nobles and increased his own status. With the establishment of many markets in which *vodihena* could be levied, many more slaughterings in what were the king's *lapa* occurred:

> Formerly, the *vodihena* was not divided; all of it came to the king from the time of Ralambo. But when Andrianampoinimerina was king he declared: 'I devote half the *vodihena* to ensure the well being of the people in the markets . . . The *vodihena* may only be divided in a *lapa* . . . but a market is one of my *lapa* and you may there divide the *vodihena*' (TNA, 602).

Thus, Andrianampoinimerina combined the functions of the sacred city with those of the market-place, and established his rule of benevolent dictatorship.

Markets existed in Madagascar before the accession of Andrianampoinimerina: 'the markets are important places of exchange founded by our ancestors' (TNA, 604). Indeed, it would be surprising had the original settlers from southeast Asia not brought with them some of the marketing traditions so well developed in that region. The Malagasy settlers also brought with them the concept of the seven-day week, the names of the days being but slight corruptions for the most part of the Arabic names. Market-places were called after the day of the week on which trading took place, and in the old days were considered to be neutral ground, though paths to and from them were considered dangerous places: 'even if hostilities were in progress, it was agreed by all sides that market trade could proceed' (TNA, 580). However, this trade was limited and markets were avoided by women and children: 'in those days you could not wear embroidered *lambas* (cloaks/shawls), nor trade in cattle, nor get tasty meats' (TNA, 607). Instead, markets were where the spoils of war were exchanged, the most important items being guns, gunpowder and slaves. Sometimes, people who were captured solely for sale as slaves (as distinct from prisoners of war) were bought back by relatives at the markets. Others eventually found their way into the hands of European freebooters based on the east coast. However, Andrianampoinimerina would not allow foreign merchants into his kingdom (TNA, 581), and most of the slave trade, which continued until very late in the nineteenth century, was concentrated in Tananarive (for the convenience of the *andriana*), or in markets on the eastern fringes of the kingdom. There were few of these *fihaonana* (meaning a meeting place, but with hostile overtones), and they were ill-attended places of evil repute.

When Andrianampoinimerina reorganised the trading system he attempted to ban all trade outside his new market-places: 'if there are people who trade in the countryside and not in the market then they are thieves' (TNA, 605). He urged his subjects to

> make your purchases in the markets rather than in the village for should you buy a chicken at evening in your village you will be doing the seller, not yourself, a good turn . . . (TNA, 623).

The first great markets were thus established in the rural areas, and during Andrianampoinimerina's reign held a virtual monopoly on all trade. They were sited in open spaces often in the valleys away from the old fortified hill-top strongholds. In time, 'houses would group around the market place giving rise to villages' (Dubois, 1938, 607) and even towns of considerable size. The markets fundamentally altered settlement patterns and lessened the danger of a reversion to the anarchic petty princedoms, centred on hill forts that characterised Imerina before Andrianampoinimerina's rule (Mille, 1969). After his death, the rural traders reappeared, and by 1880 the Friends' Foreign Mission reported that 'the way for the settlement of missionaries has been somewhat prepared by native traders, who are constantly passing about the country in pursuit of their calling' (F.F.M. Review, 1880, 34).

In the urban areas, the small bazaars established by Andrianampoinimerina to meet daily needs also monopolised trade; observations by visiting Europeans are almost identical to those quoted earlier in respect of Ethiopian towns:

> There are no shops in Antanavarivo but there is an abundant supply of all the necessaries of life and of the commoner manufactured articles in some half a dozen small markets held in the open air in different parts of the city (Sibrée, n.d., 140).

> The native town has no shops. Indeed shops as an institution are unknown in Madagascar. In Tamatave as elsewhere an open market is held (Mullins, 1875, 17).

This held true in the 1870s despite Ellis' report forty years earlier of Indian traders who had 'opened a house for the sale of their goods' in Tananarive but who sold their wares by employing 'the natives to carry their articles through the city and neighbourhood for sale' (Ellis, 1838, 339).

It is important to note that the urban markets (referred to in TNA as small, permanent markets in comparison to the large, periodic markets of the rural areas) were established *after* those of the countryside. Like their rural counterparts, the urban market-places were given the rank of royal sites, and there were harsh penalties for not supporting the market trade. Political union of Imerina seems to have led to a growth in urban populations and to a growing need for permanent markets in town centres: 'if a week passes without there being a market, the people will be unhappy . . . and hungry' (TNA, 623).

The Mechanics and Reasons for Market Establishment

The first of the new rural markets or *tsena* (meaning 'you can get it'), as the *fihaonana* were eventually renamed, were established in the heartland of Imerina, Avaradrano (Fig. 4.3 and 4.4). Only when success was achieved by the first seven

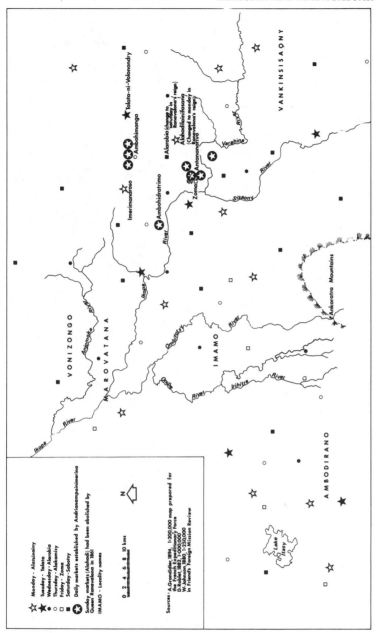

Figure 4.3   Markets of Imerina in the late nineteenth century

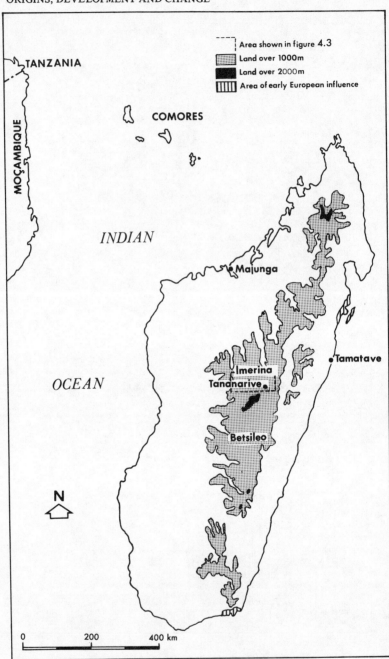

Figure 4.4   Madagascar, relief

(one for each day of the week) in Avaradrano, were emissaries sent to other areas to set up similar institutions. Each subdivision of Avaradrano was made responsible for the succes of the new markets in its daughter area.

The guidelines for a market's success were laid down by the king, and are repeated several times throughout the chronicles:

> all seven days of the week shall be market days here in Avaradrano but I shall not place the markets too close to one another, since, if there are many, this will waste the people's time. It would bring down prices and not contribute to the markets' growth. I will place them at sufficient intervals to allow you time for a return journey and to ensure that you may sell your produce every day . . . (TNA, 583).

When the Marovatana people came to the king and asked for a market to be held on Thursday because they were impressed by the success of the Thursday markets *(Alakamisy)* at Ambohimanga and Ambohidratrimo he replied:

> Yours shall be held on a Sunday as at Alahadilanifasana; I will not give you an Alakamisy lest you and the Tsimahafotsy come to blows, for you would become their rivals; . . . your markets will thus form a chain . . . (TNA, 597).

These guidelines would have been judged successful by at least one nineteenth century observer of Malagasy markets:

> They are the most favourite places of resort for all classes. There is not only a market containing a general assortment of goods held daily at the capital, but three or four large markets are also held at different distances from Antananarivo and from each other *(sic)*, every day in the week in rotation in different parts of the province (Ellis, 1838, I, 332).

These markets might be attended by as many as thirty thousand persons.

Clashes occasionally occurred, especially as some of the bigger markets, notably the Friday market just south of Tananarive (the Zoma), began to extend their hinterlands at the expense of their neighbours. Thus Alasora market did not do very well and its nobles were hard pressed to escape the king's wrath:

King: Why does the Anjoma at Alasora not flourish?

Rafiara: Be blessed, oh Andrianampoinimerina! It is because it is in competition with that at Fiadanana (the original location of the Zoma).

King: Rafiara, art not ashamed before Rabefiraisana? The seven he has created do exceedingly well and why not yours also, pray? Methinks ye know not how to govern your people. Alasora stands at no less a rank than Ambohimanga. He who is incapable of giving life to a market, is no noble but a peasant!

Rafiara forebore to directly inform the king that Ambohimanga was somewhat further from Tananarive than Alasora. However, he did point out that

> Both are Anjomas but the reputation of Tananarive is so much greater; also the people living far away prefer to go to Ambohimanga and Tananarive (TNA, 590-1).

Thus was the concept of hierarchical ordering of central places brought to the attention of the great king.

This pattern of markets spaced regularly in time and distance on every day of a seven-day week was unfortunately marred on 21 February 1869 when Queen Ranavalona II was converted to Christianity. Subsequent to this event 'the various markets formerly held on that day (Sunday – the Alahadi) were ordered to be changed to some other day and proclamations were made throughout the country (doubtless via the market-places) to the effect that the Queen commanded the people to abstain from all work on Sunday' (L.M.S. Review 1861-1870). A wholesale re-arrangement of market days does not appear to have taken place, and many of the aberrations in the present patterns of markets may be attributed to this spectacular triumph of the London Missionary Society.

The most important and oft stated reason for the careful and imaginative planning of the new markets was to improve the standard of living of the poorest of Andrianampoinimerina's subjects:

> I am establishing markets where the people may sell all the produce they can, and where those who have none may buy (TNA, 583).

Thus, even rules governing the rights of street urchins to scraps of offal were clearly laid down and the people were encouraged to sell the lowliest of produce, 'even cassava':

> all that which the people use to feed themselves with will be brought there: cooked cassava, cooked sweet potatoes, cow heels and rice, for many will have left home
> without having eaten. Even water to quench the people's thirst will be brought and those who have nothing else to sell, will here be able to sell water. Nothing will be given to drink without being repaid for in this way the poor will earn their bread (TNA, 599-600).

That this goal was achieved is confirmed by Sibrée's comment in 1870 that 'the necessaries of life . . . are certainly more easily procured by the very poor in Madagascar than in England' (Sibrée, n.d., 230).

A second set of reasons concerned the role of the market as a public meeting-place, that is the development of functions similar to those mentioned by Lefebvre in Ethiopia and quoted above. One of these functions was to enable the king's decrees to be circulated rapidly by their proclamation in the markets:

> I will cause a gun to be fired in the market place so that you might make ready for a kabary (meeting) and hear my orders which you will carry away and guard in your hearts so that you may pass them on to your wife and children (TNA, 600).

Items of lost property were to be placed on frames of wood to await reclamation by their owners (TNA, 601). The market-place became a recognised venue for the arrangement of marriages (Dubois, 1938, 395), for the carrying out of executions, and bull-fighting became a popular form of entertainment associated with the markets (F.F.M. Review, 1880, 15).

The unstated reasons (unstated, that is, in the chronicles), seem to have been far more important. Markets, in fact, seem to have been one of the chief means available to Andrianampoinimerina for the destruction of the economic power of any possible rival. By creating markets and placing the responsibility for their success upon the *andriana*, the king achieved the second of Meillassoux's two conditions for market trade: 'commerce can only result from contacts between . . . agents who are in a social position which frees them from involvement in prestation and gift exchange' (1971, 82). By placing restrictions upon the use of *vodihena*, the king reduced the power of his nobles, but he demanded their attendance at the market:

> He sent to each market people whose mission it was to spy out which persons of note had gone there. If anyone said, lying, 'I myself have contributed to give life to the market,' without having been there, then Andrianampoinimerina gave the order to assemble the people and would say to the offender, 'I have my informants *(maso ivoho* — eye in the back) and I see those who have supported the markets.' And such liars received no part of the rewards given by Andrianampoinimerina (TNA, 586).

A far worse fate awaited any noble who attempted to force the common folk to give him gifts or pay him tribute (TNA, 615), or who actively undermined the success of the markets. The offender, whether from the royal family, the nobles or a commoner, was liable to be put to death, his family being sold into slavery; 'history will retain no record of his good deeds' (TNA, 619).

By ensuring the aristocracy's attendance at and support for markets, the king also ensured a partial redistribution of wealth and the removal of much traditional economic support for any noble contemplating revolt. It is not without significance that the section of the chronicles dealing with markets also contains what at first appears to be an unnecessary digression discussing the unorthodox but overwhelmingly successful military tactics and prowess of Andrianampoinimerina's personal troop, the Manisotra (TNA, 591-7). With this force at his command, the king was able to proceed with his economic plans with little fear of rebellion amongst the *andriana* (whose strength he was gradually and skilfully sapping). The tradition for the *andriana* to attend the markets as frequently as any other class was often noted by foreign observers. In his encyclopaedic work on the Betsileo, Dubois referred to the fact that the Malagasy aristocracy were conspicuous in the markets (1938, 607).

Weights, Measures, and Currency

The King introduced measures for rice *(vata)*, controlled interest rates, and had balances made (TNA, 600). The last named were used primarily for weighing money. Although coinage was in short supply and of diverse origins (arriving in Imerina from the pirate Europeans on the coast), a workable if rather bizarre arrangement was achieved. Coins were chopped up into pieces as small as one 720th of the original piastre. Thus five *variraiventy* made one *varidimiventy* of which 144 literally made up one piastre. This was a superior currency to salt, and the system remained long in use (F.F.M. Review, 1880, 18).

As rice was the basis of the Malagasy diet, specific prices were laid down and merchants were told that 'If these prices please you not, then do not sell in the market. Leave the place to those who understand the poor and their needs' (TNA, 623). A more general guide to price setting was also laid down by the king:

> If you sell, do not sell too cheap nor too dear. Fix a middle price so that people may buy. For those who sell and those who buy cheaply are, the one as much as the other, thieves. When the one buys cheap and the other sells likewise, they are robbers. For the one is a fence and the other a cutpurse . . . Keep a watchful eye on these for . . . they are the grandmothers of thieves (TNA, 627).

The layout of the markets was also the subject of legislation:

> As for the foodstuffs which are sold in the markets, they shall be placed in sections and none shall take the place of another. Meat will not be served in the section reserved for rice, nor cloth in that of meat. Cattle shall not be placed in the area set aside for small goods, lest they injure the people (TNA, 625).

For every rule that Andrianampoinimerina laid down he gave a reason. In this the logic was that 'if the place for selling goods is not arranged in an orderly fashion, and if the people are caused to search hither and thither for what they want, they will wander haphazardly. Whilst, now, when you go to market, each may go straight to the places he seeks' (TNA, 626).

Certain articles were banned from the market-places of Imerina, notably liquor and pigs (as was the smoking of hemp) although outside specified limits in Betsileo, to the south, and in the coastward regions attitudes were more relaxed (TNA, 610). If anyone imported prohibited goods across the stated boundaries, they risked death, 'for they insult the realm; in smoking hemp, sensible people become stupid, acting like dogs'. Other articles were licensed, and gunpowder vendors had first to apply for royal permission (TNA, 691). Because of fears of sorcery, each seller of medicine had to undergo a test *(tanguin)* so that malpractices might be avoided and so that Andrianampoinimerina could assure the people:

> Only those potions sold in the markets will be good *(ody sahy lapa* – remedies of proven worth); no impure remedies will be on sale there (TNA, 700).

The certified sellers of medicines were known as the Andriamadio (the purified nobles).

Markets Without Traders?

In remarkable contrast to the role played by traders and their routes in the stimulation of market development in Ethiopia, there is virtually no mention in the chronicles of traders save in a very limited and negative sense. The exclusion of foreign traders has already been mentioned as has the attempt to repress trading outside the confines of the market-place. No other direct mention is made of traders. It is difficult to believe that these markets could prosper without traders, yet there is ample indirect evidence in the chronicles to support the contention that Imerina commerce did indeed flourish in the almost complete absence of foreign merchants and with the inflow of only very limited quantities of goods.

Imported white salt or even sea salt was available in Imerina only from the reign of Radama (1810-1827). In Andrianampoinimerina's era, *tarao*, a salt made from the ashes of plants, was in use (TNA, 693), indicating how weak links with the outside world must have been. A little imported cambric is said to have been available (TNA, 694), yet cotton goods were generally conspicuous by their absence. Indeed, Andrianampoinimerina decreed that the Merina should cultivate cotton themselves as it was 'easy to grow' (TNA, 707). Cotton cultivation in fact ceased almost immediately after the first major penetration of the Malagasy market by European-manufactured cotton in the reign of Rasoherina. Even such trinkets as mirrors, soap and silk, gaudy trappings on the fringes of European commercialism, were unknown(TNA, 695). There were pearls in circulation that must have been derived from Arab sources (TNA, 692); however, on the east coast it was not until after 1850 that Reunionese and Mauritian traders became significant at Tamatave (Lacaze, 1881, 8). The fact is that Madagascar was far more remote from the world at large than Ethiopia and became steadily more remote as the influence of European links with India began to replace that of the Arabs on the east African coast. To some extent, the Merina aversion to foreigners must also be held responsible; this was almost certainly reinforced by the presence of European slavers clustered along the eastern coasts of Madagascar in Andrianampoinimerina's time. Even coastal Malagasies were included in this aversion; Andrianampoinimerina forbade the wearing of square, woven hats in Imerina 'because, he thought, this was the headdress of the coastal people' (TNA, 695).

To explain the success of these markets, recourse must be had to the internal geographical diversity of Imerina which created complementarities in the production of scarce goods. An immense variety of goods was to be found in the markets, and to a large degree this reflects the varied environmental conditions within a few miles of Tananarive. However, it also reflects the advanced state of the handicraft industries of Imerina pre-colonially. The Ankaratra mountains stretch southwards from the Malagasy capital towards Betsileo, reaching to 2,800 metres (9,200 feet) less than 60 km (37 miles) from Tananarive whilst the Imerina plateau starts its rapid descent to the east coast less than 50 km (31 miles) eastwards. On the plateau itself, the drainage of swamps undertaken in Andrianampoinimerina's reign opened up vast tracts of land for paddy rice cultivation contemporaneously with the extension of Imerina control into the grasslands of Imamo and the lands to the west. Some specialisation of production already existed before the new markets were established and some sites were chosen specifically to serve such local specialities. Thus, Alatsinainy-ambazaha became the most important market for fine quality *lamba mena*,[7] centred amongst the Zanak'antitra (TNA, 597). There were eventually many such specialist regions: pots came from Marovatana, silk from Betsileo, wooden goods from Vakiniadiana, raffia and wood fuel from the west, iron goods from Vakinsisaony, and honey from Betsileo and from Avarandrano's forest areas where the Tanala people lived. Tananarive remained famous for its slaves (TNA, 706).

There is scarcely a mention of how these goods were traded between the different areas mentioned. However, there is little doubt that these local traders were the Merina themselves, especially those from the core area around Ambohimanga and Tananarive. It was the Merina who travelled into the newly conquered or affiliated regions to act as traders, and the picture painted by Dubois is probably applicable to many newly-won areas besides Betsileo:

> The Merina . . . have profited from trade more than the autochthonous population who are little given to financial speculation or retailing activities . . . Just as the Merina has a passion for selling, so the Betsileo has one for buying and idling away his time (Dubois, 1938, 80 and 605).

In separating the economic power of surplus goods accumulation from the political position of the aristocracy, and in creating a middle class of Merina traders, Andrianampoinimerina assured the continuing success of his programme of unification.

Conclusion

These two extensive areas of eastern Africa had developed highly sophisticated and effective marketing systems many years before exposure to European commercialism. In both societies the market-place had a virtual monopoly on commerce. In both cases the very large markets which often numbered attendances in tens of thousands tended to be dissociated from pre-existing settlements (despite the fact that they eventually became more closely linked with other urban functions). Both marketing systems were organised regularly and efficiently in time and in space, although in Ethiopia the dominant thread of spatial organisation was the network of trading caravan routes. Both satisfied important social needs.

However, in Ethiopia, markets were dominated by outsiders, their caravan routes, and their currency. In Madagascar, trade depended on indigenous produce and on a 'home-grown' currency system, and largely excluded foreigners. Ethiopia has long been a society of rented land, prestation and gift exchange, yet it has supported a dense network of markets due largely to the Islamic outsiders and their caravan routes and, to a lesser degree, to Ethiopia's vast range of environments. In Madagascar, Andrianampoinimerina undermined traditional systems to free at least part of the surplus production for regional marketing which resulted in greater specialisation. Also, markets were a political tool in his hands. In Ethiopia, markets in many ways were a stabilising feature, but one controlled by largely alien interests, overlying a highly fragmented and changing political structure. In Madagascar, trade was part of an internal political drive for unity, from which aliens were necessarily excluded, and in which 'political ideas which will contribute to the happiness of the people were nourished' (TNA, 617).

[1] Author's translation from the French original text.

[2] Caravans from Massawa to Gondar, a journey of some 550 km (340 miles) took up to five months en route (Pankhurst, 1964, 58).

[3] Even so, when the author visited a remote area in 1968, his party was warned that it might be advisable to take salt.

[4] It is still on sale in Gemu markets as an animal lick (Russell, 1969, 72), but is of poor quality.

[5] It was under Andrianampoinimerina that many of the great land reclamation and swamp drainage schemes of Imerina were undertaken. These resulted in a greatly expanded area of terraced paddy rice fields which are the chief characteristic of the landscapes around Tananarive today.

[6] All quotations from the chronicles are the author's translation. Page numbers refer to the Chapus and Ratsimba translation.

[7] *Lambas* had a high value not only as everyday dress but as shrouds for the dead. Each year at the ceremony of *famadihana* held in June, the remains of ancestors would be wrapped in new shrouds at family tombs throughout the country.

5 Periodic Markets in the Caspian lowlands of Iran

J. Keith Thorpe

In recent years considerable attention has been given to periodic markets in the tropics but there have been very few market-place studies in the Middle East. This may be partly due to the fact that the conditions necessary for the existence of closely integrated systems of periodic markets are fulfilled in only a few localities[1] (Coon, 1951, 179; Benet, 1961, 88). Much of the Middle East is characterised by harsh environments with meagre and unevenly distributed soil and water resources. In the few regions which produce a substantial agricultural surplus, there is a long tradition of commercial exchanges associated with long-distance trade routes. Their fairly abundant water supplies and fertile soils support comparatively dense populations, sometimes with large tribal elements. Where markets have arisen, they are frequently not located within an established settlement but rather at an open site, marked by few permanent buildings, which becomes the focus of economic, social and even political activity for the surrounding area one or two days each week.

Only in the rural Maghreb have such internal trading systems been documented to any degree. In a number of studies, the origins, distribution, functional organisation and internal patterns of weekly markets or suqs in Morocco and Algeria have been investigated (Fogg, 1932, 1935, 1939; Benet, 1957; Mikesell, 1958), and central place concepts have been applied to suq systems in northern Morocco (Schmitz, 1973a, 1973b). Considerable scope still remains for further studies of these phenomena in similar regional environments of the Middle East where systems of weekly rotating markets are present: the Nile valley and delta; the Tihama, Najran and Hadramaut regions of Saudi Arabia; the Al Hasa oasis; the Yemen; the Black Sea coast of Turkey; and the sub-tropical Caspian littoral of Iran.

This essay is concerned with periodic markets on the plain of Gilan, in the Caspian littoral. This area provides an empirical testing ground for a number of hypotheses that recur in current market-place research, as yet unexamined in a Middle Eastern context. Indeed, several hypotheses have been advanced in recent years to explain the principles governing the relationship between the temporal and locational spacing of periodic markets (two characteristics that are shared by

* I wish to acknowledge the award of travel grants under the Hayter Award Scheme which made the field work in 1972-73 possible.

all market systems), and to reconcile these principles with some of the propositions of central place theory (Smith and Hay, 1970). Most of the theoretical notions formulated are normative; they are largely efficiency notions serving as a framework from which to measure the extent of any deviations exhibited by reality. The initial proposition considered is essentially temporal, though with spatial implications; it concerns the question of whether there is an even distribution of market meetings on the seven days of the week,[2] or whether major, minor, or even minimal market days can be distinguished (Symanski, 1973, 262-266). Observations are based on both the numerical incidence of markets and the volume of market activity as measured by the number of sellers present in markets held on different days of the week.

The second proposition to be considered is that the temporal and locational spacing of periodic markets is complementary. This implies that there is an efficient space-time synchronisation of weekly market sequences (Berry, 1967, 94; Bromley, 1971, 128), a characteristic that appears to be common to most systems of cyclic markets. Market days of neighbouring communities are staggered temporally to permit even the most remote elements in a dispersed rural population the opportunity of visiting at least one market each week. This temporal and spatial arrangement in turn facilitates the movement of mobile traders making their weekly rounds of markets. Consumer and trader hypotheses provide an additional means of examining whether or not a direct relationship exists between periodicity and locational spacing. Finally, the proposition that periodic markets are space competitive is examined, using nearest neighbour analysis to test for the presence of spatially organising effects in a point pattern of markets. In almost every case, data for 1915 and 1973 are used; hence change is an implicit concern of the study.

The plain of Gilan is situated by the south-west corner of the Caspian Sea. The Caspian littoral reaches its greatest width of just over 30 km (19 miles) at this point. Gilan consists essentially of an alluvial lowland formed by the delta of the river Sefid Rud, which breaches the Elburz mountains to the south, and smaller rivers entering the Mordab lagoon. It has the most extensive system of periodic markets of any part of the Caspian coastlands; they occur all along the coast of neighbouring Mazanderan, particularly where the plain broadens out again in the vicinity of Babol, Sari, and Shahi (Thompson and Huies, 1968, 219) and on the edge of Gorgan to the more steppe-like eastern borders. Water, soil, and vegetal resources are abundant throughout this zone in contrast with the more arid Iranian plateau. This coastal region is densely populated, with average densities in many localities in Gilan and Mazanderan frequently exceeding 80 persons per square kilometre (210 per square mile), which is well above the critical threshold for periodic markets (Hodder, 1965, 50). On the Gilan plain population densities in excess of 250 inhabitants per square kilometre (650 per square mile) are not unusual, particularly in the areas of intensive rice monoculture on the left bank of the Sefid Rud and in parts of Fumenat. Indeed, the heavily populated plain and the region termed Gilan are almost synonomous in popular Iranian usage, although the administrative province (Ostan) includes large areas of mountainous, sparsely-peopled country within its boundaries.

Temporal Patterns of Market Periodicity in Gilan

The presence of the Islamic seven-day market week in Gilan is of great antiquity, introduced into the region following its gradual colonisation after the Arab conquests. Activity in these seven-day periodic market systems is subject to diurnal rhythms as well as variations in the volume of activity on different days of the week. Most of the markets in Gilan are day-long affairs, although dealings in livestock and local peasant produce (rice, fruit and vegetables, eggs, etc.) are usually completed by mid-day, particularly in the summer months. Itinerant merchants remain on market sites until late afternoon or early evening which is often their busiest time of the day.[3]

Variations in the weekly periodicity of market meetings have received some attention in current work on periodic markets. In two recent studies using evidence from West Africa (Hill and Smith, 1972) and Latin America (Symanski, 1973), hypotheses have been proposed to account for the differences in the numbers of markets held on different days of the week. These hypotheses will be tested using evidence from the plain of Gilan in 1915 and 1973. By using data for different time periods, generalisations about what is essentially a dynamic system can be made. However, as is so often the case in historical reconstruction, availability of data frequently determines the choice of time period. Few areas of the developing world with rural marketing systems have any documentary materials that contain information about past patterns of local markets, although there are a few notable exceptions such as in the gazetteers of rural China (Skinner, 1964, 3-43). Data on market periodicities in Gilan were available in a detailed collection of information about the province compiled by the British Vice-Consul in Gilan on the eve of World War I (Rabino, 1913, 1915-16, 64-5). In addition, several markets known to exist at this time but not enumerated by Rabino were identified after interviewing and cross-checking with senior key informants.[4] The material for the present was obtained during field investigations. Information from these two sources on the frequency of market meetings on different days of the week is presented in Table 5.1.

The first hypothesis to be considered is that there is a specific day of the week that is the most important market day (Symanski, 1973, 262). In a study of four Hausa Emirates in northern Nigeria, Hill and Smith (1972, 346-7) advanced the hypothesis that in an essentially Muslim area, Friday should be the most popular day for market meetings. This arrangement would enable those customers in attendance to make market sales and/or purchases and visit the Friday mosque, which would appear to be a common feature of most large Friday markets in Hausaland. Indeed, an above-average number of larger markets was held on Friday in each of the four Emirates, although for only two was the chi-square value significant. Friday again proved to be the major market day when, for one area, the number of cement stalls present in different market-places was used as a measure of market activity.

Market-day frequencies in Gilan do not support this hypothesis (Table 5.1). In both 1915 and 1973, Friday has a below-average number of market meetings per day, particularly in 1973 when only three markets (7 per cent) are held on a Friday. The proposition that there is an even distribution of markets throughout the week was tested using chi-square for both time periods, but in neither case was chi-square significant. In fact, the temporal periodicity for 1915 demonstrates a relatively even distribution. This dispersal of market days throughout the week may have been encouraged by the presence of well-developed market cycles with close temporal synchronisation. Apart from Friday and Monday, all days of the week have an above-average number of markets. Sunday and Thursday with nine markets each have the highest number, with Tuesday, Wednesday

Table 5.1 Frequency of market meetings on different days of the week 1915 and 1973

Day of the week	Number of market meetings[a]			
	1915	% of weekly total	1973	% of weekly total
Sunday	9	16.7	6	14.0
Monday	5	9.2	9	20.9
Tuesday	8	14.8	4	9.3
Wednesday	8	14.8	7	16.2
Thursday	9	16.7	8	18.6
Friday	7	13.0	3	7.0
Saturday	8	14.8	6	14.0
Total number of market meetings	54	100.0	43	100.0
Chi-square	1.48[b]		4.37[b]	
Mean number of market meetings	7.70		6.10	
Number of market-places	46		36	
Mean number of meetings per market-place	1.17		1.19	

Source: Rabino, 1915-16, 64-65 and interviews with key informants for 1915; field survey for 1973.

[a] Because two market meetings occur at some market-places each week, the total number of market meetings exceeds the number of market-places for each year.

[b] Not significant.

and Saturday each having eight markets. By 1973 the total number of market days had declined from 54 to 43 meetings with an apparently less even temporal distribution. Friday and Tuesday both have below-average numbers of markets, with Saturday and Sunday equal to the market-day average. However, Monday now appears as the major market day with nine meetings, with Thursday (eight markets) and Wednesday (seven markets) not far behind.

On the basis of these findings, the hypothesis that a significantly greater number of markets occur on Fridays in this area of Islamic culture must be rejected. Symanski's proposition that there is a major market day can be accepted tentatively for the contemporary situation, but the existence in the past of two and possibly more market days cannot be ruled out. Along the western Caspian littoral, only one other Friday market (Motelghu) operates. It is over 150 km (93 miles) from the study area and functions during the summer months.[5]

Some notable changes in periodicity have occurred in the last sixty years in Gilan, the most significant being the decrease in the number of Tuesday markets (from eight to four) and of Friday markets (from seven to three). However, Monday meetings have increased from five to nine to make Monday the major market day. Other days have changed less: thus, there are fewer Saturday, Sunday, Wednesday and Thursday markets, with the latter two declining by only one.

Table 5.2 Market day meetings and the numbers of sellers 1973

Day of market	Number of market meetings	Total number of sellers present in markets occurring on this day	% of total	Mean number of sellers per market meeting
Sunday	6	681	10	114
Monday	9	1210	19	133
Tuesday	4	966	15	242
Wednesday	7	755	12	108
Thursday	8	996	16	125
Friday	3	695	11	232
Saturday	6	1083	17	181
Total	43	6386	100	149[a]

Source: Field enumeration, August-September, 1973.

[a] This is the mean number of sellers at each market meeting; there were on average 177 sellers at each market-place in a typical week.

The data in Table 5.2 on the total number of sellers attending market meetings on each day of the week for 1973 can be used to evaluate the major market day hypothesis. Monday again appears as the most important market day with almost one-fifth of all sellers, followed by Saturday, Thursday, Tuesday and Wednesday in that order. Sunday and Friday attract the smallest total number of traders. However, even Monday would not appear to achieve the same dominance exhibited by the major market day in certain areas of West Africa (Hill and Smith, 1972, 347) or Latin America (Symanski, 1973, 262-4). This may be explained partly by the growing importance of permanent service centres in Gilan, particularly the regional primacy of Rasht, which is gradually reducing dependence on some of the traditional weekly markets.

Analysis of total seller attendance for each market day, broken down into size categories according to the number of sellers present at each individual market meeting (Fig. 5.1a), shows that on Tuesdays and Fridays (the two days with a below-average incidence of markets), there is a tendency for the actual size of markets (by number of sellers) to be well above average. Saturday also enjoyed an above-average number of larger markets. Smaller markets with less than 100 sellers occur largely on Mondays, Wednesdays, and Thursdays (the days with the highest frequencies of market days), although some markets with more than 150 sellers occur on these days also.

Several of these smaller markets have been established quite recently, mostly in a spontaneous fashion by a few itinerant traders seeking more profitable outlets for their goods on the busiest market days.[6] Consequently, evidence from the plain of Gilan fails to confirm the observations made in the Hausa Emirates (Hill and Smith, 1972, 346-7) where there is a tendency for the most important market day in numerical terms also to contain most of the largest markets.

Just as a temporal dispersion of market activity occurs throughout the week, there is some differentiation of market activity in a hierarchical sense. When the information on different market day activity is assembled for the whole week, there is a clear tendency for the numbers of sellers present to group into distinct size categories (Figure 5.1b). Such a hierarchical tendency would appear to be consistent with the logic of one of the main propositions of central place theory

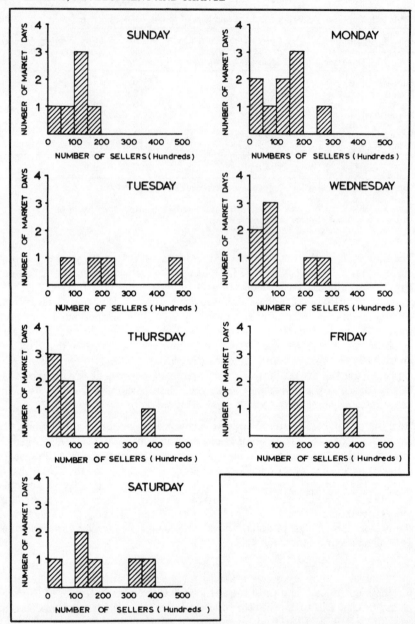

Figure 5.1a   Number of market meetings and sellers by day of the week, Gilan Plain, 1973

(Smith and Hay, 1970, 15-16). Furthermore, broad temporal patterns may be distinguished within this hierarchical context. In general, on those days when there are very few market meetings in Gilan the markets that do occur frequently are well above average in volume of activity. In contrast, there is an above-average incidence of small markets with less than the mean number of sellers on those days with the largest concentration of market meetings. This situation is

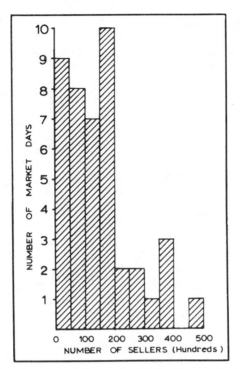

Figure 5.1b   Number of market meetings and sellers for the market week, Gilan Plain, 1973

different from that prevailing in Hausaland (Hill and Smith, 1972, 346-7), where the most important market days in numerical terms also tend to include most of the largest markets.

There are a number of possible explanations for the generally low incidence of Friday markets on the Gilan plain and the decline in their numbers since 1915. Friday markets are completely absent from urban centres in both time periods. Such markets usually occur in villages not associated with a Friday mosque. In the urban market centres, Friday closing is enforced by most major trades but especially those trades in which traditional guilds are still important (for example, goldsmiths, coppersmiths and drapers). Traders in these fields who wish to engage in business on a Friday must travel to village markets where no such restrictions apply. Moreover, the authority of the Islamic clergy (mullahs) is strongest in urban areas and they sometimes have the power to influence the choice of a market day. Thus the bazaar of Astaneh, which is held on land owned by a Holy Shrine, was a Friday market for some years until 1942 when clergy and prominent local leaders managed to have it changed to Thursday because of an emerging conflict of interest between the day of prayer (namaz) and the increasingly busy market day. A more recent phenomenon has been for a growing number of traders to make Friday a rest day. With the higher population densities and purchasing power of Gilan compared to other rural areas in Iran, there may be economic as well as religious reasons for this behaviour.[7]

It is difficult to account for the importance of Monday as the major market day in 1973, both numerically and by amount of activity. Monday marks approximately the middle of the Islamic week and in that sense is furthest removed from the two other busiest market days of the week, Thursday and Saturday. The rise in its popularity since 1915, when it was the minimal market day, is also most noticeable. Three bi-weekly markets now have meetings on Monday. A mid-week market in this context would appear to be as convenient for most peasants and traders as any other day in a temporally well-integrated system of markets.

Saturday and Thursday are relatively popular days both by the number of markets held and the number of sellers present: Saturday sees a resurgence of business after the 'day of rest', with Thursday preceding it. Thursday is considered a good day in Iran to visit holy places, and at least two Thursday markets (Astaneh and Seysharafshah) are held on land adjoining important shrines.

The minor market day hypothesis (Symanski, 1973, 264) should also be considered. This proposes that where a market is held more than once a week on the same site, it is possible to distinguish between a major market day and at least one minor market day. The evidence from Gilan is somewhat limited, although there are seven bi-weekly markets in existence at the present time.[8] In all but one market (Pir Baste Loulman), a major and a minor market day can be distinguished on the basis of seller attendance. This is especially the case with the Monday and Thursday markets where Monday is invariably the minor day. The other combinations of days are Sunday and Wednesday, and Tuesday and Saturday.[9] There has been a tendency for the temporal spacing between market meetings to increase: in 1915, four of eight bi-weekly market meetings were separated by just a day, whereas in 1973 there were five market-places with a two-day separation of meetings one with a three-day separation.

The minimal market day hypothesis (that the lowest volume of market activity in a week will occur on the day immediately after the major market day) was almost impossible to test. It was only really applicable to the larger urban markets, such as Astaneh, Langarud, and Fumen, with both major and minor market days. Many itinerant traders based in these town markets sell there only on market days and spend the rest of the week visiting markets in surrounding villages. Non-periodic functions that are present for the whole of the week tend to cater for demand on non-market days, so that the amount of activity is not subject to any great daily fluctuations.

There is almost no evidence to support the notion of a wholesale market day, in which the day preceding the major market day in large markets will be devoted mainly to wholesaling. The only exception is the Thursday livestock market that precedes the Friday bazaar held at Gourab Zar Mikh. Usually, however, the wholesale buying and bulking of produce such as rice, fruit and vegetables, eggs, etc., takes place on a normal market day.

The Space-Time Synchronisation of Periodic Markets

The organisation of market-places into weekly schedules or cycles involves a spatial dimension. As Ukwu has pointed out, 'competition between periodic markets is thus partly spatial and partly temporal' (Hodder and Ukwu, 1969, 159). There must be a relatively efficient space-time interlocking of market meetings if each market site is to succeed in attracting the necessary threshold population, and the observations of the British Vice-Consul in Gilan in the early 1900s are of interest: '[the] bazaars called gurab are places where markets are held periodically . . . [they] are only found in Gilan and western Mazanderan and, as a rule, they should be at least four miles distant from one another' (Rabino, 1913, 435). On another occasion he mentions the bi-weekly bazaar of Dehshal, which was formerly held on a Saturday and Tuesday, but which was changed to a Sunday and Wednesday because of competition from the newly established Tuesday and Thursday bazaar of Astaneh only nine km (six miles) away. There have been several attempts to provide a sound theoretical base for the study of this aspect of periodic market cycles. The classic example is that of Stine (1962), who provided an essentially economic explanation for the existence of periodic markets. This was based on the central place concepts of the threshold and the maximum range of a good. In an economy characterised by low levels of consumer demand and lack of specialisation, firms must frequently become mobile if they are to stay in business. By concentrating demand for production at certain localities on specified days of the week and grouping these selected markets in a coordinated schedule, mobile firms can conduct a sufficient (threshold) amount of trade in several places in a market circuit to remain viable, whilst consumers lessen the physical distance they must travel to obtain goods and services needed (maximum range). Thus, 'the consumer by submitting to the discipline of time is able to free himself from the discipline of space' (Stine, 1962, 70). However, there are options open to a trader other than becoming periodic: he can engage in part-time marketing to complement the time spent in producing or processing the goods traded (Hay, 1971, 395-6).

There have been few attempts to test the hypothesis that cyclic market systems are spatially and temporally synchronised. Using data on Ghanaian periodic markets, Fagerlund and Smith (1970, 342-3), examined the proposition that there was an inverse relationship between locational and temporal spacing. This hypothesis implies that the average distance between markets held on the same day of the week is greater than that between market meetings separated by one or more days in time, and involved measuring the distance from each market in a set of periodic market-places to the closest market held on the same day, pre- and post-adjacent days and on one full day earlier or later or two full days earlier or later.[10] The mean distances for each set of measurements were then calculated to give locational spacing values for these different data sets. Similar analyses have been applied to periodic market systems elsewhere in West and East Africa (Smith, 1971a, 328-35, and Good, 1972, 212, respectively) but apart from a recent contribution by R.H.T. Smith (1972, 592-3), few attempts have been made to apply this analysis to areas outside tropical Africa.

The data presented in Table 5.3 provide partial confirmation of the hypothesis that there is an efficient temporal and spatial synchronisation of markets in Gilan, although neither is in complete accord with the proposition. Markets meeting on the same day in both cases have the largest average locational spacing, almost twice as great as markets held on pre- and post-adjacent days. A trend towards a decline in locational spacing values with increasing temporal separation is also evident, except for meetings separated by one full day earlier or later, where there is a slight increase in locational spacing. An almost identical anomaly is present in the market cycles of two other Islamic areas subjected to similar analyses: Katsina Emirate, northern Nigeria, and part of the old Spanish zone of Morocco (R.H.T. Smith, 1972, 592). The reasons for this anomaly, apart from the obvious one of inaccurate data sources, are unclear, and further testing of the

Table 5.3 Temporal and locational spacing of markets in the Gilan Plain

Temporal spacing (days)	Locational spacing[a] (kilometres) 1915	1973
Same day	17.6	21.8
Pre- or post-adjacent day	9.8	11.2
One full day earlier or later	10.6	12.2
Two full days earlier or later	7.4	7.2
Nearest market (regardless of day of meeting)	6.2	6.7

Source: for 1915, Rabino (1915-16); and field survey for 1973.

[a] Measurements are based on straight line distances between markets, and while this could lead to possible underestimation, especially for 1915 when local communication networks were a little more circuitous than nowadays, it was desirable to use the same measurement scheme for the two time periods.

hypothesis in contrasting areas of Islamic culture is necessary. Markets in the Gilan plain were, in general, rather more closely spaced in 1915 than in 1973. This is a reflection of the poorer transport facilities in the former period and also of the growing importance of permanent service centres at the present time (particularly of Rasht, the regional metropolis).

In Table 5.4, the mean locational spacing of same-day markets for the seven days of the week is recorded along with the frequency of market meetings. Although the mean for the overall locational spacing has increased since 1915, some rather marked changes in the separation of markets on different days of the week are concealed (this is, of course, partly related to the changes in the temporal frequency of market meetings). The most dramatic change is for Tuesday markets: the average distance between market-places has more than doubled as the number of meetings has been halved. However, there is no consistent relationship between changes in the temporal incidence of markets and changes in locational spacing. The number of Friday meetings declined from seven to three between 1915 and 1973, but their spatial separation has hardly altered. The distances separating Thursday markets was over twice as great in 1973 as in 1915; the number changed little through the selective decline of some markets and the establishment of others on new sites. Apart from the decrease in Monday market spacings with the addition of new meetings, most other changes in locational spacing have been rather less important.

The existence of either a direct or an inverse relationship between market periodicity and locational spacing is related to the question of which group of market users, traders or consumers, is the more influential in determining the optimum spatio-temporal coordination of a market system. Traders vary greatly in their degree of mobility: some are part-time farmers or craftsmen who visit only one or two markets weekly, returning to their village after each market day; others are travelling salesmen who visit all the markets in a particular schedule in order to minimise movement costs (subject to the constraint of maximising consumer attendance). Between these extremes there is a range of sellers who circulate around different combinations of market-places in a sequence but do not visit every market occurring in the market week. Consumers are usually rural dwellers who visit markets mainly to satisfy subsistence needs, but they may also engage in trade. They must balance the movement costs of travelling to another

Table 5.4   Mean locational spacing of same day markets and number of market meetings
1915 and 1973

Day	Mean locational spacing (kilometres)		Number of market meetings	
	1915	1973	1915	1973
Sunday	19.0	17.9	9	6
Monday	31.5	20.0	5	9
Tuesday	18.7	43.6	8	4
Wednesday	15.8	15.7	8	7
Thursday	8.5	20.1	9	8
Friday	13.7	14.5	7	3
Saturday	16.3	20.5	8	6
Mean locational spacing of same day markets	17.6	21.8	–	–
Number of market-places	–	–	46	36

Source: Field Survey, 1972-73; Rabino, 1915-16; Table 5.1.

nearest market day (in time) in a cycle against the cost of waiting for another meeting up to two full days earlier or later than the day in question.

Data limitations do not permit the use of highly sophisticated techniques of analysis in this problem, but a simple test was developed by R.H.T. Smith for what he refers to as the travelling trader and consumer hypotheses (R.H.T. Smith, 1971b, 1-4; 1972, 352-3). The trader hypothesis proposes that there is a direct relationship between periodicity and locational spacing of markets, whilst the consumer proposition suggests that an inverse relationship is appropriate. Locational spacing values must be computed for each hypothesis: for the consumer hypothesis mean distances between neighbouring periodic markets for the different time lags separating their occurrence must be obtained (same day, pre- and post-adjacent day, etc. as in Table 5.3); for the trader hypothesis only the distances between post-adjacent markets were recorded on the assumption that a trader, in order to minimise distance, will look forward in time to the next market to be visited in a schedule.

The results of these calculations are presented in Figure 5.2. For both time periods, the recorded values would appear to support the consumer hypothesis with a reduction in locational spacing as temporal spacing increases. However, in each case there is a slight reversal of the trend between pre- and post-adjacent days and pre- and post-adjacent plus one days. In both 1915 and 1973 (but especially for the latter period), the spacing values for travelling traders were larger than those for consumers. Moreover, the tendency for trader locational spacing to decrease with separation in time, which runs counter to the trader hypothesis, is more pronounced for 1973 up to the post-adjacent day plus two. After this there is a sharper, though inconsistent reversal in spacing compared with the earlier period. The evidence seems to suggest that there is greatest support for the consumer hypothesis: market meetings are synchronised more to meet the needs of consumers than travelling traders.

In 1915 travelling trader schedules involving visits to several market-places before returning to home base appear to have been more common. Nowadays the use of motorised transport permits most sellers to return home after every

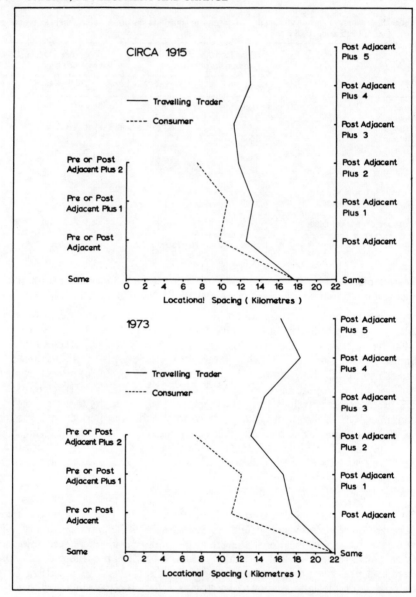

Figure 5.2   Temporal and locational spacing in 1915 (a) and 1973 (b), Gilan Plain

market meeting. Rabino cites an instance of the itinerant pedlars or 'Bazaarmadj' who, in the early part of this century, travelled by boat or 'keredji' from Enzeli (Bandar Pahlavi) to the Tuesday, Wednesday, and Thursday markets of Talesh Dulab (Fig. 5.3) returning, via the Friday meeting at Koupourchal, to Enzeli for its Saturday bazaar (Rabino, 1915-16, 141). Today the markets of Talesh Dulab are linked by a sealed motor road so that the circuitous route is no longer necessary.

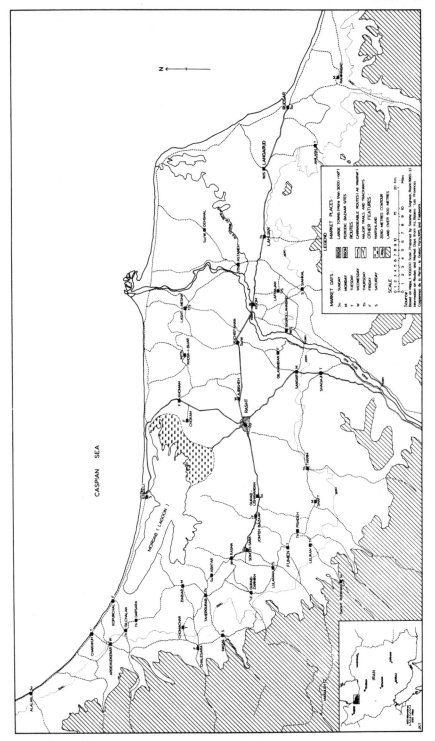

Figure 5.3   Periodic markets on the Gilan Plain, 1915

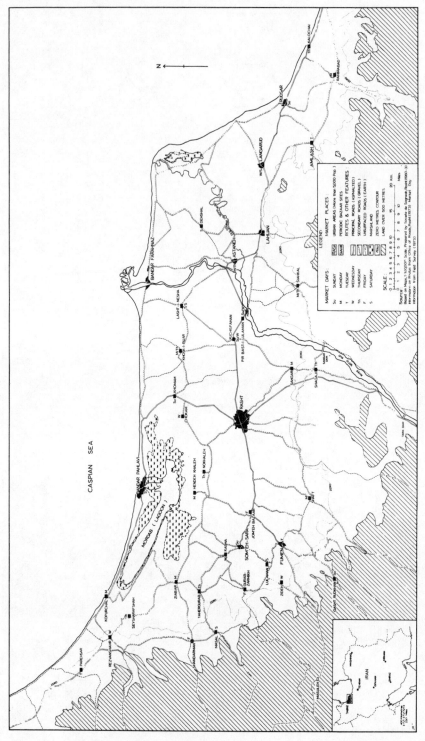

Figure 5.4   Periodic markets on the Gilan Plain, 1973

Spatial Competition and the Location of Periodic Markets

The distribution of periodic markets on the plain of Gilan is shown in Figures 5.3 (1915) and 5.4 (1973). The distribution of market-places in 1915 shows a greater linear disposition than in 1973. Markets in the first period are associated with a broadly dendritic pattern of transport routes focussing on smaller coastal centres but on Rasht in particular, which was the chief bulking point for the rice, silk and timber exported to Russia. By 1973, no weekly markets were located within a 12-15 km (8-9 miles) radius of Rasht owing to its improved accessibility, and the selective decline in markets in other parts of the plain suggests a still rather irregular spacing between those remaining. The same subjective conclusion is reached in a study of rural markets in Bangla Desh by Patel, who argued that the propositions of central place theory, regarding a uniform spacing of centres, did not apply (Patel, 1963, 151). However, nearest neighbour analysis (King, 1969, 100) of the pattern of market-places yields results which suggest that this conclusion should be challenged. The mean distance measurements for Gilan in 1915 and 1973 involved 46 and 36 market-places, respectively, in an area of 4,470 square kilometres (1,730 square miles).[11]

The nearest neighbour values for the market system in Gilan in 1915 and in 1973 (Table 5.5) are based on distances measured from each market-place to its six nearest neighbours regardless of day of meeting. In both years and for all six neighbours, the R_n values indicate a distribution that tends towards uniformity. In the context of central place theory, this would appear to provide evidence for the existence of forces of spatial competition, but several caveats should be noted. In general, the R_n values are higher in 1973 than in 1915, and this could be attributed to improvements in transportation and increasing population densities which have intensified the effects of spatial competition between market-places. In fact, R_n values in 1915 record a decline for the first three nearest neighbours before this trend is reversed; for 1973 R_n values, there is a

Table 5.5   Nearest neighbour statistics for periodic market-places on the Plain of Gilan, 1915 and 1973

| Neighbour (k) | 1915 | | 1973 | |
	Near neighbour statistic[a] (R_n)	Type of distribution[b]	Near neighbour statistic[a] (R_n)	Type of distribution[b]
1	1.2640	Uniform	1.2349	Uniform
2	1.1470	Uniform	1.2851	Uniform
3	1.1080	Uniform	1.2071	Uniform
4	1.1501	Uniform	1.2185	Uniform
5	1.1888	Uniform	1.2530	Uniform
6	1.1849	Uniform	1.3082	Uniform

Source: calculations on distances between market-places in Fig. 5.3 and 5.4.

[a] Ratio of the observed average distance to kth nearest neighbour (r_0) to the expected average distance to nearest neighbour r_e, where $r_e = \dfrac{0.26136}{\sqrt{n(\frac{n}{a})}}$,

n = number of market-places, a = area of study region .

[b] These are descriptive labels, as significance tests were not applied.

general rise (from 1.23 for neighbour 1 to 1.30 for neighbour 6). In the few instances in which nearest neighbour techniques have been applied to patterns of market-places, the first nearest neighbour has usually been selected (Fagerlund and Smith, 1970, 345; Good, 1972, 214; Jackson, 1971, 38; Smith, 1971b, 339). Of course, the selection of first nearest neighbours is essentially arbitrary and time-saving; the choice of second, third, or nth nearest neighbours can provide more information about a pattern and can occasionally yield different results. The R_n value provides no more than a numerical description of the spatial form of a pattern, and it should, if appropriate, be qualified by the calculation of a z-score (Clark and Evans, 1954, 448)[12].

Same day markets have the widest average spacing (Table 5.3), which suggests that there is a space-competitive process in operation. Nearest neighbour analyses of the spatial patterns of markets meeting on each day of the week were conducted, but because the number of market-places was very small (ranging from three to nine, see Table 5.1), the results are not recorded in detail here. It is worth noting that in both 1915 and 1973, there is a tendency towards a uniform distribution of markets on four days of the week when distances to first nearest neighbour were used; these figures rise to five days and six days, respectively, when a second nearest neighbour is considered.[13] Friday is the only day of the week that fails to conform to this trend for all neighbours for both periods. It approaches a random distribution in 1915 but tends to aggregation in 1973 when only three Friday markets remain. Thursday in 1915 is the only other day that shows any tendency to aggregation although it registers a random distribution when the second nearest neighbour is taken.[14] On both Thursday and Friday in 1915 a number of closely spaced sets of markets held on the same day can be distinguished on the map (Fig. 5.3). However, the nearest neighbour statistic is unable to distinguish between a single and a multi-clustered pattern. Other anomalous results occur for Wednesday markets on both occasions and for Sunday meetings at the present time although a uniform arrangement is indicated when second (and third) nearest neighbours are examined.

Thus, there is an overall tendency towards uniformity of market spacing for both 1915 and 1973 in over half the days of the week when the first nearest neighbour is taken and in more than two-thirds of days when second and third neighbours are chosen. This indicates at least a partial confirmation of the hypothesis that the effects of spatial competition are greater than those of spatial variation (or aggregation) in generating market distribution patterns in Gilan.

Conclusion

Periodic markets are an almost universal feature of rural exchange economies in less developed countries, but the study of the spatial and temporal characteristics of these important institutions was neglected until quite recently. The Middle East is an area with a number of regional exchange systems involving periodic markets, and it too has not received the attention it deserves. The first group of hypotheses examined concerned temporal variations in the periodicity of market meetings grouped under the headings of major, minor, minimal, and wholesale market days. Evidence was found to support the first two notions although Friday failed to emerge as the major market day as might have been anticipated in an Islamic area (Hill and Smith, 1972). There was no support for the last two propositions. Examination of temporal and locational spacing confirms the existence of efficiently synchronised market networks. The analysis of consumer and trader hypotheses of market location favoured, in spite of a slight inconsistency, the conclusion that market spacings served the needs of consumers rather than travelling traders. Analysis of the Gilan plain data in connection with the last proposition that periodic markets are space competitive, suggested that there is a general tendency towards regularity of spacing both for the overall market system and for the majority of same day markets. The study of changing market place systems has been described as a sensitive index of modernisation (Skinner, 1964, 3). Analysing the spatio-temporal relationships of markets in various places at different times can thus assist in testing developments in the role and efficiency of a marketing system. The varied environments and cultures of the Middle East offer considerable scope for further research on this problem.

[1] However, elements of such systems are latent throughout the Middle East in the way that the products of rural areas tend to arrive in city bazaars on appointed days of the week. An example is the Saturday market or 'Shambe Bazaar' of Kerman in south-west Iran, when a mart is held for livestock and beasts of burden. The Sunday bazaar of Shahpour in west Azerbaijan attracts sellers of sheep and goats from a 40 km (25 mile) radius and buyers from as far away as Tehran.

[2] The 'market week' and the seven-day Islamic week are, of course, identical.

[3] This would appear to be in contrast with the markets of central Mazanderan, where market activity has usually ceased by early afternoon. Morning markets, sometimes called matinee, are also common in large areas of Islamic North Africa: Morocco (Fogg, 1932, 260), Algeria (Benet, 1957, 194), and Libya (Blake, 1968, 26).

[4] A number of scattered references to the periodicity of some markets is available in the accounts of earlier travellers (Fraser, 1838, 482; 1826, 225-6; Monteith, 1833, 18; and Melgunof, 1868, 236-60).

[5] There is little detailed information available on market periodicities in other parts of the Middle East to use in further tests of these hypotheses. Of 38 markets in the Spanish zone of Morocco, Friday and Saturday possessed well below-average numbers of markets, with Monday and Thursday being the major market days (Fogg, 1938, 431).

[6] Examples of spontaneous market creation within the last five years include markets such as Hendeh Khaleh (Monday), Nokhaleh (Thursday), and Zideh (Wednesday).

[7] A recent survey of rural household expenditure by the Iranian Statistical Centre showed that total average expenditure by rural households in Gilan was almost 67 per cent higher than the average level for the rest of the country (Rural Household Consumption Survey, 1350, 117). (The year 1350 of the Iranian calendar corresponds approximately with 1971 in the western calendar.)

[8] The bi-weekly markets both now and in 1915 were located in the vicinity of the right and left banks of the Sefid Rud. This area has long possessed the most reliable irrigation network in Gilan and consequently the most intensive rice culture and highest population densities.

[9] Similar combinations of days for bi-weekly markets would seem to be common in other Islamic areas: Bangla Desh (Patel, 1963, 143), Afghanistan (Centlivres, 1972, 126), and Morocco (Fogg, 1938, 431).

[10] In the case of a seven-day market week, the maximum possible separation between market meetings is two complete days before or after any chosen market day.

[11] This area included all land below the 500 metre (1,645 feet) contour, minus the area of the Mordab lagoon and associated marshes which are uninhabited and of which large areas were under water in 1915. The actual land area for 1973 may still be slightly larger than sixty years ago owing to the outbuilding of the Sefid Rud delta. However, for purposes of comparability the present area is used in both cases.

[12] Such scores are not recorded here, because these calculations are based on all the market-places in the Plain of Gilan, not on a sample. Further, inferences are not made to the network of market-places elsewhere in Iran (of which the market-places in the Gilan Plain might be construed a sample).

[13] Dacey (1963) provides a discussion of the problems raised in the analysis of bounded areas and their effect on R_n values. Some difficulties were encountered owing to the artificially high R_n values for some days resulting from a boundary effect. The location of markets on these days of the week near the edge of the study area gave excessively large r_o values. In the measurement of observed mean distances (r_o) to nearest neighbours the boundary of the study area was practically ignored in order to reduce possible bias. The distribution of markets within the plain of Gilan is such that only three measurements across the boundary were necessary.

[14] When the third nearest neighbour is taken it approximates to a uniform spacing, bringing the number of market days with patterns approaching uniform to six for both time periods. Friday is again the exception on both occasions, tending to a random distribution in 1915 and aggregated pattern in 1973.

6 *Maket raun:* the introduction of periodic markets to Papua New Guinea
R. Gerard Ward, Diana Howlett, C.C. Kissling, and H.C. Weinand

In most countries where periodic markets are found, they have existed for centuries as part of the traditional socio-economic organisation. In Europe, such markets pre-date the rise of industrialism and in most parts of the Third World they existed before the penetration of European forms of mercantilism and colonialism. With increasing urbanisation periodic markets often declined in relative importance. Transport improvements, and rising densities of population with greater disposable personal income, allowed firms to command threshold populations from central places without resorting to itinerant trading.

Planners have tended to overlook the advantages provided by periodicity of service, and periodic markets have been seen as part of the pre-modern economy in developing areas. The common assumption that 'modernisation' requires extensive transformation of traditional systems has led to neglect or rejection of some features of the pre-modern economy which could be integrated into the modern sector. The relative decline of periodic markets in Europe has tended (perhaps indirectly) to reinforce the view of Western planners' that such institutions in developing countries are likely to wane. The fact that periodic marketing is unimportant in North America where much central place and development theory has been enunciated may help account for the relative neglect of these systems of distribution as possible agents of development. Yet their very persistence in both developed and developing areas indicates that they play an important economic and social role.

The Papua New Guinea Context

In Papua New Guinea the pre-colonial society consisted of myriad small, undifferentiated, self-sufficient, non-monetary communities. Trading was rarely a specialised occupation and, in the absence of other prerequisites, had not led to the development of urban central places. However, commerce was a prime motive for penetration by the colonial powers. Central places were essential for the pursuit of the colonial administrative and economic goals. The colonial towns were exogenous, small, few in number and widely spaced. They were dependent on high technology transport by sea and air. Their links were directed towards the external, overseas economy and a very high proportion of the basic consumer goods, including food, required by the expatriate communities was imported. Initially, indigenes did not participate in the towns except in menial and unskilled capacities. Towns provided few services, other than administration, to the surrounding villages, and were not dependent on their rural hinterlands for their viability.[1]   Urban-village articulation was very weak and the gap between the traditional and modern sectors was (and remains) exceptionally wide.

Improvement of the level of living in rural areas depends on narrowing this gap and increasing the efficacy of urban-rural linkages. Until recently planning strategies have tended to reinforce the dichotomy between the two sectors. In the interests of achieving the maximum rate of economic growth, emphasis was placed on major projects, the formal sector, and the expatriate-dominated enclaves. Planners did not seek improvements through small changes compatible in scale and organisation with the traditional sector. Yet small changes which can diffuse readily through indigenous information networks may produce more far-reaching effects than elaborate multi-faceted proposals which are too complex for ready adoption.

With the establishment of self-government in 1972, the Government of Papua New Guinea began to re-orient the country's development strategies. The eight basic goals set out in the Improvement Plan for 1973-74 (Central Planning Office, 1973) include commitments to decentralisation of economic activities; emphasis on small-scale activities; more equal distribution of services throughout the country; and greater participation in the monetary sector by Papua New Guineans. The achievement of these goals required considerable reorganisation of the country's spatial structure. Locations once assumed to be most suitable for industries, service centres, road systems or government establishments under the former development philosophy of maximum possible rate of national economic growth are not necessarily compatible with the achievement of the new goals of self-reliance, greater participation and better levels of living for the majority of Papua New Guineans. Compared with many developing countries, Papua New Guinea has relatively few small service centres. One of the goverment's proposed strategies for improving conditions in rural areas is to encourage the development of 'rural growth centres' (small towns), which would bring a range of services closer to the village population and thereby provide some stimulus to monetary activity in their hinterlands.

In late 1973 the Papua New Guinea Central Planning Office invited several groups of geographers and planners to examine prospects for establishing rural growth centres in a variety of districts. The study on which this paper is based (Ward et al., 1974a and 1974b) was conducted in the Eastern Highlands District (Fig. 6.1), an area of relatively densely settled montane basins at elevations of above 1,500 metres (5,000 feet) in the central cordillera. The District has approximately 250,000 people engaged primarily in subsistence cultivation and coffee growing. The all-weather Highlands Highway, which crosses the northern part of the District, links an extensive network of feeder and minor roads of variable trafficability (Fig. 6.1).

In and near the two main towns of Goroka (1971 population 12,065) and Kainantu (2,124), scope exists for expansion of a variety of processing industries and commercial and service activities. Nevertheless, such development is unlikely to have much effect outside the immediate vicinity of the towns, except as a magnet for migrants. By encouraging concentration, this pattern of development, regardless of its economic rationality, may be directly antagonistic to rural

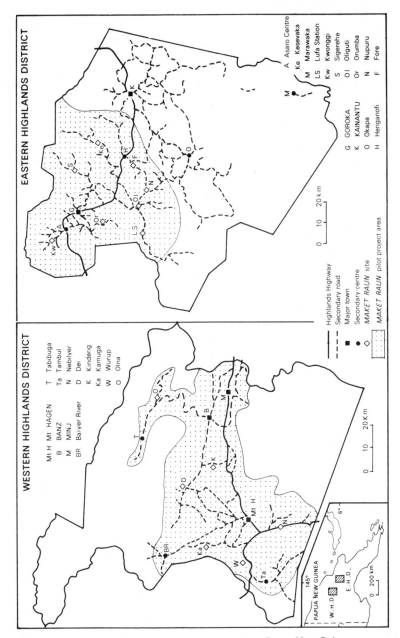

Figure 6.1   Western and Eastern Highlands Districts, Papua New Guinea

improvement. The establishment of scattered small centres with health, education, law and order, extension and basic retail services might appear to offer an
alternative to concentration in the two towns. However, the crucial dilemma is
that the provision of any service requires a market of sufficient population or
buying power to make that service viable. In most parts of Papua New Guinea

average cash income and population density are low. As a result, only urban areas of some size or a few restricted, populous and relatively wealthy rural areas have the required threshold population or purchasing power within a reasonable radius to support higher order services at fixed locations. Smaller centres can offer only a restricted range of low threshold services. The consequent smallness of such centres limits their role as purchasers and consumers of rural produce, and as stimulators of rural growth.

As higher order services are only provided in the larger centres people requiring them must either travel considerable distances at relatively high cost, or do without. Furthermore, if the potential consumer does get to town he is forced to seek services in an alien institutional context. Unfamiliarity with quantities, suppliers, store practices and terminology inhibits the full utilisation of higher order services and thus reduces the benefits such services should bring.[2] Conversely, because such services are unfamiliar and obtainable only in a context largely foreign to the consumer's experience, their benefits are not obvious to many potential users. Their power to motivate people to seek means of obtaining them (through, for example, increased cash crop production) is thus reduced. Given these circumstances, it seems likely that a 'rural growth centre' strategy based on fixed-point services could provide only limited benefits to a relatively small proportion of the rural population. An alternative is to provide services on a mobile basis.

Mobile Services and the *Maket Raun*

A mobile service expands its market by fulfilling demand at a series of points on successive days. It is thus able to offer higher order services and to reach a large proportion of the rural population. At present a number of mobile services operate in the District, including maternal and child care clinics, coffee and firewood buying, sale of secondhand clothes, agricultural extension, and some wholesaling. These services are not coordinated in time or space. Such coordination is essential if the maximum advantage of mobility is to be obtained. The coincidence of a range of activities at a periodic market-place will attract more people, thus giving the benefits of concentration of consumers to the sellers, while the consumers have the opportunity to compare and choose between sellers, goods and services.

Legal, capital and institutional prerequisites inhibit participation by Papua New Guineans in the urban formal sector (Goldring, 1973). On the other hand, participation in existing markets, commercial dances and parties and other informal commercial activities in the Eastern Highlands District shows that people are eager and able to engage in monetary sector activities, provided that the initial scale and entry requirements are not too high (see also Moulik, 1974).

Therefore, the establishment of a system of periodic markets, coordinated with visits by mobile government services was recommended (Ward *et al.*, 1974a). The name *maket raun*[3] has been proposed for the system. Through the *maket raun*, higher order goods and services offered in a familiar context should act as a motivating force for increased cash crop production through more thorough harvesting, greater planting or use of improved agricultural techniques (Ward *et al.*, 1974a). Provided that regulation of participation is kept at a minimum, the *maket raun* would afford opportunities for local people to engage in commercial activity on an occasional, and educative, basis. An increased flow of information is essential for rural improvement and research in West Africa suggests that in a semi-literate society the market-place is the most effective place for transmitting information (Johnson, 1974). The *maket raun* can also be used for extension work and informal adult education (Adler, 1973, 4). The coming together of people from a number of villages will increase the inter-village exchange. Any local specialisation in production might then be encouraged. The presence of outsiders (government personnel and commercial sellers) would bring potential purchasers into the rural areas because visitors must be fed and perhaps housed and entertained.

A system of periodic service centres appears to be the most promising means of slowing the current trend of economic polarisation; such a system should facilitate the more intensive urban-rural and rural-rural interaction that will be necessary if improvement innovations are to reach beyond the major towns and into the fabric of the traditional sector. The periodic markets should obviate many of the visits to town which are costly for villagers in both time and money and for which no alternative exists at present (Weinand, 1975).

Possible Functions of the *Maket Raun*

A detailed feasibility study of the *maket raun* proposal, setting out proposed functions, manpower, vehicle and other requirements, suggested sites, and indicated probable costs and benefits, is contained in Ward *et al.*, 1974b. If the *maket raun* is to be successful it must provide an attractive range of services: these should include advisory, welfare and educative services; purchasing of agricultural produce; sale of consumer goods; provision of tertiary services; and entertainment. A good mix of services is desirable to cater for all segments of the rural community.

Government services might include those of a generalist administrative officer and a community development advisor. One important role of these officers would be to advise villagers how and where to seek specialist services when required. The existing maternal and child care service should be integrated with the unit and would help attract women and children to the *maket raun*. A post office agency has an important role in encouraging spread of information. Local Government Council services might also be represented. It would be desirable, however, not to encumber the *maket raun* in the initial stages with the more restrictive or less welcome aspects of government, such as tax collecting and law enforcement.

A recent study of the highlands' pyrethrum industry stresses the need for banking facilities to be available when produce is sold (Scoullar, 1973, 22, 29-30). Many highlanders have small savings accounts but find it almost impossible and uneconomic to operate them because of the absence of local banking agencies. These should be provided at the *maket raun*. It is also desirable that advice on sources of development finance be available, through a business development or development bank representative. In the Philippines, rural credit advice and services are provided on a mobile basis and this has the advantage of bringing the advisors into wider contact with potential borrowers.

Government might sponsor initially a range of other services to be handed over later to local, private sector operators. These include a mechanic, whose initial role would be preventive maintenance on village-owned vehicles and education of their drivers; a letter-writer/clerk to assist in formal and informal communications; a veterinary officer, licensed to slaughter cattle for local sale in the *maket raun* and who could also provide instruction in butchering techniques; and an information and adult education officer to show films or run short classes. Initially, the justification for several such activities lies in their educative role. The resources of local educational institutions could be utilised most effectively in this context.

It is important that the *maket raun* be used as a selling point for agricultural products. People in the eastern part of the District already seek the establishment of regular coffee markets to which coffee buyers would come. The *maket raun* could provide the site and occasion for coffee buying, and the presence of an audience (and the ease of checking scales) should counter many of the current complaints of malpractice by buyers. Additional produce, such as pyrethrum, European potatoes, and other vegetables, could be sold to itinerant buyers at the *maket raun*.

Wholesale and retail outlets would obviously provide much of the customer appeal of the *maket raun*; they might include the sale of foodstuffs, beverages, clothing, hardware and agricultural supplies. It might be argued that mobile traders would destroy the market for village stores. However, the fact that each would handle different orders of goods, and given that one provides periodic and the other permanent service would render the two systems complementary. Those stores at or near the *maket raun* should benefit from the increased number of people visiting the site. Local residents would have an opportunity to establish stalls for fresh and cooked foods. The demonstration effect might also encourage some local women to sew and sell clothing.

Once the *maket raun* is established, some of the traders and visitors could well wish to stay overnight at the site. This would require provision of simple hostel or rest house accommodation but could have the advantages of prolonging activity into the evening, providing a market for food and restaurant services offered by local people, and giving some employment to residents.

The attractive power of periodic markets is increased by the entertainment offered. The *maket raun* could provide a venue for recently established groups of professional travelling players, while film and videotape programmes and traditional dances could also be presented. Raffles and simple games of chance, already popular in urban markets, can be organised by residents or visitors.

To establish the *maket raun* system it is necessary for government to provide the initial core of services and basic structure around which private sector activities can cluster. It was proposed that two pilot projects be set up, differing in location, scale and complexity of organisation (Ward, *et al.*, 1974b). Government would provide general administration, health care, agricultural extension, banking and postal facilities, information services and a vehicle maintenance unit. A coordinator would manage the unit vehicles, schedules and general liaison, and encourage private sector participation in produce trading, wholesaling, retailing, entertainment and other functions.

Locations, Sites, and Periodicity

The central problem in the selection of market locations is to identify, in the absence of existing market networks, a set of places that will constitute a viable system, reach the greatest possible number of participants and have the greatest impact as points of diffusion. The number and location of sites to be served by a *maket raun* unit is governed by the purchasing power and distribution of the population; accessibility; the location of alternative central places; the unit's operational constraints; and local physical and socio-economic conditions.

In the Eastern Highlands District estimated cash income per capita in rural areas ranges from less than $A5.00 per annum to over $A50.00. Few areas outside the immediate urban environs have annual per capita incomes in excess of $A20.00. This scale of purchasing power influences the spacing of sites and the frequency of *maket raun* visits; thus, it was proposed that sites should be served on a fortnightly cycle. At present, it is unlikely that the market could sustain more frequent provision of higher order goods and services, while an interval longer than two weeks between visits would be inadequate for the people's needs.

The location of sites is restricted to localities with all-weather road access to ensure regularity. Sites must be within an economic travelling time from the unit's base, but beyond the economic shadow of existing towns. To be viable, each site must be accessible to a sufficient threshold population.

An important operational constraint is the institution of a five-day working week for government personnel. As at least one day will be required for vehicle maintenance and base activities, the unit can only operate in the field for four days a week. Consequently, the maximum number of sites which can be included in a fortnightly schedule is eight.

In selecting sites to be served by the pilot units, a location-allocation heuristic was devised to take into account all the above constraints, the details of which have been described elsewhere (Kissling and Weinand, 1975). Sensitivity testing showed that the model yielded stable solutions with altered conditions of accessibility, demand and periodicity.

In practice, any site within a limited radius of the theoretically derived points will meet the basic requirements. The choice of actual sites must finally depend on local conditions and on community acceptance of the pilot projects. These conditions include the prior existence of any modern sector services such as schools, medical aid posts, police posts, coffee-buying points and informal markets. People are already accustomed to visiting such focal places and the addition of a *maket raun* to their existing functions will reinforce and increment the role of these rural centres. The traditions of social organisation and cultural affiliation of groups around each potential site must be considered to ensure that the sites are acceptable meeting places. The site must have sufficient flat land, vehicle access from the highway, and preferably be strategically located in relation to networks of walking tracks as well as roads.

Each *maket raun* site will vary slightly according to terrain, community preference and the presence of any prior fixed services. The basic layout for a *maket raun* site is shown in Figure 6.2; this takes into account the need for vehicle and pedestrian access to stalls and space for off-vehicle selling and pedestrian movement.

Once agreement has been reached on the location of sites to be served, several scheduling options are available. Units may either return to base each evening or stay overnight at some or all of the *maket raun* sites. Neighbouring sites may be visited on consecutive days or in alternate weeks in order to give some

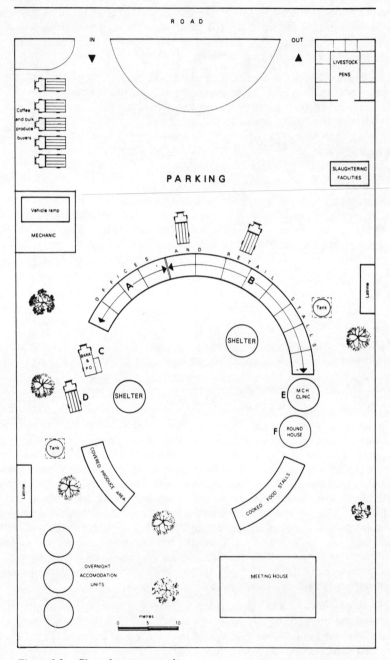

Figure 6.2   Plan of *maket raun* site

consumers the possibility of more frequent access to services. The actual schedules adopted by the pilot units will depend on local conditions and may be subject to an initial period of trial and error.

Benefits and Costs

The *maket raun* was proposed as a means of attaining desirable social and economic goals by stimulating improved conditions in rural areas. Time and data constraints prevented a comprehensive benefit-cost analysis of the proposal being conducted. For example, it is considered likely that private sector operators will join the unit in increasing numbers but it was not possible to estimate their costs, their benefits or the likely multiplier effects. Groups who will benefit from the establishment of the *maket raun* system include villagers, vehicle operators, coffee and produce buyers, village trade store owners, petty traders, itinerant traders and the government. Although not all benefits can be quantified, most of the sources of benefit can be indicated. Values can be estimated for some of these, and three examples may be quoted.

Proposals for two pilot units operating from Goroka and Mt Hagen, in the Eastern and Western Highlands Districts respectively, were prepared. The Goroka unit would serve eight points and the Mt Hagen unit six. In the Goroka area, 64 per cent of the total rural population of the pilot project area (102,000) would be closer to higher order services than they are at present. The equivalent figures for the Mt Hagen project area are 41 per cent or 146,000. Not all these people will take advantage of the new services. In estimating likely attendance at the *maket raun* sites, a conservative distance-decay function (Kissling and Weinand, 1975) was used which suggested that the Goroka unit would have a fortnightly clientele of 15,500 in dry weather and approximately half this in wet weather. The Mt Hagen unit would serve 16,500 in dry weather.

The establishment of the *maket raun* sites changes the cost of access to services dramatically. Figures 6.3 and 6.4 show the differences in the transport cost surfaces which should result from the introduction of the *maket raun* system in the two pilot project areas. In the Goroka case, if all those people likely to attend the *maket raun* were required instead to use the existing fixed site service centres each fortnight, their total annual travel costs would be $A1,042,000 or $A2.74 per capita per round trip, compared with a mean round trip fare of $A0.97 to the *maket raun* sites. The difference in travel costs indicates why so few rural people at present enjoy higher order services.

In the Eastern Highlands District, only 25 per cent of village-owned vehicles survive to be registered for a second year. This represents a severe drain on capital. Even if the *maket raun* mechanic can save only ten additional vehicles for a second year, approximately $A25,000 would be released annually for purposes other than vehicle replacement.

The *maket raun* will include representatives of at least five government departments. Sharing of vehicles will yield significant transport 'savings'. At present, interdepartmental coordination of field days is rare. If the same number of field days which the *maket raun* will give were provided without coordination, five rather than three vehicles would be required. The cost of hiring the additional two vehicles from the Plant and Transport Authority to provide a level of service similar to that proposed for the *maket raun* would be at least $A8,000 per year.

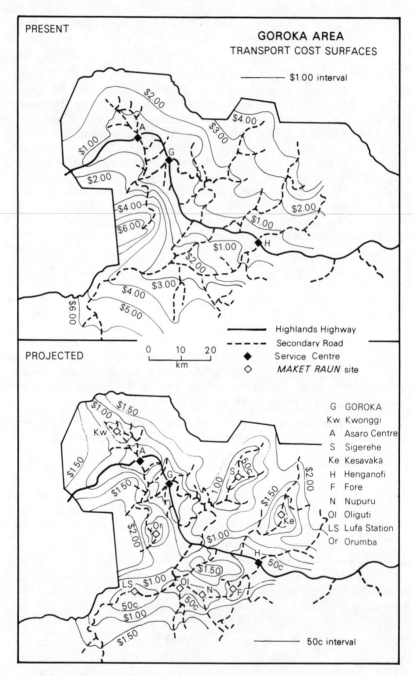

Figure 6.3   Present and projected transport cost surfaces around Goroka

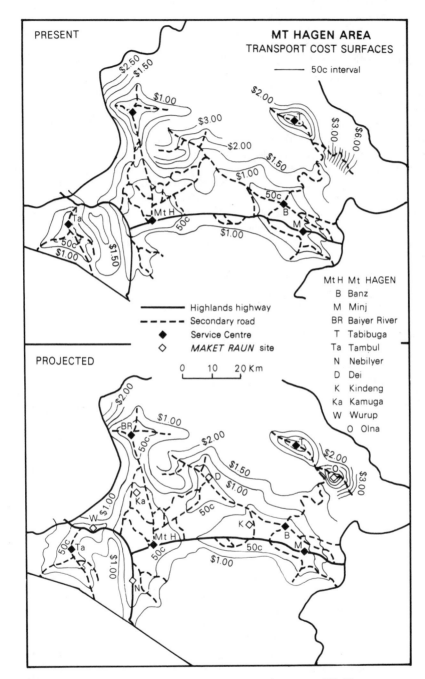

Figure 6.4   Present and projected transport cost surfaces around Mt Hagen

Substantial benefits should also accrue to coffee buyers through a reduction in their daily travel; to village retailers who will be able to buy from itinerant wholesalers; to villagers who will have new opportunities to engage in informal monetary activities; and to agriculturalists who will not have to transport their produce to the urban centres for sale.

Perhaps the greatest benefits to government and people will come from an increase in people's exposure to a wider range of government services and from greater effectiveness of the contact between villagers and government officers. At the *maket raun* field officers will be able to contact greater numbers of people than is normally possible in one day in the field. Rural improvement depends upon an increase in technical and other knowledge available to villagers. The presence of extension officers, advisors and adult educators should accelerate the flow of such information. The availability of a much wider range of consumer goods, in an informal market context, should make it much easier for villagers with limited experience of urban institutions to improve village life. Better access to credit, as well as the ability to save through a bank or a savings and loan society, should act as a further stimulus to improvement.

The total net cost of establishing a *maket raun* pilot unit in the Goroka area of the Eastern Highlands District, as at 1 May 1974, was calculated as $A49,600. This expenditure would cover twelve months' operation, plus the costs of the preparatory period. The figure does not include the costs of services already provided but which would in future be attached to the *maket raun*. Allowing for contingencies (but *not* for inflation) it was recommended that a sum of $A55,000 be allocated to initiate this pilot project. It was thought that a Western Highlands District *maket raun* need not duplicate all the features of the Goroka unit, which was designed to demonstrate a wide range of possible functions from its inception. Rather, there is much to commend the establishment of an additional *maket raun* in the Western Highlands District and elsewhere, organised by District staff and councils, financed largely from existing resources, and with only a modest central government input. Accordingly, it was recommended that a special grant of $A25,000 be made to launch a Western Highlands District *maket raun*. Staffing would be entirely by secondment, coordination would be the responsibility of District or local government staff and some vehicles would be made available by re-scheduling existing vehicle allocations. Individual sites would be prepared mostly through community self-help participation.

Conclusion

Providing services for the rural population of Papua New Guinea from a few fixed points has proved inadequate for rural improvement. The economic rationale of periodic marketing lies in the fact that it enables traders (and government) 'to aggregate "the day's demand" for each commodity' (and service) at each site and allows customers a greater choice of goods (Kirk *et al.*, 1972, 10). The regular gathering of people provides increased opportunities for information exchange. Periodic markets should not be viewed as relict features in a modern commercial structure, but in appropriate circumstances can be encouraged by government as a dynamic means of promoting rural development.

The proposals outlined here have been accepted by the Government of Papua New Guinea and two pilot units will begin operation in 1975. One of the roles of these units is to demonstrate to other rural communities the value of periodicity on a regular basis in provision of goods and services. The principle can be applied to the scheduling and organisation of existing activities to increase their impact. It is hoped that the basic concept will diffuse to other parts of the country as the economic and social advantages of the system become apparent.

[1] Where towns were linked with their hinterlands, the links tended to be with the expatriate-controlled mining and plantation enclaves rather than with the villages.

[2] Crocombe and Hogbin provide a good example – 'No agricultural extension workers had visited Inonda during the twelve months. . . . People can, of course, consult extension officers in Popondetta at any time, but as a result of language difficulties and social distance the Inonda people do not take advantage of this facility' (Crocombe and Hogbin, 1963, 86).

[3] In Neo-Melanesian the term *raun* conveys the concepts of both mobility and shape.

PART TWO
Urban market-place systems and mobile vendors

A formidable amount of retail exchange takes place daily in every large city of the world. This is an inescapable impression in the teeming metropolises of lesser developed countries: streets are crowded with vehicles of all kinds carrying people and goods; vendors roam the sidewalks seeking customers for such items as cooked foods, ball-point pens and wrist watches; modest little specialty shops selling cloth, local handicraft products, etc. stand cheek by jowl with large department stores and supermarkets more characteristic of western cities; and there are few cities without at least one large market or bazaar where locally grown fruit and vegetable products (as well as other local and imported goods) are offered for sale in a more traditional context. These three components (mobile hawkers, established shops, and traditional market-places) of the retail structure of cities in lesser developed countries account for variable shares of retail trade, and it might be argued that the proportion of retail exchange handled by established static commercial outlets is an indication of the degree of modernisation. However, the notion of a neat transformation from 'traditional' market-place retail trade and mobile vendors to 'modern' shop-based retail exchange is too simplistic by far. The three (or four, if one distinguishes between small, predominantly family-owned and run specialty shops and larger department stores) components co-exist and, indeed, may complement each other, especially in the cities of Africa, Asia, and Latin America.

The four essays in this section are not concerned with the spatially-fixed retail establishment component of the urban exchange system; rather, the focus is on market-places and hawkers in Hong Kong, Lagos, Mexico City and Singapore. In several of the essays there is an explicit concern with policy matters, especially where traditional activities impinge upon the functioning of the city. McGee and Ho ask whether the urban hawker's propensity to be spatially mobile is related primarily to elements of the economy of the city or whether it represents a response on the part of vendors to a more complex and diverse institutional environment. The somewhat remarkable extent of hawking as an established and accepted feature of the retail scene of Hong Kong–Kowloon is documented, and then two case studies illustrating aspects of hawker mobility are presented. In the first case (Jardine's Crescent), spatial mobility is induced by a legal prohibition on hawking activities in a particular area; hawkers recognise the enormous concentration of potential customers and take elaborate measures to circumvent the equally determined efforts of the authorities to prevent hawkers from selling in the area. That the hawkers understand the economy is beyond question; the reasons for their mobility are related more to public attitudes to traffic and pedestrian congestion. The second case study illustrates daily and weekly patterns of spatial mobility of Mongkok hawkers: hawker concentrations tend to be adjacent to public retail markets; hawker numbers vary systematically throughout the day and the week, at least partly in response to the number of potential customers present; and these peaks and troughs tend to be related also to the types of goods offered.

McGee and Ho note that the spatial and temporal adaptability peculiar to mobile vendors should be seen as a major economic advantage, as rapid adjustments to changes in the market and institutional environments can be made. While urban authorities frequently seek to prevent mobile hawkers from operating, largely because of a concern for traffic congestion (and also perhaps because hawking is a traditional, non-modern activity?), McGee and Ho argue that given imaginative planning, a good case can be made for the encouragement of mobile retailing in the cities of lesser developed countries.

Certain aspect of the *tianguis* (periodic markets) of Mexico City discussed in Jane Pyle's essay are not unlike the hawker concentrations in Hong Kong–Kowloon. The *tianguis* occupy a distinctive niche in the city's retail structure; Public Daily Markets and static retail establishments also exist, but the *tianguis* seem to cater particularly to the urban poor in areas of low population density especially on the fringe of Mexico City. While *tianguis* are officially discouraged by the authorities, they are tolerated because they provide a useful service in areas in which a Public Daily Market has not been provided. Pyle describes the main characteristics of *tianguis*, and it is clear that they are not unlike periodic markets elsewhere in the world. Although they are highly informal gatherings, there is a substantial degree of organization: there are, for example, unions of traders (organised both by commodity and by location), and leaders of these groups collect taxes which are paid directly to the Mexico Federal District Treasury (*not* to the Department of Markets which administers the Public Daily Markets), and select new sites for *tianguis* (this becomes necessary when a *tianguis* is replaced by the construction of a market building). Pyle suggests that there is a developmental sequence from *tianguis* to a street market, to a public market building, but the relatively recent inception in 1955 of the programme to construct public market-places makes it difficult to confirm conclusively the existence of this sequence. The similarities to the situation in Hong Kong–Kowloon are obvious: *tianguis*, like hawker concentrations, are surviving elements of the traditional urban trading scene. However, it seems that *tianguis* trade in Mexico City is grudgingly tolerated by the authorities until a market building is constructed near the *tianguis* site; in Hong Kong–Kowloon, the authorities seem less willing to recognise the important role played by hawkers in the city's retail exchange system.

In Singapore, night markets or, as they are called locally, *pasar malam*, have emerged during the last twenty years, and Yeung's essay thoroughly documents their origins, the characteristics of hawkers and customers, and aspects of the spatial and temporal organisation of *pasar malam*. There are almost seventy travelling night markets in Singapore (fifty-seven of which Yeung surveyed in 1970). It seems that they were established originally by energetic entrepreneurs who capitalised on the market provided by indigenous and expatriate employees of military bases. The boom in public and private housing estate construction in the 1960s occasioned the widespread development of night markets, mainly because the provision of normal static shopping facilities lagged well behind housing construction. Thus the *pasar malam* occupied a niche in the city's developing retail structure.

Approximately eight travelling markets operate each night of the week with anything from fewer than ten to more than 200 stalls, and there is apparent an attempt to reduce spatial competition. Small scale of operation is the norm, with almost all stalls being manned by no more than two hawkers; Chinese also dominate the ranks of hawkers in the *pasar malam* and constitute the main patrons. A classification of *pasar malam* into six types, based on hawker characteristics suggests that the mobility of hawkers is related to age, sex, transport ownership, and specialisation.

The question of spatio-temporal synchronisation of *pasar malam* is taken up in the final section of Yeung's essay. The urban travelling markets conform in general to the well established trend of locational proximity implying temporal separation, but this does not hold for rural *pasar malam*. Yeung observes that the *pasar malam* must operate within quite rigid spatial and functional limits; in particular, the night markets have to serve a set of customers some of whom also patronise daytime static and mobile units. This, of course, narrows locational choice, but *pasar malam* operators can reduce wasteful competition by manipulating the frequency of meetings. Yeung identifies the policy options available to urban authorities in the matter of mobile marketing elements: these might be termed active and passive, with the latter being the rule in Singapore. When a viable *pasar malam* emerges, the city provides basic support services (such as marking of hawker pitches, policing of market areas and, where necessary, resiting of markets). Authority assumes a low profile and in this respect it is in marked contrast to the situation in Hong Kong–Kowloon. Of course, if *pasar malam* sites were to be sought in busy city thoroughfares rather than in areas of obvious need in housing estates, this benign attitude could well be modified.

The essay by Sada *et al.* is less concerned with the activities of hawkers than it is with the relationship between urbanisation and periodicity of market meetings in a metropolitan environment. Sada *et al.* argue that systematic changes in the marketing environment occur as one proceeds from the centre of the metropolitan area to the periphery; the periodicity of market-place meetings changes, as does the order of goods offered and the income density surface. They also suggest that four different kinds of market-places can be distinguished on the basis of periodicity. These propositions are examined in the context of Lagos, Nigeria, a million city in which four of the thirty market-places meet on a periodic basis. The daily component (i.e. the number of people present on non-market days) in the four periodic markets is relatively larger the closer the market-place is to the city centre. The four surviving periodic markets each have markedly different functions, which are not unrelated to their location within the city.

Traders in Lagos markets are quite specialised, and more than 90 per cent attend markets six days in seven; a large proportion arrive at the market-place by 8 a.m., and remain until after 6 p.m. which suggest an enormous labour input, considering that few have lock-up facilities in the market-place and must therefore carry goods to the market-place in the morning and remove their unsold wares at the end of each day. Only a few Lagos markets obtain a large proportión of their goods from regional (long distance) sources, and these market-places tend to emphasise wholesale distributive functions. There does not appear to be any systematic difference between periodic and daily markets in the degree of commodity specialisation. Such differences between market-places as do occur with respect to this characteristic seem to be related more to size; the number of different commodities offered in a market-place increases quite rapidly up to a market size of 1,000 traders at which point the rate of increase levels off.

The degree of public intervention in street and market-place trade has traditionally been limited in West Africa, most probably because this trade was and is such a pervasive feature of everyday life. Policy issues are not raised explicitly by Sada *et al.*, but there are obvious implications of some of their findings about market-place trading in Lagos. Thus, if the city grows further, it could well be advisable to limit the size of existing and newly established markets, given that the basic range of goods seems to be available when approximately 1,000 traders are present. Also, the tendency towards functional specialisation of periodic markets located in different parts of the city might also provide some planning guidelines.

Policy issues assume a position of considerable importance in this section; in particular, the spatial mobility of vendors is examined in three of the four essays. The similarity between Hong Kong–Kowloon, Mexico City and Singapore in the matter of mobile vendors is quite remarkable. However, the contribution by Sada *et al.* on Lagos is no less appropriate in the section because, while the authors do not discuss policy matters directly, there are clear policy implications to be drawn from their essay, and especially from the relationship between distance from the city centre and periodicity of market-place meeting.

7 The spatial mobility of vendors: hawkers in Hong Kong
T.G. McGee and S.F. Ho

When Webber and Symanski stated that 'it is, therefore, necessary to decide which characteristics of an economy cause some sellers to be mobile, others to be immobile, and others to be both immobile and full-time' (Webber and Symanski, 1973, 214), they raised an issue that has become of major concern to a growing number of social scientists concerned with marketing distribution systems in the less developed countries of the world. While it is possible to find early geographical accounts of mobile retailing activity (Allix, 1922; Fogg, 1938), it was not until the beginning of the 1960s that the work of Hodder (1961) and Stine (1962) began to focus the attention of geographers upon the theoretical and empirical aspects of mobile retailing activity. At the same time, there was a parallel surge of activity among anthropologists stimulated by the collection of studies on Africa edited by Bohannan and Dalton (1962), by the work of Mintz (1959) in the Caribbean, and later by Dewey (1962) and Geertz (1963) in Indonesia.

Much of this research, especially in geography, has concentrated upon a major element of the rural retailing structure of the less developed countries, namely, the systems of periodic markets which occur in many parts of Africa, Latin America, and Asia.[1] By comparison the amount of research into the spatial aspects of retailing within the cities of the less developed countries has been relatively small, and a cursory analysis of the geographical literature reveals only a few articles on this subject. Among them, those of Mukwaya (1962) in Uganda, Mabogunje in Lagos (1964), Dutt (1966a and 1966b) in India, Hodder (1967) in Ibadan, Mushtaq (1968) in Pakistan, Temple in Uganda (1969), Pyle (1970) in Mexico City, Ho (1972) in Hong Kong, Yeung in Singapore (1973), and McGee (1974) in Hong Kong have all attempted to delineate elements of the retailing patterns of the Third World city.

Perhaps because of the apparent dominance of static retailing units, little attempt is apparent in this literature to delineate the mobile elements of this retailing structure. This trend is further accentuated by a theoretical perspective reinforced by the work of Stine (1962), Berry (1967), and Skinner (1964), which lays great emphasis upon central place theory as the explanatory framework for the transition from mobile to static retailing patterns. Thus their models suggest that the low population density and low per capita income characteristic of the hinterland of cities in less developed countries favours the periodic market system, while the high density, higher per capita income situation of the Third World cities favours static retailing. In fact, mobile vendors play an important role in retail distribution systems in many of the cities of the less developed world. Of course, such an assertion needs careful definitional and statistical support, as well as some understanding of the complex retailing structure of these cities in which one finds a bewildering variety of retail outlets ranging from the department store to the itinerant vendor who sells such items as shoelaces and cigarettes. It is unfortunate that in the Asian context at least, there have been no comprehensive surveys of the total range of these outlets; thus, one can only guess at the structure and contribution of this wide variety of outlets to total retail turnover.

The retail structure of Asian cities has four main components: first, the department store or supermarket offering a wide variety of products from one static location or series of locations; secondly, the ubiquitous retail store, ranging from such highly specialised types as tobacconists to the neighbourhood store (restaurants fall into this category); thirdly, sellers who sell from rented spaces in enclosed and roofed public market areas; and finally, vendors who sell goods and offer services from public space, most frequently streets. These latter sellers, or *hawkers*, are distinguished from the previous category simply by the locations from which they sell, and in fact, their scale of organisation and operation may be little different from market sellers.

While there are exceptions (as when a supermarket despatches mobile vendors to sell icecream), it is generally true in the Asian context that only among the last category of hawkers does any substantial spatial mobility characterise their mode of operation. There is nothing remarkable in this statement, for hawkers have the best opportunity to be mobile in that they occupy space often designated for other purposes, and over which they have no permanent legal claim. Unlike the other types of retailing unit, they do not own the land upon which they sell their goods, and therefore apart from the intrinsic value of the selling site as a *location* (including their locational goodwill), they have the capacity for mobility. This may be enhanced by economic advantages that can accrue from selling in different locations.

Reliable data on the proportion of total retailing outlets made up by hawkers in Asian cities do not exist, but estimates suggest that hawkers account for more than 50 per cent of the outlets in some of the cities. Thus, hawkers made up 53 per cent of the total retail outlets in the urban area of Hong Kong Island in 1971 (Lu, 1972; Wong and Sum, 1971).[2] In Hong Kong there appears to have been a sizeable expansion in retailing stores far in excess of that of some of the other larger Asian cities such as Bangkok and Jakarta. Even if the importance of hawkers in the total retailing outlets in other cities is less than in Hong Kong, their numbers are substantial, ranging from an estimated 100,000 in Jakarta to as few as 16,000 in Kuala Lumpur (McGee, 1970; McGee and Yeung, 1973).

Because of their numerical importance in the retailing distribution network it is not surprising that spatial mobility among these urban hawkers is of major theoretical and practical interest. It is useful to specify the major types of spatial mobility that occur among urban hawkers. On the basis of research in Hong Kong and other south-east Asian cities, it is possible to distinguish three types of hawkers on the basis of spatial mobility: itinerant hawkers, semi-itinerant hawkers, and location-specific mobile hawkers. *Itinerant hawkers* are very similar in their patterns of spatial mobility to a periodic market system which exhibits regularity in time and space. In the urban situation, they tend mostly to be individual hawkers moving from street to street in a repetitive pattern, calling out the type of goods sold or playing a musical instrument. Sometimes, they even have specific households to which they sell on their route. Such hawkers typically convey their goods by foot on a carrying pole with baskets at both ends. In many cities, these hawkers now use motor bikes and sometimes even small vans. Far less common are groups of hawkers who come together at a certain place at regular times to sell particular commodities. The system of night markets in Singapore described by Yeung in this volume is an example of this form of itinerant hawking, and in Jakarta there is an elaborate system of periodic markets for particular commodities such as bicycle parts.

Semi-itinerant hawkers are those who vary the location of their business throughout the day. Cooked-food hawkers who frequent locations with large numbers of potential customers are typical of this type, and in Hong Kong sizeable numbers of cooked-food hawkers cluster around playgrounds, cinemas, and schools. Typically, these hawkers sell their wares from wheeled push carts or baskets on the ground. There is considerable fluctuation in their numbers, both diurnally and weekly.

Location-specific mobile hawkers go to the same location each day to sell. Although they may not occupy the same pitch within the cluster of hawkers, they will stay at their chosen pitches for the duration of business and then move away with their goods. Often they bring their goods by push cart or display them in baskets on the ground or on benches made out of the boxes that held the goods. Many of these location-specific hawkers are parasitic on already existing concentrations of hawkers, taking advantage of the customer attraction which the existing hawker-core has developed. It might be argued that there is an additional type of mobility among hawkers which is related to their participation in seasonal fairs. For instance, in Hong Kong some hawkers who normally trade at other locations move to the seasonal fairs where the city government has designated space for hawkers. This category is, however, excluded from the following discussion.

Of course, not all hawkers are mobile in the sense described above. Many have established permanent lock-up stalls in streets or other public space such as parks to which they return reach day. Results from a series of surveys conducted in south-east Asian cities in 1973 indicate that well over two-thirds of the hawkers in Manila City, Jakarta, and Kuala Lumpur were characterised by some degree of mobility (McGee and Yeung, 1973) as compared to 42 per cent for the Hong Kong–Kowloon urban areas (Lu, 1972, 36).

It is worth asking whether the hawkers' propensity to be spatially mobile is solely related to the economies of these cities as Webber and Symanski suggest (1973, 214), or whether it represents an assessment by hawkers of how they must operate in order to cope in a wider, more complex institutional context. In order to answer this question, case studies of spatial mobility among hawkers in two districts of the urban area of Hong Kong–Kowloon[3] are presented; they raise questions about determinants of mobility far beyond a simple reaction to economic circumstances.[4]

Hawkers in Hong Kong

While figures on the number of hawkers in Hong Kong are often unreliable because of enumeration difficulties, a recent estimate suggests that there were 34,187 operative hawking units in 1971 (Tse, I, 1974, 16). With a mean figure of 1.5 hawker operatives per hawker unit there were approximately 54,000 hawkers operating at that time (Lu, 1972). These can be divided into three main types: *fixed-pitch stall hawkers* who sold their commodities from permanent lock-up stalls erected on footpaths and in resettlement estates (57.5 per cent of the

Table 7.1   Hong Kong—Kowloon Hawkers by Type of Commodity Sold, 1971

Raw Foodstuff	16,032	46.2
Emporium Goods	5,115	14.7
Other Food, Confectionary, etc.	3,003	8.6
Cooked Foods	2,982	8.6
Services	2,416	7.0
Household Wares	1,952	5.6
Newspapers	1,340	3.9
Toys and Books, etc.	1,072	3.1
Others	800	2.3
TOTAL	34,712	100.0

Source:Chinese University of Hong Kong Social Research Centre, 1971.

Table 7.2:   The Number and Percentage of Operative Hawking Units by Census District in Hong Kong—Kowloon, 1971

District	Number of Hawker Units	Percent of[a] Hong Kong—Kowloon Hawker Population	1971 Population	Percent of[a] Total Population
Central	484	1.4	22,794	0.7
Sheung Wan	1,566	4.5	67,907	2.1
Western	1,612	4.7	146,202	4.6
Mid-Levels	12	*	47,112	1.5
Peak	4	*	8,241	0.3
Wanchai	1,584	4.6	142,884	4.5
Tai Hang	665	1.9	94,040	3.0
North Point	1,468	4.3	176,492	5.6
Shaukiwan	1,788	5.2	162,456	5.1
Aberdeen	983	2.9	109,116	3.4
Hong Kong Island	10,166	29.5	977,244	30.8
Tsim Sha Tsui	2,855	8.3	73,988	2.3
Yaumati	1,904	5.5	203,749	6.4
Mongkok	2,752	8.0	172,006	5.4
Hong Hom	1,933	5.6	188,572	5.9
Ho Man Tin	90	0.3	77,125	2.4
Cheung Sha Wan	3,884	11.3	259,431	8.2
Shek Kip Mei	1,112	3.2	190,138	6.0
Kowloon Tong	28	*	21,403	0.7
Kai Tak	5,574	16.2	555,543	17.5
Ngau Tau Kok	2,592	7.5	230,571	7.3
Lei Yue Mun	1,297	3.8	222,331	7.0
Kowloon	24,021	69.7	2,194,857	69.1
Hong Kong—Kowloon	34,187	100.0	3,172,101	100.0

Source: Tse, I, 1974, 16.   *Less than 0.1%

[a]Totals may not sum due to rounding

total); *fixed-pitch pedlars* who returned to the same pitch each day (19.6 per cent; some were location-specific hawkers); and *mobile hawkers* (22.9 per cent), which group included both semi-itinerant and itinerant hawkers. The wide variety of commodities and services sold by Hong Kong hawkers is indicated in Table 7.1; raw foodstuff, particularly vegetables and fruit, was the major commodity sold, with emporium goods, principally clothing and textiles, next in importance.

These hawkers were not distributed evenly throughout the urban area, and Table 7.2 shows that over 45 per cent of the hawkers were concentrated in the six census districts of Sheung Wan, Western, and Wanchai in Hong Kong, and in Yaumati, Mongkok and Cheung Sha Wan in Kowloon. These six districts account for 30 per cent of the urban population, and are amongst the most densely populated districts of the urban area (Table 7.3 and Figure 7.1). Most of these hawkers were licenced (84.9 per cent) (Lu, 1972, 33) by the Hong Kong Urban Services Department to sell goods from only one specific location, although it seems likely that the survey did not record all the illegal hawkers who understandably exhibited considerable reluctance to stand still and be counted. In fact, many of the licenced hawkers sold illegally from other locations because the return from the licenced location was inadequate. The licence fees were low and varied considerably according to the conditions under which a hawker could operate (McGee, 1973). The hawkers were supervised by the Hawker Control Force and the Police Force but both were too understaffed to control efficiently

Table 7.3:   Hong Kong and Kowloon Urban Areas: Hawker Unit and Population Density per Hectare, 1971

District	Area (hectare)	1971 Population	Density per hectare	Number of hawkers	Hawker density per hectare
Central	104.94	22,794	217.21	485	4.62
Sheung Wan	68.96	67,907	984.88	1,619	23.48
West	152.54	146,202	958.45	1,607	10.53
Wanchai	88.05	142,844	1,622.31	1,586	18.01
Tai Hang	354.57	94,040	265.22	655	1.85
North Point	403.84	176,492	437.03	1,438	3.56
Shaukiwan	481.87	162,456	337.14	1,826	3.79
Hong Kong [a]	1,654.77	812,735	491.15	9,216	5.57
Tsim Sha Tsui	180.75	73,988	409.34	734	4.06
Yaumati	158.39	203,749	1,286.38	3,979	25.12
Mongkok	110.94	172,006	1,550.44	2,820	25.42
Hong Hom	202.23	188,572	932.46	2,081	10.29
Ho Man Tin	243.31	77,125	316.98	90	0.37
Cheung Sha Wan	473.16	259,431	548.29	3,883	8.21
Shek Kip Mei	342.42	190,138	555.28	1,216	3.55
Kowloon Tong	250.02	21,403	85.61	30	0.12
Kai Tak	1,290.83	555,543	430.38	5,846	4.53
Ngau Tau Kok	566.01	230,571	407.36	2,590	4.58
Lei Yue Mun[b]	741.81	222,331	299.71	1,228	1.66
Kowloon	4,559.87	2,194,857	481.34	24,497	5.37

Source: McGee, 1973, 78 and 82 (in Table 4.5, p.82, the entry for Cheung Sha Wan is omitted)

[a] Aberdeen, Mid-Levels, Pokfulam and Peak included

[b] Lei Yue Mun excludes Tertiary Unit 833

all the hawkers. However, periodic raids on illegal hawker locations were
mounted with the result that illegal hawkers were fined and moved on. Two
areas in districts with large hawker populations were chosen to illustrate aspects
of hawker mobility: the Jardine's Crescent hawker agglomeration in Wanchai
(Hong Kong urban area), and the area formed by Tertiary Units (TU)[5] 2.2.3 and
2.2.4 in Mongkok (Kowloon urban area).

Jardine's Crescent Hawkers: A Case Study in Spatial Mobility Induced by Illegality

The district in which the Jardine's Crescent hawkers are located is approximately
one and a half kilometres (one mile) from the Hong Kong Central Business
District; it had been primarily residential although there were some warehouses

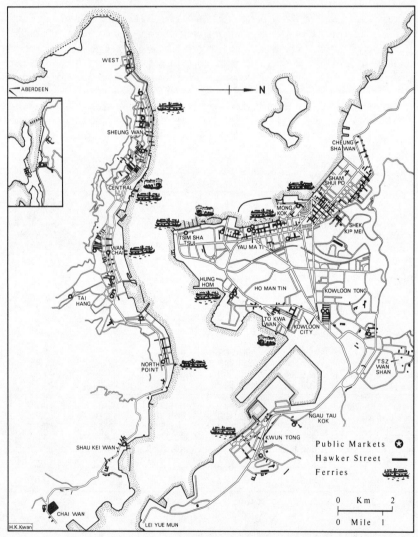

Figure 7.1   Hawker distribution in Hong Kong–Kowloon metropolitan area, 1960

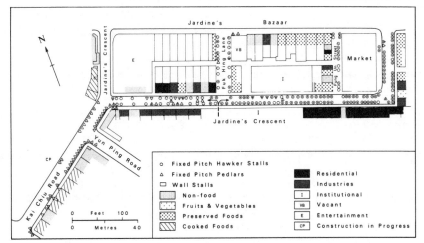

Figure 7.2a   Hawker distribution and adjacent landuse in Jardine's Crescent (1969; morning)

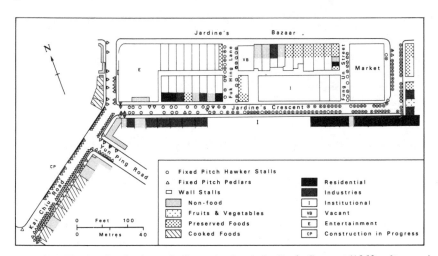

Figure 7.2b   Hawker distribution and adjacent landuse in Jardine's Crescent (1969; afternoon)

only a short distance away. In the 1950s this warehouse area was sold for high-rise development offering retailing and residential possibilities, and the whole area began to develop rapidly with the growth of cinemas, restaurants and other recreational facilities. Today this Causeway Bay area is the second largest entertainment and shopping centre on Hong Kong Island. Within its boundaries are located five large cinemas, a major Japanese-owned department store, and many retail stores and restaurants. Since the opening of the Cross-Harbour Tunnel in August 1972 and the completion of three major tourist hotels, it is rapidly becoming a tourist-orientated district as well. At the time of the hawker survey in 1969 (McGee, 1973), it was still largely a shopping and entertainment area for local Chinese residents.

The location of the Jardine's Crescent hawkers (Figures 7.2a and 7.2b) suggests that the hawkers fell into three locational clusters: firstly, those located in

Jardine's Crescent East who consisted mainly of fixed-pitch stalls selling vegetables and preserved foods, closely related to the Tang Lung Chau Public
Market; secondly, in Kai Chiu Road where there were fluctuating numbers of
fixed-pitch pedlars selling textiles (numbers increased markedly in the afternoon
and early evening); and thirdly, a transitional zone in Jardine's Crescent West and
Fuk Hing Lane in which vegetable sellers merged into textile and other
commodity sellers.

The activities of the second group of hawkers are of most immediate relevance
here for they were forbidden by law to sell from their Kai Chiu Road location.
The hawkers who invaded Kai Chiu Street came to tap the very large number of
potential customers attracted by cinemas and shopping, and who flowed into
the adjacent Causeway Bay district. As this was a major route for both pedestrian
and motor traffic, the authorities had declared hawking in this district illegal.
This did not deter the hawkers and they came prepared with wheeled push carts
from which the goods were sold and with an elaborate system of guards alert
for the pending arrival of enforcement agencies. During 1969 and 1970 the
hawkers of Kai Chiu Road were frequently raided by the police and the Hawker
Control Force; the hawkers either rapidly dispersed into the maze of streets
surrounding the area, or they were arrested, fined and had their goods
confiscated. Thus their efforts to establish a stable selling concentration were
thwarted constantly by the authorities. Their assessment of the area's potential
selling possibilities showed considerable understanding of the economy, but the
institutional assessment of their contribution kept them in a condition of
enforced mobility.

Mongkok Hawkers: A Case Study of Daily and Weekly Patterns of Spatial Mobility

The hawkers of Mongkok (Fig. 7.3) have experienced little institutional harass-
ment, although even here the area of maximum selling potential in Nathan Road
(the main thoroughfare forming the western boundary of TU 2.2.1) was
patrolled by police, and hawkers did not often occupy it. Mongkok is one of
the urban districts of Kowloon with a large number of hawkers. It has an area of
approximately 166 hectares (410 acres), and it is located two and a half kilometres (one and a half miles) from Tsim Sha Tsui, the Central Business District
of Kowloon. The landuse pattern of Mongkok has one common characteristic:
there is a predominance of shops selling high-order goods (clothing, watches,
jewellery, etc.), restaurants, cinemas and office buildings along such main
thoroughfares as Nathan Road, Shanghai Street and Prince Edward Road. It is
also an area of high-density residential housing. In a similar fashion to Causeway
Bay, it lies along the main east-west axis of the major communication route of
Kowloon, Nathan Road, and is a major retailing and entertainment centre.

In Mongkok, hawkers were found in twelve major concentrations of some 4,000
hawkers in 1969 (Fig. 7.3). Three of these offered specialty goods such as
textiles, secondhand books, metal wares and machine parts, attracting customers
from a large area. The remaining nine concentrations sold food and daily
necessities such as vegetables and fruit. These clusters occurred at 300–400
metre (330–440 yard) intervals, serving the different segments of Mongkok
district, more or less coinciding with areas of dense population, heavy pedestrian

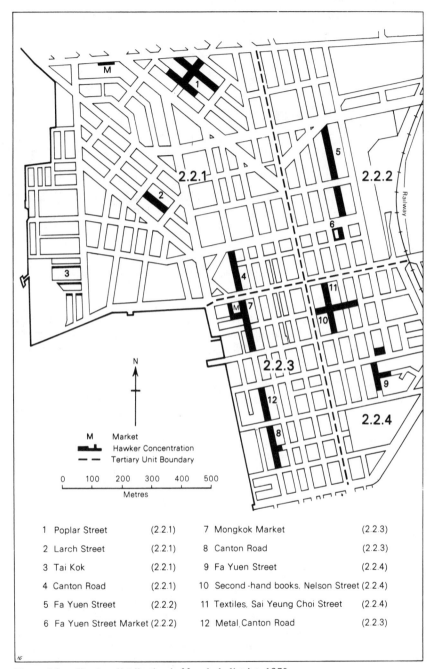

Figure 7.3   Hawker distribution in Mongkok district, 1970

flow, and prosperous neighbourhood business; they tended to be adjacent to *public retail markets*. In some concentrations, especially those found along Canton Road in the heart of Mongkok, the density of hawkers was as high as 215 stalls per 100 square metres (1,100 square feet). In general, the eastern

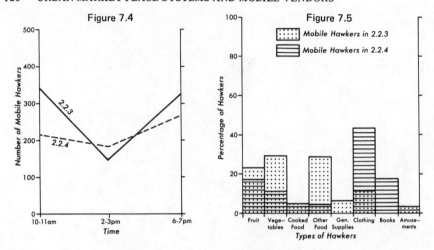

Figure 7.4   Diurnal variation in the number of mobile hawkers (T.U. 2.2.3 and T.U. 2.2.4)

Figure 7.5   Percentage of different types of mobile hawkers in T.U. 2.2.3 and T.U. 2.2.4

fringe of Mongkok (a region of mainly institutional buildings, open space and special services such as car repairing) had very few hawkers. Along thoroughfares such as Nathan Road, Prince Edward Road and Boundary Street, the hawker density was also quite low because hawking was illegal and most hawkers doing business were illegal pedlars.

Mobile hawkers tended to gravitate to these locational nuclei of static hawker concentrations, the *location-specific mobile hawkers* forming a major proportion. Thus they exhibited significant mobility in their temporal occupance of locations while not always occupying exactly the same pitch within a location. Field observations involving daily counts at different times were made for one week in two of the sub-districts which contained a major part of the commercial and retailing activity (TU 2.2.3 and TU 2.2.4, Fig. 7.3). The number of mobile hawkers varied significantly during the day: they were most numerous in the morning (10–11 a.m.) and in the evening (5–6 p.m.), and least numerous in the early afternoon (1–2 p.m.) which was lunch-time (Fig. 7.4). In TU 2.2.3, the number of mobile hawkers at peak hours in the morning and early evening exceeded 300, but declined to half this number between 2 and 3 p.m. This was because in TU 2.2.3 the mobile hawkers were mostly vegetable hawkers located close to the market and their busiest hours coincided with the marketing times of the housewives. In TU 2.2.4 the two peaks were less marked: the number of mobile hawkers was lowest at lunch-time but there was a marked increase in the number of mobile hawkers in the evening (270–280). This may be explained by the fact that in TU 2.2.4 about half of the mobile hawkers sold specialty goods such as secondhand books and emporium goods (stylish clothing, cosmetics, and ladies' wear) (Fig. 7.5), and their peak hours stretched from 2 p.m. to 9 p.m.

Thus, different types of hawkers had different peak and slack hours throughout the day. Mobile hawkers are more immediately affected by this peaking than static hawkers because the former group have no fixed stalls for displaying or storing their goods; they must remove everything, including goods and stalls, from the business locations at slack times.

Of the different types of mobile hawkers, those associated with the vegetable hawker bazaars were most numerous in the morning and evening. The morning concentration was slightly greater because housewives usually made their daily purchase after breakfast (Fig. 7.6a). In the early afternoon (1–3 p.m.) the hawkers dispersed for lunch, resulting in a marked shrinking in the pattern of concentration. These hawkers complemented the vegetable bazaars and sold vegetables, preserved food, cheap clothing and general supplies. Other mobile hawkers were locationally associated with shopping centres, restaurants and cinemas. Usually these central facilities were visited by customers in the afternoon and evening, and rarely in the early morning. Thus the mobile hawkers around these types of land use were more numerous after 2 p.m. (Fig. 7.6b), but their numbers decreased towards the late evening because of inadequate lighting facilities. These hawkers sold textiles, general supplies, secondhand books, toys and fruit.

Mobile hawkers selling fruit (near the former Mongkok Ferry Pier), cooked food (around cinemas and playgrounds), and cloth and clothing (around department stores in Mongkok), were most numerous in the evening. These were associated with areas of heavy pedestrian flow around playgrounds, shops, the waterfront, recreational open space, cinemas, restaurants and parks; all of these were frequented by people after work (Fig. 7.6c), and the mobile hawkers usually had lighting facilities.

Figure 7.6a-b-c   Daily spatial variations of mobile hawkers in T.U. 2.2.3 and T.U. 2.2.4

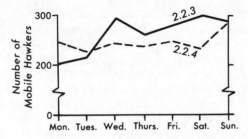

Figure 7.7   Daily average number of mobile hawkers in T.U. 2.2.3 and T.U. 2.2.4

There was considerable fluctuation in the trading patterns of mobile hawkers during the week. Observations in TU 2.2.3 and TU 2.2.4 suggested that there was usually an increase in the number of mobile hawkers towards the end of the week (Saturdays and Sundays), especially after 2 p.m. On Mondays and Tuesdays the number of mobile hawkers was the smallest (Fig. 7.7). This may be explained by the fact that most mobile hawkers spent Mondays and Tuesdays replenishing their stocks. The number of mobile hawkers did not fluctuate greatly on the remaining three week-days. In TU 2.2.3 the hour of greatest hawker activity throughout the week was 10–11 a.m., many of these being food hawkers; a similar concentration occurred daily at 6–7 p.m. (Fig. 7.8). By contrast, 6–7 p.m. was the time with the greatest number of hawkers throughout the week in TU 2.2.4 (Fig. 7.9). Here the mobile hawkers sell mainly emporium and specialty goods. On Saturdays and Sundays there was usually an increase in mobile hawkers near the shopping centres along Nathan Road.

The various types of mobile hawkers had markedly different patterns of weekly

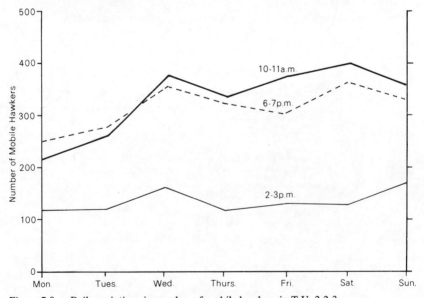

Figure 7.8   Daily variations in number of mobile hawkers in T.U. 2.2.3

attendance. Mobile hawkers catering to daily needs (i.e., sellers of vegetables, fruit, preserved food, general supplies and newspapers) have a relatively even distribution throughout the week (Fig. 7.10); this is also the case for hawkers of certain goods for which, while there is not a steady daily demand, such demand as exists is not confined to any one day (e.g. sellers of toys and of secondhand books in TU 2.2.4).

Another group of mobile hawkers is most numerous on Saturday afternoon and on Sundays when large numbers of customers buy goods from hawkers as part of a more general shopping expedition to the area. These mobile hawkers include those who sell cloth and clothing near the department stores, and fruit hawkers

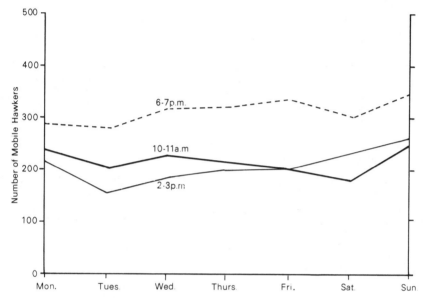

Figure 7.9   Daily variations in number of mobile hawkers in T.U. 2.2.4

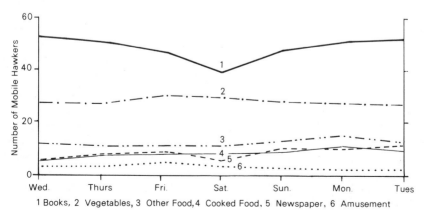

1 Books, 2 Vegetables, 3 Other Food, 4 Cooked Food, 5 Newspaper, 6 Amusement

Figure 7.10   Types of mobile hawkers with even daily distribution in T.U. 2.2.3 and T.U. 2.2.4

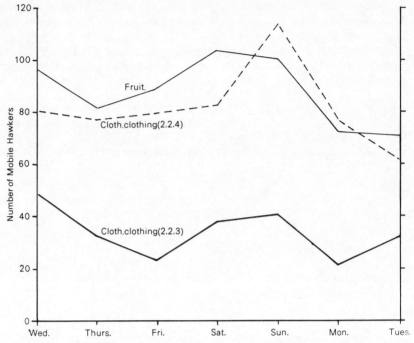

Figure 7.11 Types of mobile hawkers with uneven daily distribution in T.U. 2.2.3 and T.U. 2.2.4

and hawkers selling ice-cream and confectionery near cinemas and restaurants (Fig. 7.11).

It seems that if the demand for goods sold is inelastic (e.g. fruit and vegetables) the number of mobile hawkers concerned fluctuated little throughout the week. If the demand of the goods sold is more elastic (e.g. cloth, clothing, cosmetics), the number of mobile hawkers selling these goods had much greater weekly variations. Their reasons for not doing business may be bad weather, shortages in the supply of stocks, the desire to rest for a few days after a busy day, and special occasions such as festivals and family occasions. Of these variations, those induced by bad weather were of major importance. Within these sub-districts of Mongkok, the mobile hawkers exhibit a considerable degree of spatial and temporal mobility for a variety of legal, economic and even climatic reasons.

Conclusion

These two case studies of mobile hawkers in the Hong Kong–Kowloon Urban Area indicate that even in a city with one of the highest population densities in the world, with large numbers of static retailing outlets and rapidly rising per capita incomes (Hopkins, 1971), spatial mobility persists among some retailers. While this spatial mobility occurs only at a micro-scale (that is, generally occurring temporally within a broad hawker concentration), it is an aspect of retailing activity which has important theoretical and practical consequences.

In theoretical terms it is possible to argue that certain characteristics of the economy encourage mobility among these Hong Kong hawkers. Thus in both case study areas the mobile hawkers are taking advantage of the generative power of existing sedentary activities which attract potential customers. At the same time they are cutting overheads such as rent and power costs by operating from public streets. Most significantly, their mobility allows them to choose locations which maximise contact with customers. Even within established concentrations of hawkers, mobile pedlars will often switch their pitches in an effort to increase the number of potential customers. Thus their capacity for spatial mobility gives them marked economic advantage in situations of considerable retail competition. There are, of course, differences in the temporal and locational aspects of this mobility according to the types of commodities sold: vegetable hawkers congregate near public markets throughout the week and textile vendors stay as close to static retailing and entertainment complexes as possible, particularly on Saturdays and Sundays. This spatial and temporal adaptability can be construed as a major economic advantage for it is possible to make adjustments quickly to changes in the market situation, weather, and arrival of law enforcement authorities. Thus peddling is a very rational mode of economic operation in the cities of many Third World countries.

However, on the practical level it is the mobile hawkers who are seen as posing the major problems of obstruction and congestion by city authorities who wish to keep the streets of their cities clear for traffic and pedestrians. Consequently, the mobile hawkers, particularly those selling in street concentrations, are often declared illegal and are harassed by city authorities. Thus, as was the case of the Kai Chiu Road hawkers, they are operating under conditions of *enforced mobility*, whereas their reaction to the economic situation would be a desire to remain as static as possible. In this manner institutional factors cause mobility in addition to the characteristics of an *economy*.

A good case may be made for encouraging mobile retailing within the urban areas of the less developed countries. The economic advantages to the mobile vendor in terms of low overheads and greater locational adaptability, and to the customer in the form of cheaper goods and locational convenience, are obvious. In addition, as Yeung's study of the Singapore night markets elsewhere in this volume shows, it is possible to make use of space in a multi-functional manner at different times of the day leading to a more efficient and less wasteful use of city space. While the problems posed by mobile selling are real enough, imaginative planning which uses the obvious advantages of mobile sellers and provides space for their activities will enable the economies of the Third World cities and the welfare of their citizens to be considerably enhanced.

---

[1] Much of this extensive literature is referred to in other parts of this volume, and it is not cited here.

[2] Unfortunately, statistics on the total value of retail turnover generated by the different retail outlets are not available. Such data would enable a more accurate assessment of the relative contribution of the various types of retail outlets.

[3] This includes the urban areas of Hong Kong on Hong Kong Island and Kowloon and New Kowloon on the Kowloon peninsula which are now linked by the Cross-Harbour Tunnel.

[4] These case studies are based on fieldwork carried out by Ho Seck-Fun and T.G. McGee, and are dealt with more fully in Ho Seck-Fun, 1972, and in McGee, 1973.

[5] Spatial units composed of several census blocks used by the Census and Planning authorities in Hong Kong.

8 *Tianguis:* periodic markets of Mexico City
Jane Pyle

In Mexico City, periodic market-places are known as *tianguis*, and they are a well established component of the retail structure of Mexico City, despite efforts by government authorities to eliminate them. They are informal sector activities *par excellence*, being characterised by small scale operators, lack of rigid internal control, and great spatial and organisational flexibility. *Tianguis* are patronised by people from all walks of life, but they cater mainly to low income earners in recently settled areas on the fringe of the city. In many cases, the presence of a periodic market foreshadows the establishment of a permanent market building at a later time; there appears to be a developmental sequence from periodic outdoor market, to daily street market, to the permanent facilities of a government-sponsored daily market. It is not clear whether (as is the case with many markets in rural areas) a system of periodic markets exists within the city, based on a hierarchy of meeting places, with synchronisation to avoid conflicts in meeting times. In this essay, the characteristics of Mexico City's *tianguis* will be discussed, and the organisation and operation of *tianguis* will be described. A central theme of the essay is the relationship between *tianguis* and daily markets.

Characteristics of the *Tianguis*

The word *tianguis*[1] is used to distinguish the periodic markets from permanent daily markets, whether the latter are housed or in the streets (Fig. 8.1). All *tianguis* have certain features in common: rough grouping of goods into sections, such as clothing, drygoods, hardware and dishes, pottery, fruits and vegetables, and prepared foods; ambulatory vendors of various goods; vendors of local products, if any, behind the more raucous professionals, on side streets or in odd corners; and *sombras* or squares of cloth for shade, supported by intricate tracings of rope, string and miscellaneous bits of lumber or sticks.

The layout of an individual *tianguis*, other than one built into a market, is shaped by existing structures; that is, a compact cluster of vendors results when the *tianguis* meets in an empty lot or field, while a straggling effect is evident when it occupies the streets in a built-up area. Existing building and street patterns are taken into account by those selecting sites for new *tianguis*. While a compact grouping is preferred, few large spaces are left in the areas where enough people live to attract the *tiangueros* (vendors in the *tianguis*, also known as *tianguistas*). In the villages outside the city that are frequented by *tiangueros*

132

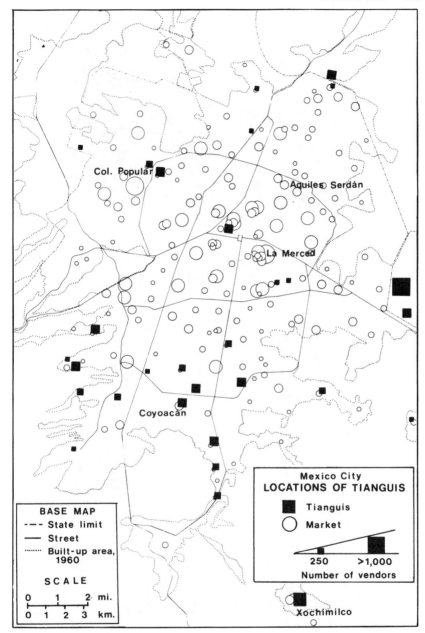

Figure 8.1   Location of *tianguis* in Mexico City

from Mexico City, the *tianguis* spreads around the permanent market building into adjacent streets. The market building often fronts on the main square and the *tianguis* may engulf the plaza on market days.

Five of the public market buildings in Mexico City have been designed with outdoor annexes for the weekly *tianguis*. Deserted during the week, and in some

Figure 8.2   *Top: Tianguis* in Colonia Popular; *middle:* street market in Aquiles Serdan; *bottom:* accommodation for *tianguis*, Coyoacan (see Fig. 8.1)

cases closed off from the daily market stalls, these annexes have the appearance of the common *tianguis* in the streets except that they are equipped with concrete benches for display of goods and have pavement underfoot (Fig. 8.2). No new market buildings are being planned with provision for *tianguis*. This is one of the means used by the Department of Markets of the Federal District to discourage actively the continued meeting of travelling vendors.[2]

Of the network of *tianguis* in and around Mexico City, only the *tianguis* of Xochimilco could be called a specialty market (and the term is used with reservation). The permanent market building in Xochimilco is located adjacent to the central plaza. On the opposite side of the market from the plaza is a permanent enclosure for *tianguis*, but many vendors have established themselves there to sell daily. On Saturdays and Sundays, in addition to these permanent vendors and the customary *tianguistas*, who overflow to the sidewalk east of the enclosure, additional vendors of flowers and plants arrive to offer their goods from stalls set up on the north sidewalk and in the parking lot. In no other market does the number of sellers of plants rise so high, and this kind of specialisation is not evident in other *tianguis*.

The map of the *tianguis* at Coyoacán market illustrates the arrangement of goods, number of vendors, and general proportions of men and women selling in one of the larger *tianguis* (Fig. 8.3). Usually, the clustering of goods into sections is not so pronounced as to allow an observer to identify precise boundaries, but broad groupings are evident. Fruit, vegetables, grains, and chiles are found in the same general vicinity and each is more or less localised. Dry goods appear together without further grouping into shoes, women's clothing, or men's clothing. Occasionally one may see a vendor 'out of place', such as a blanket salesman among pottery vendors, for example. This may be explained by the recent acquisition of his booth (in which case he is obliged to occupy an area newly opened to the *tianguis*), or by the fact that rates were reduced at the location because it was away from the main stream of traffic.

Preferred positions for various goods are difficult to assign from observation since ease of access to *tianguis* does not vary from the several different directions. Although markets in buildings are planned with flower vendors at the main entrance, flower stalls are less in evidence in the *tianguis*, where the first salesmen met often are offering fruit. Meat, poultry and fish stalls have less preferred positions in housed markets, but these types of stalls are not common in *tianguis;* instead, they are found in permanent booths near the edge of the *tianguis*, or in the market building. An exception to both these generalisations is one of the larger *tianguis*, which meets on Fridays, where there are several vendors of fresh fish, one of whom occupies a prominent position close to the main street from which many of the buyers arrive.

Roughly two-thirds of the vendors sell foodstuffs, both perishable and staple dried foods (such as grains or chiles), and prepared foods (such as tortillas, barbecued meat or sauces). This proportion decreases only slightly in the larger *tianguis*, where there are more dry goods vendors. Few goods are sold in *tianguis* that are not available in at least some of the daily markets; however, live animals are more likely to be found in a *tianguis* than in a market. Chickens, turkeys and rabbits are common, and pigs, sheep and, occasionally, cows are available in small numbers. The administrators of market buildings discourage steady trade in live animals because they are a nuisance.

There appears to be no special division of labour in the *tianguis*, as there is none in the markets. Both men and women sell goods, and neither men nor women predominate consistently as sellers. Women are more likely to be selling surplus

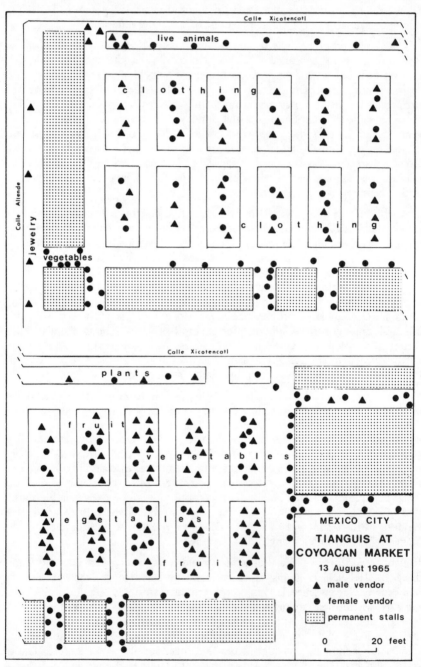

Figure 8.3   *Tianguis* at Coyocan market, Mexico City

country goods such as local pears, peaches, apples, avocados or mushrooms, but male vendors of these goods are also seen. In any event, country people selling small surpluses represent a small proportion of the total number of vendors and occupy the least preferred places. They are often found on the outer edges of the *tianguis*, or in doorways and along walls behind the makeshift display tables of the professional vendors.

The rhythm of business in the *tianguis* is well established. Vendors start arriving as early as 8 a.m. and continue to arrive to set up their benches and *sombras* until about 10 a.m. The late start may be owing to the distance some of the vendors travel. Many sellers claim to make daily trips to the wholesale markets, especially La Merced, before travelling to the outlying *tianguis*. Buyers may also start arriving as early as 8 a.m. but most come later. Trading starts in earnest about 10.30 or 11 a.m. and continues until about 2 p.m., unless interrupted by rain. Business does not cease for midday dinner but slackens from 2 p.m. until about 4 p.m. Some vendors of dry goods pack and leave during this interval, but most vendors stay. There is a slight increase in activity just before the *tianguis* closes about 7 p.m. There is some evidence to suggest that prices decrease as vendors try to dispose of perishable goods at the end of the day.

Almost all methods of transportation are used by *tianguistas*. Many own cars or trucks, which may be either unloaded and parked away from the marketplace or parked near the margin of the *tianguis* and used for display of goods. One of the unions of *tiangueros* owns a fleet of trucks to transport the goods of its members. Taxis are often used for moving goods for smaller enterprises in the city. Buses and streetcars are more often used by buyers than by sellers, partly because the seller has bulky items to handle and partly because he is now charged extra for his bundles whereas formerly he was not.

Organisation and Operation of *Tianguis*

Two levels of organisation interact in the *tianguis*, one for the operation at an individual site and the other for cooperation among vendors of similar items. Some eighteen unions represent vendors in *tianguis*. They are organised both by place of meeting and by goods sold (e.g., Unión de Comerciantes Tianguistas del Mercado Xochimilco, and Unión de Comerciantes Tianguistas en Pollitos Recién Nacidos). Although several unions may be represented in a given *tianguis*, one man is usually regarded as the leader, and through him a loosely organised form of internal control is maintained in a given location. The leader collects fees and coordinates welfare projects. Fees, or 'market taxes', are collected by the leader, who issues receipts to the vendors. The money collected is delivered directly to the Federal District treasury and not to the Department of Markets, which collects fees from vendors in permanent markets. In *tianguis* meeting outside the city, fees are sometimes paid directly to a local official rather than to the leader. Fees are charged on the space used for display of goods and not on the type of goods sold, as is the practice in the markets.

An important function of the leader is to help select a new site for the *tianguis* when this becomes necessary (as it does when a *tianguis* is suppressed subsequent to the construction of a market building). Site selection is based on personal knowledge of areas with growth potential and lack of competition. One leader reported that the vendors seek a concentration of population, near a church if possible, where retail facilities are not already available. These locations are increasingly difficult to find within the Federal District, so that new *tianguis* are more likely to be found toward the north and east in the State of Mexico.

Despite the loose organisation of the *tianguis* through a leader and the existence of unions, the operation of *tianguis* appears to be highly individualistic. Routes followed by *tiangueros* are not standardised, and the same group of *tiangueros* does not attend a single circuit of markets. The routes of individuals are fixed, however, and they rarely change unless a *tianguis* is disbanded at one location. Figure 8.4, showing several of the routes followed by *tiangueros*, illustrates the diversity of circuits followed in the vicinity of Mexico City.

From the independence of *tiangueros* in selecting the periodic markets they attend and the consequent failure of the individuals to move together from one meeting to another, it follows that the weekly calendar of *tianguis* conforms only partially to a neat theoretical pattern of spacing (Fig. 8.5). On most days the *tianguis* are far enough apart to avoid direct competition, but on Fridays, when the large, out-of-town *tianguis* meet (e.g., Toluca, Pachuca, Chalco and Santiago Tianguistengo), four *tianguis* in the city are concentrated in one area. When asked what *tianguis* were best, many vendors cited Toluca as the largest and busiest of markets, even if they did not attend themselves. Sunday is usually claimed to be the best day for selling, and *tiangueros* attend the market they judge is best on that day. No less than nine *tianguis* meet on Sundays; there is a gradual increase from four on Mondays to eight on Thursdays, after which there is a marked fall off, to two on Saturdays.[3]

With the exception of recent direct planning and construction of markets in government housing projects, a developmental sequence of market growth in Mexico City appears consistently to explain present market locations (Pyle, 1968). As an important early element in the sequence, *tianguis* are found in the areas of urban expansion away from the city centre (Fig. 8.1). These areas, characterised by low population density (Table 8.1) and low socio-economic level (Table 8.2), have both more *tianguis* and more vendors than other areas of

Table 8.1: *Tianguis* **and Population Density**

Characteristic	Density classes (thousands of inhabitants per square kilometre)				
	>40	20—40	10—19	>10	Total
Area (square kilometre)	26	56	44	175	301
Families (thousands)	195	251	153	250	849
Number of *tianguis*	3	4	10	16	33
Number of vendors	430	400	2,500	4,400	7,730

Source: Pyle, 1968, 58

Table 8.2: *Tianguis* **and Socio-Economic Level**

	Socio-economic level			Total
	High	Middle	Low	
Area (square kilometres)	9	101	191	301
Families (thousands)	16	364	469	849
Number of *tianguis*	0	11	22	33
Number of vendors	0	2,280	5,450	7,730

Source: Pyle, 1968, 63

the city, and leaders of *tianguis* seek new locations in these areas. As a *tianguis* flourishes, it attracts permanent vendors.[4] When at least a hundred vendors have established themselves to sell daily, they may petition the Department of Markets for the construction of a building. This is a fairly recent development, following a building programme initiated by the Federal District in 1955 to

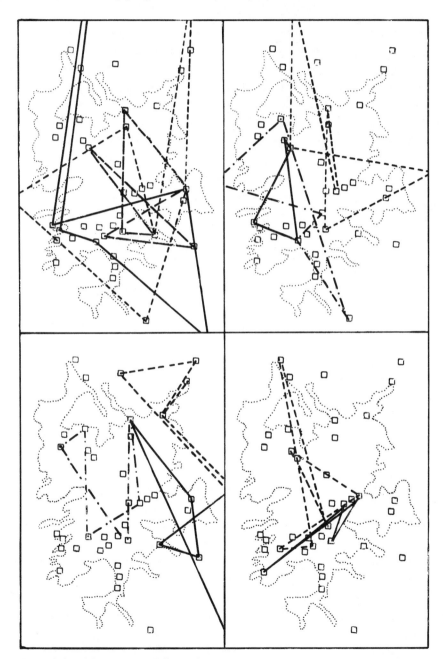

Figure 8.4   Selected routes followed by *tiangueros*

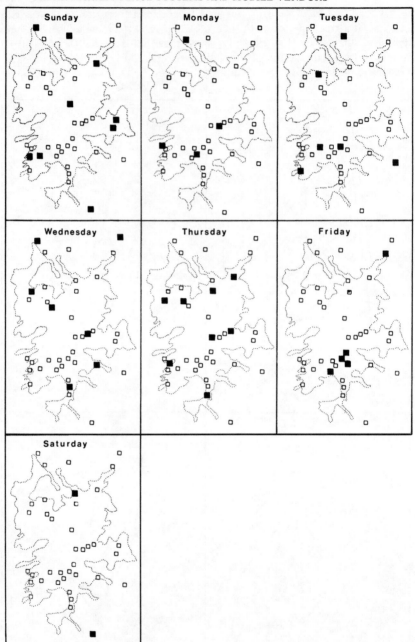

Figure 8.5   Calendar of *tianguis*. Vendors from Mexico City attend *tianguis* in many villages just outside the immediate vicinity of the city, such as Toluca (Friday), Pachuca (Monday and Friday), Chalco (Friday), Amecameca (Sunday), and Ozumba (Tuesday and Friday)

replace street markets. Since the programme of construction started, the policy of the Department of Markets has been to discourage *tianguis* because they often block traffic, lack sanitation, and are difficult to control. As a result, when a building is constructed the *tianguis* is suppressed and vendors must seek out a new location.

The developmental sequence — *tianguis*, street market, building — cannot be fully verified, although there is a considerable amount of supporting historical evidence (Pyle, 1968). Locations of former *tianguis* cannot be mapped, for as one vendor said, 'Before 1955 Mexico City was just one big *tianguis*.' Although the administration officially discourages *tianguis* by forbidding their continued meeting after construction of a market building and by regulating pedlars, with whom *tiangueros* are often associated in the minds of administrators, the government does not take responsibility for planning new market locations but merely reacts to congregations of vendors when they become large enough to be problems in sanitation and control. *Tianguis* are officially discouraged because of problems of control, but they are tolerated at least partly because they perform a useful service.

Conclusion

Tianguis are a surviving element of the traditional urban scene. Their essentially parasitic relationship to public markets renders them a natural object for concern by government. However, they perform a very important function by providing basic, low-order goods for large numbers of low-income people, especially in the peripheral growing parts of the city, and they also serve a useful purpose in selecting new locations for permanent markets.

[1] The word *tianguis* is derived from the Aztec (Nahuatl) word *tianguixtle,* meaning a market (Galindo y Villa, 1925, 63). It is not in widespread use throughout Mexico, and even in Mexico City it is used more by vendors in the *tianguis* than by anyone else. Its apparently local use may be the result of revival of an indigenous expression; such a revival is being attempted by the merchants of Mexico City, who are using the Aztec symbol and word *pochteca* in a loose sense of merchant or trader in their promotional activity. It seems more likely, however, that the word *tianguis* lost ground in competition with the Spanish word *mercado*, or that it was never widely accepted. Earlier, *tianguis* referred solely to Indian markets and some prejudice may have worked against its continued respectable use because of this connotation. The word *tianguis* may be little used simply because there are fewer periodic markets now than formerly, and because many markets have replaced former *tianguis*, a change that further reinforces the use of the word *mercado*.

[2] Organised within the Treasury Department, the Department of Markets is charged with the regulation of markets and ambulatory vendors. It issues vending permits, regulates the installation and maintenance of stalls, administers markets in buildings, fixes places and times when *tianguis* may meet in the public markets, and enforces regulations pertaining to the markets. It does not regulate the *tianguis* except to permit or forbid them in permanent market buildings.

[3] It is interesting to note that Sunday and Thursday have maximum temporal separation (cf. Hill and Smith, 1972, 348-49).

[4] Rarely are these *tiangueros* who have decided to settle down, although some may establish their wives or children in a permanent location and continue to travel themselves. Some *tiangueros* expressed the sentiment that following a route was a way of life that they did not want to change. Others said that sales were faster in the *tianguis* and thus it was more interesting to be on the move. Those interviewed denied that they had to travel in order to make a living. Stine (1962, 73) bases his theoretical treatment of periodic markets on an assumption of the profit maximizing motive. Although this motive can hardly be dismissed in a Mexican context it is perhaps revealing that it was not articulated by any *tiangueros* interviewed.

9 Travelling night markets in Singapore
Yue-man Yeung

In many rural areas of the world, periodic markets and fairs constitute a familiar landscape feature closely bound up with transportation technology, levels of living, and methods of economic organisation (Allix, 1922; Hodder, 1961; Skinner, 1964; Spencer, 1940; and Yang, 1944). In the city there are normally enough static marketing elements to discourage the existence of periodic markets. Indeed, many scholars believe that urban retail units represent the end product in an evolutionary process from mobile to static modes (Berry, 1967, 111-14). For instance, Hodder (1971) and Scott (1970, 127-41) suggest two paths periodic markets can take in their development: shops, and specialised wholesale daily markets. Much of the literature deals with periodic markets in a rural context; Singapore's travelling night markets are explicitly urban phenomena and therefore are of special interest and significance, particularly as they display a distinct cycle of periodicity. A similar orderly system of periodic markets is also found in Mexico City (Pyle, 1970; and Pyle, in this volume).

There have been several recent surveys related to travelling night markets in Singapore (Nanyang University Geographical Society, 1973; Lim, 1973),[1] and in 1970 the author conducted a comprehensive survey of night markets (Yeung, 1973, 7). This essay is concerned especially with the mechanics of the present night market system, and with their spatial and temporal distribution. In addition, the origins of the system will be discussed and a typology of the markets will be presented.

Origins of *Pasar Malam*

Although they are now widespread, travelling night markets (or *pasar malam*, as they are called locally), are a relatively recent phenomenon (Fig. 9.1). Despite the early operators' knowledge of periodic markets in China, Singapore's system seems to be an independent development, more in keeping with local conditions

---

* I wish to extend my sincere thanks to students of the Geography Department at the University of Singapore for their active participation in my survey of night markets; to the Geographical Society of Nanyang University for the release of night market customers data; and to Mrs Charlotte Lim for the use of unpublished survey data on market operators.

than as the result of conscious transfer of techniques. Chao (1962) noted that the first night market was started in 1953 in Jalan Kayu by a group of enterprising hawkers whose mode of operation had hitherto been associated with opera troupes and followed their itinerant performing schedules. Higher profits connected with hawking at these opera sites spurred the pioneers to look for a more dependable clientele than that attracted by erratic performing schedules. Early night markets were explored in Sembawang and the Keppel Harbour area, where not only fewer shops existed in relation to the population but, perhaps more importantly, weekly markets were scheduled to coincide with the pay day of the workers in the military establishments in the vicinity.

Growth of night markets initially was slow. At this incipient stage the *pasar malam* were nurtured by indigenous and expatriate employees of the military bases in different parts of the island. Growth became more rapid with the beginning of the present phase of accelerated public housing construction in 1960. The development in the early 1960s of public and private housing estates, in which shopping facilities were insufficient to meet demands, contributed to the mushrooming of night markets at this stage. By 1962 the basic framework of the present system of night markets had crystallised, with forty *pasar malam* operating in different parts of the island in a week. Markets established later tend to fill the interstices of a pattern already formed, and many gravitated towards the western Alexandra—Queensway corridor where substantial population increases associated with public housing have since taken place. Not all of the original forty market sites are shown in Figure 9.1 as more than ten sites have since been abandoned or resited. Many of those abandoned market sites are in close proximity to the new sites that have subsequently been opened. This serves to underline the limited maximum range of many *pasar malam*, a feature related to the role and nature of the markets themselves.

The Present System of *Pasar Malam*

There are sixty-six recorded night markets in Singapore: several usually operated with less than ten stalls, and fifty-seven markets were covered in the author's night markets survey (Yeung, 1973). The survey recorded a total of 4,853 stalls and 8,787 hawkers; the mean number of stalls, functions and hawkers were 86, 22 and 156 respectively. *Pasar malam* vary considerably in size and, to a lesser degree, in function. In size, they range from an agglomeration of less than ten stalls to over 200. In all cases, however, the markets operate well below capacity which is fixed by the number of licenses issued and pitches marked. Hawkers pay a license fee on the basis of the number of occupied unit pitch each measuring three by one metres (six by four feet), and each operator can occupy as many as four units.

The system of travelling night markets is characterised by a regulated cycle of about eight markets per night, with the peak trading period stretching from about 7 to 10 p.m. On the same night, individual markets are never sited close to one another, thus minimising competition. The week-long spatio-temporal pattern is portrayed in Figure 9.2, which shows that when all markets in the week are considered, they occur most frequently at a distance of from two to eight km (one to five miles) from the city centre (i.e., within the urban area, Fig. 9.1). Within this zone, markets meeting on the same night rarely are more than one km (half a mile) apart, and in many cases spatial separation is considerably less. Market size also varies considerably, with the smallest and some of

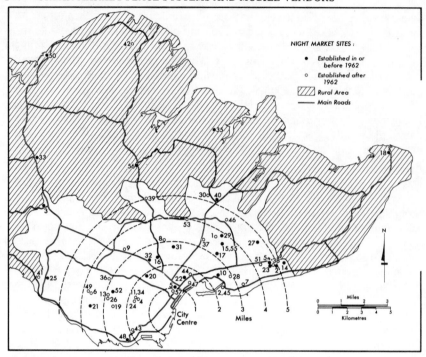

Figure 9.1

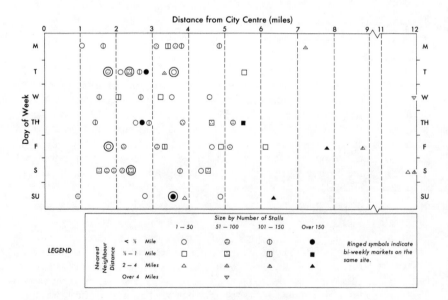

Figure 9.2   Spatio-temporal pattern of travelling night markets

Figure 9.1   Travelling night market sites in Singapore. Key to market code numbers (see text for explanation of types):

Code	Market	Code	Market
Type I		*Type II*	
2	Frankel Avenue	1	Aljunied Lane
3	Jalan Jurong Kerchil	5	Prinsep Street
7	Tanjong Katong	13	Jalan Rumah Tinggi
9	Dunkirk Crescent	16	Thompson Road
10	Guillemard Road	19	Hocksan Estate
12	Jalan Batu	21	Stirling Road
14	Opera Estate	23	Still Road
18	Changi Village	27	Jalan Eunos
20	Tanglin Road	28	Kallang Estate
22	Hamshire Road	31	St Michael's Market
25	Clementi Road	54	Changi Road
29	Macpherson Road		
30	Lorong Chuan	*Type III*	
32	Kg. Java Road	4	Jalan Bukit Ho Swee
33	Bukit Panjang Village	6	Queen's Crescent
35	Jalan Kayu	11	Indus Road
37	Tai Thong Crescent	24	Beo Crescent
39	Thompson Road	26	Commonwealth Avenue
40	Upper Serangoon Road	34	Indus Road
41	West Coast Road, 8½ m.s.	36	Margaret Drive
42	Chong Pang Village	52	Alexandra Road
43	Cantonment Road		
44	Kampong Kapor	*Type IV*	
45	Jalan Batu	15	Pesiarian Keliling
47	Sumbawa Road	17	Aljunied Road
48	Telok Blangah Road	46	Industrial Road
50	Woodlands, 14¾ m.s.	55	Pesiarian Keliling
53	Braddell Road	*Type V*	
56	Sembawang Road	38	Telok Kurau
57	Short Street		
		Type VI	
		49	Tanglin Halt
		Ungrouped	
		8	Balestier Road
		51	Everitt Road

the largest markets being found here. Nevertheless, in the more outlying and rural area, markets not only tend to be larger; beyond the eleven-km (seven-mile) limit, the nearest[2] markets are without exception, the farthest apart as well. The markets occur in closer proximity to each other in centres of population concentration. Markets are held on new sites on each night of the week, and only where exceptionally favourable conditions prevail are markets held on the same site more than once a week.

The preference for unique sites on different days of the week to repeated use of the same site is a consequence of an at once self-imposed and self-regulating mechanism. Chao (1962) reported that in the cases of at least four sites, attempts were made to operate for a second night; quarrels ensued when business in the first night declined, and latecomers were persuaded (sometimes coerced) to look for a new site. This is consistent with an observation made by Yap (1972, 35) who recently found that the locus of hawker mobility in relation to other *pasar malam* can be identified by groups. *Pasar malam* operators trading in rural centres do not usually choose public housing sites for other nights' activities. In addition, Yap noted that the choice of market sites (at least for a significant proportion of hawkers) was governed by proximity to home so as to minimise transport costs and time. In general, the less 'local' the night market, the greater the distance travelled and the mobility of hawkers. Urban markets are thus characterised by typically short-distance movements of their operators, whereas the converse is true of rural markets.

In the present system, the cycle of periodicity among the market sites is complete in one week. Night markets occur every night of the week but, judged by the number of markets and stalls (Fig. 9.2) and, by inference, the level of activity, Wednesday and Sunday nights are, in relative terms, the slack evenings of the week. In a sample of *pasar malam* operators, Lim (1973) found that more hawkers traded every night of the week than those who reported not selling in any night of the week. She also found that in three nights of the week, Monday, Tuesday and Wednesday, more hawkers took a rest than in the other nights.

As Table 9.1 indicates, the majority of the stalls in night markets are manned by one hawker (42.0 per cent) or two hawkers (40.1 per cent), with a progressively smaller proportion of the stalls operated by up to five or more hawkers. The dependence on one or more operators seems to vary with the nature of stalls; eating places have the largest proportion of single operators, whereas for the clothing and personal furnishing group stalls with two hawkers predominate. This latter group ranks first in total number of stalls, with 2,644 of 4,853 (55 per cent). The remaining four retail categories have an approximately equal number of stalls, ranging from 10 to 12 per cent of the total. However, service functions are conspicuous by their absence, and there are only three stalls in this category. This observation distinguishes Singapore's travelling night markets

Table 9.1: Business Functions by Stall Size in Singapore's *Pasar Malam*

Functions	Stalls by Number of Hawkers							Number of
	1	2	3	4	5	5+	Total	Hawkers
Retail								
Eating Places	327	146	33	10	3	0	519	773
Food	211	225	96	35	12	6	585	1,185
Clothing and Personal Furnishings	978	1,146	381	97	29	13	2,644	4,956
Personal Needs	265	198	52	4	0	0	519	841
Household Goods and Furnishings	255	231	80	13	4	0	583	1,029
Services								
Fortune Telling	3	0	0	0	0	0	3	3
Total								
Number	2,039	1,946	642	159	48	19	4,853	8,787
Per cent	42.0	40.1	13.2	3.3	1.0	0.4	100.0	

Source: Author's night markets survey.

from the rural periodic fairs and markets referred to earlier, in which service and social (and occasionally political) activities loom large. It would appear that in Singapore, *pasar malam* have a rather specific and well-defined role to play: that is, they fill a lacuna in the marketing system which static retail elements have not adequately served. This role seems to be remarkably consistent throughout the year; thus, Lim (1973) found that all of her sample of *pasar malam* operators were engaged in selling the same line of goods at any time of the year, with little adjustment to meet seasonal demands. In their present form and under the prevailing social conditions, night markets do not perform any social function of significance.

Yeung (1973, 120-30) has substantiated the short maximum range of Singapore's *pasar malam*. This seems to be related to generally high levels of urban transport costs and to the predominance of low-order goods for which the demand is elastic. Conversely, the minimum range is large. Night markets in the urban area often operate in areas of medium to low population density with medium to high socio-economic status. Thus, despite high levels of disposable income, there is no sustaining demand from low population densities for a market to operate more frequently than once a week. The limited maximum range of goods in *pasar malam* is underscored when it is noted that since the relocation of Tanglin Road Market in early 1971 from its former thriving Wednesday meeting along Orchard Road a stone's throw away, business is reported to have declined.

Night Hawkers and Customers

Pasar malam are run almost exclusively by Chinese operators, and even with those participants from other ethnic groups, Chinese dialects still form the lingua franca in most transactions. The multi-lingual ability of *pasar malam* operators was also emphasised by Chao (1962). Educational attainment of most night hawkers tends to be low: the majority completed only primary education in the Chinese stream, and only a relatively small number received any secondary education (Chao, 1962). Related no doubt to the historical development of night markets, both Yap (1972) and Lim (1973) found that over 70 per cent of the operators were of at least five years' standing in their business; there have been very few entrants to the system in recent years.

The Nanyang survey reveals that the six sampled *pasar malam* attracted, on the average, 3,000 customers (Yap, 1972, 12). As there were an average of 82 hawkers per *pasar malam*, it is estimated that every hawker had about 400 customers.[3] Although not all of these people would buy, the number of potential customers is still very large. However, this potentially large clientele is not reflected in the level of earnings by each stall: Lim's data indicated that 66 per cent of the sampled operators reported net earnings of between S$4 and S$12 (US$1 = S$2.50) per night per stall. There is, of course, a high probability that the high earners are included in the minority and that operators may under-report their profits.

The night markets survey results agree well with other observations on the functions of *pasar malam* and consumer behaviour: Lim's data showed that *pasar malam*, from the standpoint of the operators, was primarily a local marketing institution (Lim, 1973), with most customers coming from the immediate neighbourhood. The proportion of regular customers is moderately high, with 32 per cent of the operators reporting 25 per cent of their business with regular customers. The notion of a local clientele is reinforced by the results of the Nanyang Survey which show that half of the customers come from within two km (one mile), arriving principally on foot (72.3 per cent). In addition, 64 per cent of the interviewed customers stated that they did not visit any other *pasar malam* apart from the one they were patronising. The modal frequency of attendance was weekly (47.8 per cent), followed by fortnightly (27.8 per cent), and monthly (14.2 per cent). Thus, almost half of the customers regularly use the weekly cycle.

The dominance of Chinese operators is matched by an overwhelming Chinese participation in patronage. The Nanyang Survey reveals that 93 per cent of the *pasar malam* clientele was Chinese, although the sex distribution favours females (in contrast to the dominance of male operators): 58.5 per cent female compared with 41.5 per cent male. Most customers came from the younger age groups: just over half of the customers were between 15 and 25 years of age, and over 80 per cent were below 35 years of age. In this respect customers resembled operators. Many of the customers spent over two hours in the *pasar malam*, but the modal length of stay was 1 to 1½ hours (37.2 per cent). Most visitors are moderate spenders, as suggested by over half of them spending from S$1 to S$20 per month. To some extent, this explains the rather low level of operators' income.

A Typology of *Pasar Malam*

The discussion so far has been concerned with the entire system, and has not focused on individual markets. Yap (1972) performed a classification of 59 markets using a number of variables, and arrived at a typology of six market types.[4] The characteristics of the six groups are summarised in Table 9.2, which is discussed below.

Type I: Non-local market

This group represents the *pasar malam* phenomenon, comprising the largest number of markets whose major characteristic is an exceedingly high proportion of the operators living outside the Postal District[5] in which the *pasar malam* occurs; operators often travel long distances to reach market sites. Most hawkers sell *general merchandise* items and the smallest number belongs to the *drinks* group. Multiple-pitch stalls are well represented.

The thirty markets of this group are widely distributed geographically, occupying sites ranging from near the city centre to the rural area (Fig. 9.1). Whereas rural markets cater largely for daily necessities, *pasar malam* in the more central localities depend on lower prices and convenience to attract customers. Although twenty-one of the thirty markets were established before 1962, this group of markets appears the most attractive to new operators to enter the *pasar malam* system. This is implied by the highest proportion of traders having less than one year of experience.

Type II: Average market

The eleven markets of this group are concentrated in five Postal Districts. Whereas the proportion of 'local' operators is higher than that in Type I markets, stall size does not seem to differ significantly. It suggests that the scale of operation and 'local' character are not necessarily linked. Many of the characteristics of Type II markets are close to the national average, hence the designation.

Type III: Local or HDB[6] market

Located exclusively in public housing estates, the nine Type III markets are confined to only Postal Districts 3 and 12. They were all developed after 1962, in response to local shopping demands. The proportion of 'local' operators is

Table 9.2: Summary of Characteristics of *Pasar Malam* Types

Market Type	I	II	III	IV	V	VI	Total
Number of Markets	30	11	9	5	3	1	59
Mean Number of Hawkers	98	77	61	88	9	107	82
Mean Number of Stalls	221	172	116	172	15	231	178
Markets (%)							
Commodities[a] General Merchandise	85.0	79.3	84.1	87.1	46.5	89.3	82.1
Food	6.7	8.8	6.3	4.9	28.9	3.9	7.9
Drinks	2.4	4.2	5.3	3.3	8.3	1.0	3.5
Fruits	5.8	7.7	4.2	4.6	16.3	5.8	6.4
Stall Size (%)[a] 1 Pitch	28.1	36.3	36.9	34.8	84.5	23.4	33.9
2 Pitch	35.5	35.7	41.4	40.0	11.8	46.7	35.8
3 Pitch	27.4	20.7	14.0	18.8	3.7	20.6	22.4
4 Pitch	9.0	7.3	7.6	6.4	0.0	9.3	7.9
Operators							
Mean Age (years)	39	39	41	40	39	38	39
Sex[a] (%) Male	80.3	81.15	76.19	73.91	88.17	80.37	79.63
Female	19.7	18.84	23.80	26.08	11.82	19.62	20.36
'Non-Local'	86.29	59.49	24.17	59.28	39.17	40.56	66.35
'Local'	13.70	40.50	75.82	40.71	60.82	59.43	33.64
With Owned Transport	55.09	57.01	56.80	43.39	63.81	47.66	54.18
Without Owned Transport	44.91	42.99	43.19	56.60	36.18	52.33	45.81
Years of Experience 1	1.4	0.5	0.7	0.4	0.1	0.0	1.5
2	7.3	7.7	9.9	8.4	3.7	2.8	7.9
3	6.7	5.1	5.1	4.4	2.5	9.3	5.9
4	7.5	6.1	4.6	9.4	5.5	9.3	6.9
5+	77.1	80.6	79.4	77.4	88.1	78.5	77.8

Source: Yap, 1972, 13.

[a] Percentage totals may not sum to 100.0 due to rounding.

unusually high and, in contrast to Type I and II markets, Type III markets tend to be smaller in terms of both stall size and total number of hawkers and stalls. The average age of the operators is marginally higher than that in other groups, which is consistent with the general observation that the older the age of operators, the more 'local' the market.

Type IV: Female operator market

Like Type III markets, the five markets of this group are all sited in HDB estates. However, since they are not in areas with the highest densities of hawkers, the 'local' tendency is not pronounced. Two features appear to set these markets apart from the other groups: the highest incidence of female participation, and the largest proportion of operators without owned transport. As with Type III markets, the stalls are generally small.

Type V: Withering or male operator market

Longest established in terms of operators' experience and distinctly 'local', the three Type V markets appear to be on their way to decline if not disappearance. Table 9.2 indicates the highest proportion of male participation, small stalls, and a distribution of commodities weighted heavily towards food and fruits.[7]

Type VI: Tanglin halt market

If it were not for the high percentage of 'local' operators, this market could be grouped under Type I market. Stalls are generally big and deal mostly in general merchandise.

The implication to be drawn from this classification of *pasar malam* is that the mobility of operators and, by implication, the 'local' tendency, is a function of the operators' sex, age, ownership of transport, and commodities traded. Operators engaged in the sale of general merchandise and fruits exhibit much greater mobility than food sellers who are quite restricted in their movements. The relationship between types of goods sold and market sites seems clear: in higher-income or European districts, general merchandise stalls, by virtue of their greater appeal, prevail. In contrast, *pasar malam* operating in lower-income areas devote greater attention to food items. It is useful to order the available information about *pasar malam* in this way, but such a classification does not clarify the interrelationship of the markets, especially those which pertain to the timing and spacing of meetings.

Spatio-Temporal Analysis of *Pasar Malam*

Such authors as Stine (1962), Hay (1971) and Smith (1971) searched for explanations of linkages between temporal periodicity and locational spacing, but a general theory of periodic markets with wide applicability is yet to be propounded. As a step towards that goal, Fagerlund and Smith (1970) suggested an admirably simple working hypothesis, that proximity in space implies separation in time. They proposed that spatial and temporal competition are complementary, and that markets located close to each other in space will be separated by longer time intervals, and *vice versa*. This section will examine this hypothesis using data from Singapore's *pasar malam*.[8] Measurements were taken from each of the fifty-seven travelling night markets (Yeung, 1973) to the

Table 9.3: Temporal and Locational Spacing of Singapore's Night Markets (kilometres)

	Temporal Separation (nights)			
	Same	Adjacent	One-night	Two-nights
By Market Group				
All Markets	3.36	1.98	2.17	2.20
Rural Markets	7.39	7.35	8.11	9.46
Urban Markets	2.85	1.35	1.43	1.29
By Night of Week				
Monday	3.57	1.53	2.04	1.27
Tuesday	2.27	1.13	1.13	1.13
Wednesday	4.15	2.56	2.48	2.43
Thursday	2.85	1.16	1.26	1.40
Friday	4.07	2.38	2.77	2.59
Saturday	2.93	3.03	3.30	4.25
Sunday	3.88	1.75	1.50	1.74

Source: Author's night markets survey.

nearest market meeting on the same night, on pre- or post-adjacent nights, pre- or post-adjacent nights plus one night, and on pre- or post-adjacent nights plus two nights. The mean distances are recorded in Table 9.3.

It is readily apparent that while the hypothesis is generally applicable, there are conspicuous anomalies. Whereas, for instance, the average spacing values for all markets and urban markets conform roughly to the postulated regularities, the rural markets do not. Rural markets whose meetings are separated by one and two nights are (comparatively) widely spaced 'on the ground'. Several reasons can be advanced in explanation. Firstly, there are only six rural *pasar malam* in Singapore (Fig. 9.1), and they provide anything but uniform coverage of the rural areas. Moreover, even temporal spacing is incomplete: no rural market occurs on Mondays or Tuesdays. Frequently, urban markets were used in the measurement of distances to nearest markets, accounting in part for the large mean distances and inversion of locational spacing of markets at one and two nights apart.

A second reason relates to the existence of factors extraneous to the night market system. The *pasar malam* operate within fairly restricted spatial and functional limits, and since they have to compete with static and day-time mobile marketing units, they are never allowed full authority in locational choice, particularly in the urban area. In other words, within the locational constraints imposed by population densities and different forms of business competition, *pasar malam* must seek out the interstices of the demand surface inadequately filled. To compensate for the relative lack of influence in choosing locations, they can more readily regulate temporal periodicity and schedule meetings the most efficient way. The self-correcting mechanism helps to rectify inefficiencies arising from excessive competition through too close temporal and locational spacing. Finally, the use of linear instead of functional distances may also contribute to the disparity between empirical results and theoretical norms.

When the temporal and locational spacing of markets is analysed by nights of the week, the results do not approximate more closely to the anticipated regularities. In fact, the hypothesis is confirmed in about half of the cases: distances separating nearly all nearest markets on adjacent nights are shorter than for those on the same night. However, when markets at one and two nights remove are considered, almost all mean distances are anomalous. With the exception of Tuesday and Wednesday markets, all markets on other nights are at greater distances apart as compared with adjacent-night markets.[9] The considerable variation in every set of distance measurements may reflect uneven population distribution and other competing marketing facilities. On the basis of the evidence adduced, it appears that the articulation of locational spacing is more difficult than temporal control in the system.

Table 9.4: Nearest Market by Temporal Separation and Nights of Week

| | Nights of Week | | | | | | | |
Temporal Separation	M	T	W	Th	F	Sat	Su	Total
Same Night	0	0	0	0	0	4	0	4
Adjacent Nights	1	1	3	2	3	1	1	12
One Night	1	3	3	4	3	2	4	20
Two Nights	6	4	1	2	4	3	1	21
Total	8	8	7	8	10	10	6	57

Source: Author's night markets survey.

Identification of nearest neighbours with respect to the same scheme of temporal spacing yielded more encouraging results, and Table 9.4 indicates that with the exception of Saturday markets, markets on every other night have a great majority of (spatially) nearest markets at one and two nights remove. That almost an equal number of nearest markets is spaced at one and two nights apart serves to show that while there must be a break of one complete night before shopping demand re-emerges, the difference between a separation of one and two nights is apparently immaterial. In a clearer way, therefore, the nearest-market analysis does give support to the notion that spatial and temporal competition are qualifiedly complementary in the system of *pasar malam*.

Conclusion

It has been the purpose of this paper to document the phenomenon of travelling night markets in Singapore, but it is also appropriate to raise several points of a more general theoretical and policy nature (Yeung, 1974). At the present time, there are insufficient urban periodic market systems documented to judge whether the operation of such systems can be explained in similar terms to those which apply to their rural counterparts. The Singapore case, however, does provide several points of departure.

The policy implication to be drawn from this study is that there appear to be two alternatives at the disposal of the city administration with respect to mobile marketing elements. One is an active strategy, in which the authorities have a decisive say in matters of the location and number of stalls and hawkers, etc. An example of this approach is Singapore's recent decision to relocate street and stall hawkers into landscaped and sanitary hawker centres. The alternative is the present system of *pasar malam*, in which the government plays but a passive role. Initially, the government exerted a minor influence on the mechanics and planning of night markets; assessment of market viability and site selection was left entirely to individual hawkers, almost invariably on a trial-and-error basis, and the government exercised greater control only after the market had started to function. The public roles are limited to the licensing of hawkers, resiting of markets when and where there is need, and policing of the market area. The experience of *pasar malam* in Singapore suggests that, given a tolerant and benign official attitude and the existence of a pool of energetic entrepreneurs, a marketing innovation can evolve.

There has recently been a noticeable decline in the fortunes of some *pasar malam*, associated apparently with the British military pullout and the departure of attendant personnel. It is perilous to speculate whether the present marks the beginning of an end of this heretofore successful institution, but the heyday of the system seems gone beyond recall. That dynamism still remains in the system is reflected in the beginning of booming *pasar malam* recently in Jurong, the industrial town in west Singapore. The *pasar malam* has been legalised on Wednesday nights in Jurong, although trading activities are carried out on many other nights of the week as well. This recent development is reminiscent of the extraordinary growth of the system in the early 1960s, when rapid development of residential estates contributed substantially to the expansion and consolidation of the system. In view of the resilience of the *pasar malam* system, and given the fact that many new towns are being developed by government authorities, the *pasar malam* should have an assured future barring official intervention to the contrary.

---

[1] The Nanyang survey was conducted in late 1971 by the Geographical Society of Nanyang University. The survey covered 1,689 customers in six markets: Jalan Jurong Kerchil, St. Michael's Market, Jalan Bukit Ho Swee, Pesiarian Keliling, Telok Kurau, and Tanglin Halt (Fig. 9.1). Charlotte Lim's hawker study included a national sample of 1,128 hawkers, 44 of whom were *pasar malam* operators. Lim's survey results are being incorporated into a Master's dissertation in Sociology at the University of Singapore.

[2] 'Nearest' is used here in a strictly spatial sense, with no reference to time of meeting. The nearest market can be any market meeting on any night.

[3] It should be noted that since the Nanyang survey included only six markets, these statistics are representative of only the surveyed markets. The Author's night markets survey (see also Yeung, 1973), suggests that the average figures in the Nanyang survey were reduced by the smaller markets surveyed; the mean hawker numbers in the two surveys are, respectively, 156 and 82.

[4] This was a 20-stage linkage tree analysis, using 20 variables in seven groups (Yap, 1972, 7-8). They were average age; sex; degree of 'localism'; percentage of hawkers with means of transport; years of hawking experience; number of stalls occupied; and kind of goods sold. It should also be noted that because of different research methodologies, there is a slight discrepancy in the number of markets in the Yap and Yeung studies. Yap collected data from hawker files on 59 markets, 55 of which tally with those in Yeung's night markets survey (see also Yeung, 1973).

[5] The Republic of Singapore is divided into 28 Postal Districts. The relationship of place of residence and market sites is the basis upon which 'local' markets are differentiated from 'non-local' markets.

[6] The Housing and Development Board (HDB) is a statutory body responsible for, among other things, the development of public housing in Singapore.

[7] This suggests that a *pasar malam* is sustained by stalls specialising in general merchandise, not by those selling food and fruit items, which appeal more to the impulsive buyer.

[8] An expanded version of this part of the paper has been presented in Yeung (1974).

[9] The standard deviations for all distance measures are very high, often as large as or even exceeding the mean, and caution in interpretation is in order.

10 Periodic markets in a metropolitan environment: the example of Lagos, Nigeria

P.O. Sada, M.L. McNulty, and I.A. Adalemo

The general conditions for the existence of periodic markets in developing areas were outlined by Stine (1962); his model provided for a change in the marketing system as the environmental conditions are altered through increasing demand density until the periodic market begins to function as a daily or permanent market. Urban population growth represents one such major change in the marketing landscape, and is synonymous with a rapid intensification of the marketing landscape; there is an increase in the density of households ('demand density' in Stine's terminology), and also an increase in the degree of household participation in the marketing process which is associated with a rise in the level of disposable income. These conditions which result from urban population growth and the transformation from a self-sufficient to a wage-earning and monetised economy have very significant implications for the functional and temporal features of traditional markets.

Markets serve a variety of economic and social functions both of which are influenced by the process of urbanisation. In Nigeria, markets are associated socially with gods, the regular worship of which is deemed to be necessary for economic well-being. A local chief is normally in charge of a market and regular worship of the market god by the chief forms an essential part of the social life of the community. The basic four-day period in Nigeria's Yorubaland (of which Lagos is a part) is rooted in Yoruba religion: 'Four is the sacred Yoruba figure and their standard unit of calculations' (Hodder and Ukwu, 1969, 60). Each of the four days is set aside for four major deities and their local variants.[1] A major influence of urbanisation is the suppression of the socio-religious ties of the markets so that the holding of a market has virtually no religious or ritual connotation. This in turn makes for easy transformation from one periodic system to another.

In terms of economic functions, markets are points of spatial articulation in the collection and distribution of goods as well as services. Initial functions of the markets are generally confined to the provision of low order goods and services, especially foodstuffs, to a limited trade area. A wider variety of goods and

* We acknowledge the generous support of the Rockefeller Foundation for this research.

services begins to be offered once demand density increases to a point where the minimum range or threshold is achieved (Stine, 1962, 77). Demand density, defined as a function of population density and level of disposable income, increases as urbanisation proceeds. With the process of urbanisation, higher order goods are added to the initial stock of lower order goods. Thus it may be argued that a large proportion of higher order goods is a concomitant of urbanisation and, further, that such functional changes will be spatially differentiated, with markets located near the centre of the city being the first to be affected.

Urbanisation also affects the periodicity of the markets. As demand density rises, market meetings occur more frequently (Berry, 1967, 96); this is accentuated by the urbanisation impulse towards occupational specialisation. Ultimately, specialised and full-time traders emerge and market periodicity ceases. Such a change in market schedules will not occur abruptly, except in those cases where the days of meeting are regulated by a controlling authority. Rather, the volume of trading on days preceding and following market day gradually increases, until it is difficult to distinguish the actual market day from non-market days. Through the intensification of demand for market products, urbanisation gives rise to daily markets.

The changing nature of the urban marketing landscape in developing areas is illustrated in Figure 10.1. A pronounced change in the marketing environment is encountered in a traverse from the centre of the metropolitan area to the periphery. At the city centre is an area of high demand density associated with the concentration of large numbers of people with relatively higher levels of disposable income. Surrounding the immediate centre is an area of somewhat lesser density of population and a lower level of income. Outside the city itself may be a suburban ring, a still lower income density area; although such suburban areas are characterised by high population densities, they are very often the poorest urban dwellers. Thus, there is a per capita income surface which declines from the centre of the city to the rural fringe. The implications of such a surface for the existence of periodic markets are that as distance from the centre increases, the range of goods offered narrows, periodicity increases, and the number of relatively small markets rises.

Periodic markets represent the spatial articulation of periodic cycles of activity intensity. The size of urban service centres is known to pulsate in a periodic manner as mobile facilities (buyers and sellers) converge on them at periodic intervals. For all practical purposes these urban markets are daily markets, but on specific days the size of the market swells markedly. Empirical evidence seems to confirm the deductive hypothesis that the magnitude of the daily component of periodic markets is strong in the urban centre and declines with distance away from the city, so that the market-place at some critical distance from the city is devoid of any marketing activity on all but the market day. A corollary of the distance relationship is that there is also a decline in both the number and range of goods and services offered; in the remote village, few if any goods or services are offered on a daily basis in the market-place.[2]

On the basis of these characteristics, markets can be classified into four groups (Fig. 10.2). The first consists of those markets with *regular (or simple) periodicity*, which meet at periodic intervals corresponding to the regime(s) which operates in the area in which they are located. They have no daily component, and any marketing transactions occurring on non-market days generally

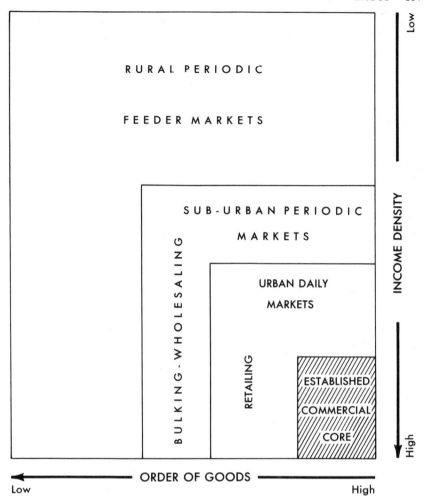

Figure 10.1   Schematic diagram of urban market structure

take place outside the market-place. Markets with *modified periodicity* have very weak daily components and are found in rural towns. The *urban periodic* market, the third category, is actually an *incipient daily market* with periodic 'bursts' of higher activity intensity. The daily component of these markets is very strong.[3] The final category includes the *urban daily* market where the level of activity intensity remains roughly the same each day.[4] They meet all day and offer a wide range of goods. The urban daily markets merge somewhat imperceptibly with the shops and supermarkets together with which they represent the increasingly stable service centre which in itself is a part of the modern urban commercial system.

The purpose of this paper is to assess some of the propositions outlined above in the capital city of Nigeria, Lagos. Like a large number of the world's cities, metropolitan Lagos is experiencing the problems associated with large scale population growth. The population of 42,000 at the turn of the century had

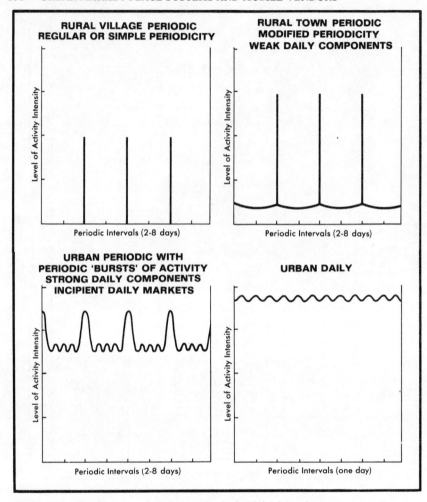

Figure 10.2   Classification of markets on level of activity intensity

trebled by 1931 and by 1963 there were more than a million people living in Lagos. While the rate of annual increase was 3.4 per cent between 1901 and 1950, it rose to 13.6 per cent in the decade 1953-63. Such rapid urbanisation has had a decided impact on traditional markets, and this paper is concerned specially with the ramifications of this impact on the thirty markets in the city (Fig. 10.3).

Periodic Markets in Lagos[5]

Of the thirty markets in the metropolitan area, seven existed as periodic markets up until 1940 (Ebute-Ero, Obun-Eko, Oyingbo, Mushin, Iganmu, Apapa, and Agege) (Sada, 1968). Of these seven markets, only Agege, Mushin, Oyingbo and Obun Eko can still be said to evidence marked periodicity. These four markets are located at varying distances from the city centre (Fig. 10.3), and therefore

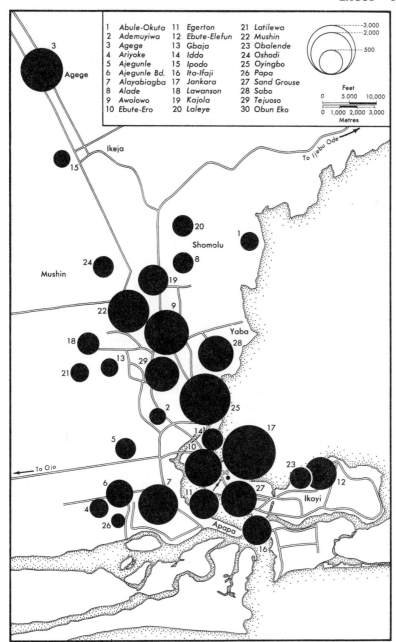

Figure 10.3   Number of traders in Lagos traditional markets

operate in somewhat different marketing environments. They represent a cross section of the marketing landscape as discussed above, and as such can be expected to differ somewhat from one another in their temporal, spatial and functional attributes. Specifically, if the evolution of periodic markets to daily markets is characterised as a continuum, Oyingbo near the centre of the city should be furthest along the continuum, Mushin would occupy a median location and Agege would be near the beginning. Of the three markets, Oyingbo usually has about 60 per cent of its market-day capacity on any non-market day. In contrast, Mushin is usually half full, and Agege has a little more than one-third of its market-day capacity (Table 10.1).

Oyingbo is the largest of the three markets, and it has a favourable location being near the Lagos lagoon (from which many 'water side' people patronise the market and make Oyingbo a special fish market), on a main highway which facilitates the transportation of foodstuffs and other agricultural products from the countryside to the market, and near the population centre of the metropolis. It has experienced such rapid recent expansion in area that several adjoining streets are officially closed to traffic and filled with traders on market days. Oyingbo functions mainly as a distributing (feeder) centre to the subsidiary markets both within and outside the metropolitan area.

The founding of Mushin market (presently located at the boundary of the city of Lagos), dates back to the middle of the nineteenth century. According to the Olu of Mushin, the market was sited at the junction of roads leading from Abeokuta, Isolo, Lagos, Shomolu and Igbobi (Odetoyinbo, 1970). It was therefore a convenient site for the exchange of products by traders from different ecological areas. The development of the market was stimulated by the opening of the railway to Abeokuta in 1901, which resulted in the frequent movement of Egba traders to Lagos with their base in Mushin. Although the market was taken over from the Olu of Mushin in 1957, the chief still performs the traditional ritual ceremony which involves sacrifices to 'Subulade', the goddess of the market located at the centre of the market in the form of a cylindrical mound almost two metres (five and a half feet) high. Mushin is a four-day periodic market with a substantial pre-market session on the eve of the market day called Ana'le (contracted from 'Anasile'). It serves principally as a distribution centre to subsidiary markets and receives consignments of such foodstuffs as vegetables, yams, gari and oil from Idogo and Ilare by rail.

Agege market also owes its growth to the opening of the railway in 1901. Because of the production of large quantities of kolanut in its agricultural

Table 10.1: Daily Components of Periodic Markets at Varying Distances from the City (Number of traders)

Name of Market	Distance from City (km)	Size on Market-day	Size of Daily Component	
			Number	% of Market-day
Oyingbo	0.0	2899	1697	58.5
Mushin	6.8	2050	1087	53.0
Agege	18.0	2192	842	38.4
Otta [a]	32.0	1235	126	10.2

Source: Authors' field surveys.

[a] This is not in Lagos proper, but it is included to complete the profile of the periodic market system in a rural-urban continuum (Adalemo, 1974).

hinterland, Hausa traders were attracted to Agege. The market serves as a collecting centre for kolanut which the Hausas bulk and consign to the northern states by railway and motor truck mammy wagons. Agege market also serves as a wholesale market for most of the vegetables consumed in Lagos. It is a four-day periodic market with a very strong pre-market session (Ana'le). The size of the Ana'le is 1,949 trading units as compared to 2,192 on the actual market day.

It is interesting to note that Oyingbo, while having a strong daily session, has no noticeable Ana'le. Mushin has both substantial daily sessions and Ana'le (both about 50 per cent of market day). However, Agege, at the rural edge of the metropolitan area has a much smaller daily session (Table 10.1) but a very substantial Ana'le. This finding suggests that increases in urban concentration of population will lead to the elimination of Ana'le which is a special characteristic of pure periodic markets.

Obun-Eko market which now has only about 160 trading units is the oldest market in Lagos and is associated with the King's Palace. Important ceremonial functions connected with the installation of the Oba of Lagos are still carried out at the Enu Owa end of the Obun-Eko market. It operates on a four-day week, and it is now a small food market with only a small variation between the real market day and the non-market session. The stagnancy of Obun-Eko is due to the re-orientation of traffic routes and, perhaps most importantly, to the conflict between traditional and modern political authority. Because of the identification of the market with the Oba of Lagos, the Lagos City Council was unable to take it over. However, responsibility was assumed for such nearby markets as Idumagbo and Ebute-Ero, which were improved and equipped with many stalls. Most traders gravitated towards these newly established markets, and Obun-Eko has been virtually abandoned.

Ebute-Ero is an interesting market centre because it is essentially a daily market which still portrays some of its former characteristics of periodicity. A large proportion of Ebute-Ero traders attend other periodic markets such as Ojo, Badagry, Ejinrin, and Ikorodu. Consequently, the market pulsates in size as mobile traders converge on it from the other periodic markets. Indeed, the daily market sessions at Ebute-Ero are named after the other periodic markets, so that the first day in the market week is Ebute-Ero, the second Abo-Badagry ('return-from-Badagry'), the third Abo-Ojo, and the fourth is Abo-Ejinrin. A survey on Ebute-Ero market day recorded 1,661 traders, but on Abo-Badagry this rose to 1,951, reflecting the return of traders from Badagry. The other two days fluctuate slightly around 1,600.

The Trader in a Changing Periodic Market System

In Stine's general model of periodic markets, the trader attains viability by moving from one market to the other. In an urban setting characterised by rising demand, the corresponding response involves more frequent market meetings and the gradual replacement of itinerant traders by traders with a permanent attachment to specific markets. Thus, one of the effects of urbanisation is occupational specialisation and this can be observed in Table 10.2 which shows that 92 per cent of the traders in Lagos attend the market for at least six days out of seven (44 per cent trade every day of the week). This contrasts sharply with the part-time periodic market trader who, in a four-day market week, spends three days on non-market activities.

Table 10.2: Market Attendance by Lagos Traders, 1970

Frequency of Attendance (days per week)	Traders		
	Number	Per cent	Cumulative Per cent
Seven	297	43.9	43.9
Six	317	47.6	91.5
Five	19	2.9	94.4
Four	7	1.1	95.5
Three	5	0.8	96.3
Two	3	0.5	96.8
One	21	3.2	100.0
Total	669	100.0	100.0

Source: Authors' field surveys.

Table 10.3: Time of Arrival at and Departure from Selected Markets

Market	Per cent of Traders Arrived by 8 a.m.	Average Time of Arrival	Per cent of Traders Present at 6 p.m.	Average Time of Departure
Ita Faji	100	7.30	65	6.00
Ebute-Ero	86	7.30	83	6.00
*Mushin	82	8.00	64	6.30
Sabo	79	8.00	82	6.30
*Oyingbo	74	8.00	78	6.00
Tejuoso	70	8.00	69	6.00
Alayabiagba	68	8.00	84	6.30
Laleye	64	8.00	86	6.30
Awolowo	64	8.30	92	6.30
Iddo	62	8.00	65	6.00
Lawanson	61	8.30	75	6.30
Kajola	58	8.00	85	6.30
Ebute Elefun	50	8.00	95	6.30
Obalende	42	8.30	73	6.00
Gbaja	23	9.00	63	5.30
All Markets	68	8.00	79	6.30

Source: Authors' field surveys.

* Periodic markets.

The magnitude of labour inputs is shown in Table 10.3; with four exceptions (Ebute Elefun, Gbaja, Obalende, and Kajola), over 60 per cent of the traders arrived in the markets before 8 a.m., and in none of the markets did they leave before 5.30 p.m. In the absence of lock-up stores, the traders return with their wares to their houses at the end of each day, and arrive at the market sufficiently early the following day to be able to set up the merchandise in the stalls before the first customers arrive.

The behaviour of traders in periodic markets such as Agege is radically different. A large proportion of the traders arrive on the eve of the market day for bulking purchases and to be able to display their merchandise for sale early enough for the first customers on the market day. By noon on market day, however, the traders have started to disperse so that by the late afternoon the market is virtually empty.

Sources of Commodities by Markets

The supply of goods in the markets follows systematic but small-scale bulking and distribution channels (Onakomaiya, 1970). From the farms or hamlets agricultural products are brought to the markets either by the farmers' wives or by forestallers. The typical farmer-producer will carry a tin of palm-oil, some yams, and some plantain, which frequently is bulked by forestallers into large lots. The distances involved range from three to twenty-four kilometres (two to fifteen miles). A second type of goods movement involves the distribution of factory products from the towns to surrounding village markets; this phenomenon may be observed in Ebute-Ero where some of the traders travel to Badagry and Ado for the sale of manufactured goods. The long distance involved in the supply channels associated with traditional markets inevitably demands periodic meetings (Onakomaiya, 1970).

Urbanisation has a significant impact on the supply system and while markets still serve as distribution points for rural products in the city, the distribution channel is much improved. There is a group of interregional traders who buy from forestallers in the rural markets and transport the goods to the city in lorry loads. While the cost per unit is thereby reduced, the trader must dispose of the perishable goods in the city; usually, he is attached to wholesalers in a few of the markets who in turn serve as the point of distribution to the smaller markets. Thus only five of the markets listed in Table 10.4 obtain more than 40 per cent of their supplies from the region; two of these (Iddo and Ebute-Ero) are developing as specialised centres for the distribution of farm products from the regions. Iddo market is located at the terminus of the railway from the western and northern states and large quantities of northern farm products are shipped to the adjoining Iddo wholesale centre where market women and other large scale food supplying contractors make their purchases. Ebute-Ero is a part wholesale, part retail centre and it serves as the distribution centre for the markets of Lagos Island (Fig. 10.3). Because of this specialisation by a few centres, many of the urban markets depend almost entirely on local sources for a large proportion of their goods, thereby ensuring easy access to supplies by traders in the metropolitan area.

Commodity Structure of Periodic Markets

The location of a periodic market within the metropolitan environment might be expected to have implications for the range and variety of goods offered. An inventory of all the commodities available in all Lagos markets was taken and no fewer than thirty-seven different commodities were identified. Observations were recorded in terms of the number of units (including stalls, counters, hawkers and sellers) offering each commodity and service. For an indication of the relative presence or absence of certain commodities, an index of concentration was computed for each of the commodities offered for sale in each market. The index shows whether a market contains more or less units offering a particular commodity than would be expected based upon its size and periodicity; it is a ratio between the proportion of the units offering a particular commodity

Table 10.4: Sources of Commodities for Selected Markets

Market	Number of Traders	Percentage of Commodities from		
		Region (long distance)	Other Markets (short distance)	Factories
Iddo	448	88	10	2
Ebute-Ero	1,761	61	37	2
*Mushin	2,050	46	43	11
Alayabiagba	1,892	44	43	13
Ajegunle	419	42	42	16
Tejuoso	1,200	36	51	13
*Oyingbo	2,899	34	55	11
Awolowo	2,165	34	60	6
Kajola	998	31	69	0
Laleye	534	30	55	15
Ebute Elefun	770	30	70	0
Jankara	3,312	23	57	20
Egerton	667	21	67	12
Oshodi	420	20	80	0
Abule Okuta	335	18	70	12
Ariyoke	350	17	83	0
Alade	439	16	68	16
Obalende	455	12	63	23
Sand Grouse	1,300	10	90	0
Ajegunle Boundary	754	7	78	15
Latilewa	320	6	94	0
Ademuyiwa	250	3	97	0
Papa	201	0	100	0

Source: Authors' field surveys.

* Periodic markets.

Table 10.5: Correlation Matrix of Market Characteristics

Variables	1	2	3	4	5	6
1	1.00	−0.41	−0.24	0.64	0.77	0.80
2		1.00	−0.31	−0.54	0.03	−0.52
3			1.00	−0.10	−0.35	0.21
4				1.00	0.46	0.62
5					1.00	0.66
6						1.00

Key to Variables

1   Total Number of Trading Units
2   Perishable Trade as a Per cent of Total Units
3   Non-perishable as a Percentage of Total Units
4   Number of Different Commodities and Services Offered
5   Number of Trading Units in Perishable Commodities
6   Number of Trading Units in Non-perishable Commodities

in a market to the proportion of all trading units found in that market (Alexander, 1958).[6] The index is greater than one when there is an above average concentration, less than one when a market has less than its share of the commodities, and equal to one when it has just its share of the commodity (based on the number of units in all of the markets). A comparison of the four periodic markets with the other twenty-six markets of Lagos did not reveal any marked differences in the index, and the magnitude of the index of concentration seems to be related more to size of the market than to periodicity. For example, the commodities and services which display a tendency towards concentration in the larger markets (either periodic or daily) are vegetables, live animals, manufactured goods, traditional medical products, sewing, blacksmiths' products, watch repairing and food selling. The smaller markets have an excessive concentration of condiments, cereals, bulky food, meat, fish, oil, barbers, shoe makers, grinders and women's hair plaiters.

This finding is further corroborated by the relationship between the range of commodities offered and size of markets; whether periodic or non-periodic, as market size increases both the number of traders offering a particular commodity and the total number of commodities increase (Table 10.5). Regression of the range of commodities on the logarithm of the market size (given by number of traders) produced the relationship shown in Figure 10.4. The correlation coefficient was +0.71, and the equation took the form $Y = -11.1 + 12.9 \log X$. The non-linear nature of this relationship suggests that as market size increases, functions are added fairly rapidly up to a market size

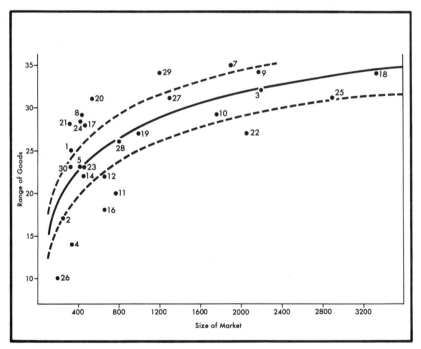

Figure 10.4   Relationship between market size and range of commodities offered

of about 1,000 traders, after which additional functions are added more slowly. This probably reflects the fact that after a certain size (approximately 1,000 traders), markets have many or most of the commodity types represented, and further increases in the number of traders represents duplication of trading units rather than the addition of new commodities.

Conclusion

Some conceptual issues relating to the temporal and functional changes in the traditional market system operating in a metropolitan setting have been examined. The evidence from Lagos markets confirms the main hypothesis that one of the major effects of urbanisation is the intensification of marketing activities and gradual development of the daily component of the businesses in the market. The data also provide supporting evidence for a theoretical profile of marketing activities in a rural-urban continuum, and the classification of marketing centres by regular periodicity, modified periodicity, urban periodicity and urban daily seems reasonable. The corollary also holds, namely that increasing urbanisation results in occupational specialisation in marketing business. There is, however, no evidence to suggest that the functions of the markets are significantly affected by the metropolitan environment, and they continue to provide outlets for convenience goods. The range of goods offered in the markets is a function of market size, which is very weakly related to urban density of population (Adalemo, 1974, 56, 125-6).

[1] The god of creation, Oduduwa or Ogun, takes the first day; Sango or Jakuta, the second; Obatala or Orishala, the third; and Orunmila or Awo or Ifa or Eshu takes the fourth.

[2] Only the fresh meat sector and the 'sauce' market component offering traditional herbs operate on non-market days.

[3] These markets are not daily markets proper, but have strong daily and periodic components. They might be better described as 'persistent periodic markets', since they were periodic markets which, having acquired a strong daily component largely because of location within the urban area, have persisted and maintained their periodicity.

[4] The only type of market similar to this in rural areas is the daily night market. The nightly market is a retail market held at specified locations within the town in the evenings, usually at a location different from that at which the periodic day market occurs. Goods in frequent demand can be purchased by people on their return from the farm outside the village.

[5] This discussion is based on almost 700 interviews with traders and detailed inventories of commodities conducted in the markets of Lagos in 1970.

[6]
$$I = \frac{X_i}{\Sigma X_{ij}} \div \frac{\sum\limits_{j=1}^{km} \Sigma X_{ij}}{\sum\limits_{i=1}^{} \sum\limits_{j=1}^{} X_{ij}}$$

where

$i = 37$ (commodities)
$j = 30$ (markets)

PART THREE
Rural periodic market systems

The literature on contemporary rural periodic market systems is large and diverse (Bromley, 1974c). However, all sets of market-places possess several features in common: location, a particular meeting frequency, size and function. There are regularities in the way in which periodic market-places are *spaced*, regardless of whether day of meeting is considered. Meetings occur at rural periodic market-places according to a temporal schedule, and a rural periodic market system operates according to a given *periodicity regime*. Markets vary in *size*, regardless of how this is measured (e.g. number of people present, number of sellers, number of goods offered, etc.). Finally, rural periodic markets perform several different *functions* (Eighmy, 1972, 299); the functions performed and the size of the market can indicate the position of the market-place in an hierarchy. These four features of rural periodic market systems (location, periodicity, size and function) are useful in any attempt at a central place theory interpretation of periodic markets. In several of the five essays in this section, this body of theory is used quite explicitly as a conceptual framework.

The Nariño area of southern Colombia provides the regional setting for Symanski's analysis of periodic market-places. Central place theory is used heuristically to investigate the hierarchical and spatial structure of periodic markets in this area of Andean Colombia. Symanski employs four criteria to establish a five-level hierarchy of periodic market-places: the volume of buying and selling (1) on major market days and (2) on additional market days during the seven-day market week; (3) the origins of buyers and sellers; and (4) the range and quantity of goods and services available on the major market days. The body of Symanski's essay comprises an attempt to validate this five-level hierarchy through a discussion of consumer travel patterns, the availability of goods and services, and production and product flows. There are distinctive patterns of consumer movement to and from periodic markets at different levels of the hierarchy, and spheres of influence are much more extensive for higher order than for lower order market-places. Not only is there a greater number and variety of goods and services in higher order market-places, but sales occur in bulk lots as well. The pattern of goods flows is related to the hierarchy of market centres (and especially to the redistribution functions of higher order markets), to regional specialisation and ecological complementarity, and to certain accessibility relationships. Symanski stops short of asking whether particular geometries of market-places and hinterlands exist (Skinner, 1964,

1965; C.A. Smith, 1972), and argues that central place theory is better used as a loose and pliable conceptual framework within which to ask questions about periodic markets in lesser developed countries.

Periodic market systems in east Africa appear to be of relatively recent origin (especially in comparison to west Africa), but in his essay on periodic markets in the Lushoto District of Tanzania, Gezann suggests that some such markets pre-dated the colonial period, and that there certainly were periodic markets in the early part of this century prior to the First World War. The primary function of the contemporary periodic market-place is to provide an opportunity for the sale of locally produced agricultural products, and a substantial amount of the activity in Lushoto periodic markets is horizontal exchange. Goods which are exotic to the local area (both indigenous foods and manufactured goods) are offered for sale in local shops and also by itinerant traders who follow regular routes around several periodic market-places. The number of these traders present in a market-place and the number of different goods they offer varies considerably and, following central place theory, Gezann argues that these two characteristics should provide the basis for an hierarchical grouping of periodic markets. A four-level hierarchy is established, service area populations are estimated, and some relationships between the spacing of markets at higher levels and population density are discussed. For seven itinerant salesmen commodities, the service area population is an adequate predictor of the number of salesmen in a given periodic market; however, for cloth and clothes, and local medicine, this relationship does not hold. Gezann's analysis implies that a periodic market system will be relatively undifferentiated functionally and spatially when horizontal exchange of local produce predominates; the introduction of exotic goods (for which threshold values differ) triggers off processes that result in the development of a market hierarchy.

In the third essay in this section, Handwerker presents the first comprehensive analysis of the periodic market system of Liberia which, like that of Tanzania, is of relatively recent origin. The question posed by Handwerker concerns the *viability* of periodic market-places: is this contingent upon market location and (possibly, or) timing, and if so, how is the spatial and temporal competition for buyers and sellers related to the locational and temporal properties of these markets? Village periodic markets are one of six types of market sites in Liberia, their principal function being to channel local foodstuffs to urban consumers. The Totota market circuit in central Liberia is used to illustrate the operation of Liberian periodic markets. One of the key participants is the *producer-seller* (often at one and the same time a *farmer-consumer*); part of his produce enters the local exchange network, but most is purchased by *bulking intermediaries* who sell bulked lots to urban market retailers. Imported goods and items exotic to the market area are sold by *professional intermediaries* (men and women) mostly to farmer-consumers. Most producer-sellers/farmer-consumers visit only one market weekly; professional intermediaries visit more, and bulking intermediaries are the most mobile. Travel costs to periodic markets severely constrain the mobility of the farm population, but a minimum number of producer-sellers/farmer-consumers *must* be present if the market is to be viable. Analysis of the spatio-temporal synchronisation of Liberian periodic markets suggests that market meetings are scheduled to serve the convenience of the producer-sellers/farmer-consumers, even though the days of meeting do not seem to have involved the careful decision making by market initiators to be expected in a competitive situation. Handwerker argues that competition occurs in a specific context: access by the farming population to markets is constrained by travel costs; interdependence of selling and purchasing strategies impose constraints on market attendance to sell local goods and to buy exotic items; and the availability of alternative purchasing sites also affects the likelihood of attendance at a given periodic market-place. He concludes with the observation 'It could well be that market initiators give little thought to the long run viability of a market, and . . . its persistence or dissolution ultimately is contingent upon the attendance decisions of various kinds of buyers and sellers.'

Periodic markets pre-dated the colonial period in Kenya, but in the early twentieth century the seven-day market week was imposed upon whatever vestiges of the traditional system remained. There are three components of the contemporary internal exchange system in rural Kenya: cooperatives and marketing boards that organise the transfer of selected cash crops to urban areas for processing and possible export; retail shops or *dukas* that supply the rural population with items manufactured in urban areas; and almost 1,000 daily and periodic market-places that facilitate the horizontal exchange of locally produced goods. Wood's essay is concerned with the latter component. The role of rural periodic markets in the internal exchange economy of Kenya contrasts sharply with the role of comparable markets in both Tanzania and Liberia. A relatively small proportion of market participants are traders (i.e. people who buy goods for resale) rather than marketers; most traders work on a part-time basis and are primarily farmers. There is now an elaborate mechanism (involving several levels of local government) for initiating new markets and also for adding extra meetings at existing markets. Every attempt is made to avoid spatial and temporal competition, and Wood's analyses reveal that in general, same-day markets are on average further apart than adjacent-day markets (a relationship that must almost always hold if the major participants in periodic market meetings are producer-sellers/farmer-consumers). The prevalence of horizontal exchange in Kenyan rural markets stems from the fact that the internal exchange functions of the three components (cooperatives and marketing boards, shops and rural markets) are quite rigidly circumscribed. Thus, a strong relationship between population density and rural market provision is to be expected, although 70 persons per square kilometre (180 per square mile) seems to be the upper limit beyond which only slight changes in mean market provision occur. The bulking and professional intermediaries of Liberia and itinerant traders of Tanzania do not provide the same cohesion for periodic market circuits in Kenya. Periodic markets coexist in close spatial and functional juxtaposition with static retail establishments, and these two components provide complementary services to Kenya's rural population.

Gormsen's essay is concerned with the system of weekly markets in the Puebla region of central Mexico. Periodic markets in Mexico were pre-Hispanic phenomena (Kaplan, 1960), and present day markets retain many features of their pre-colonial counterparts. There are two networks of market-places in Puebla: firstly, there are many small markets with fewer than 400 vendors that meet on Sunday; and secondly, there are larger regional markets that are less numerous than the Sunday markets and whose days of meeting are spread throughout the week (with some concentration on Friday and Saturday). The *campesinos* combine visits to the Sunday markets with church attendance, and there is a strong loyalty to the local market-place. The function of these small markets is fundamentally different from the regional markets, and horizontal exchange between *campesinos* is more important in the former than in the latter. Both *campesinos* and the urban population nowadays visit markets (especially the larger markets) primarily to purchase goods from full-time (frequently itinerant) traders. Because of this subtle difference in function, there is a more pronounced inverse spatio-temporal synchronisation of larger markets than there is for the smaller Sunday markets. The provision of modern transport facilities has altered accessibility relationships in the market-place system (resulting in the waxing and waning of the fortunes of given market-places), and has also broadened the scope for itinerant traders. However, in the Sierra Norte de Puebla, many people still walk to the market and visits by itinerant traders are rare. Compared with the other rural market systems discussed in this section, weekly markets in the Puebla area do not have an important horizontal exchange function. Further, they play a much more significant role in the distribution of durable manufactured items to the rural population than they do in the bulking of agricultural produce for sale in urban areas. There is here, as elsewhere, an important social dimension to the weekly market, not only because the market meeting provides a regular opportunity for social interaction, but also because the intensity of market activity is partly related to the incidence of local and national feast days.

The same set of themes is not followed consistently in each of the five essays in this section. However, each one has an at least implicit concern with the relevance of central place theory in explaining aspects of the spacing and functioning of periodic market systems. It is quite fortuitous that the market systems in all five essays meet on a seven-day schedule. The three essays on periodic market systems in tropical Africa add documentation on areas for which there is only a sparse literature. The inescapable conclusion that emerges from a comparison of the five rural periodic market systems is that there is much more cross-cultural similarity than might have been expected, and that such differences as do exist are differences in degree, not of kind.

11 Periodic markets in southern Colombia
Richard Symanski

The extensive testing, elaboration, and refinement of central place theory in the 1960s as it applies in the developed world has since been paralleled in the developing world, especially for peasant periodic and daily markets. Interest in formal central place theory generally has lagged, and has shifted to a search for behavioural postulates. Amongst scholars with a strong regional commitment to and interest in developing economies, however, there is significant activity at the level of matching predicted central place and related normative patterns with empirical findings. Although the theory was developed to explain the distribution of retail centres in a relatively developed part of the world, the most often cited best fits with predicted geometries have been in areas where periodic and daily markets are prominent. Particularly noteworthy are the studies of Skinner (1964) for rural China and C.A. Smith for highland Guatemala (1972); both authors identify hexagonal trade areas, but until a much larger number of cases is available, judgement must be reserved on the question of whether this particular form of spatial organisation is the exception rather than the rule.

In this paper, central place theory is used indirectly as a heuristic device in the identification of the hierarchical and spatial structure of periodic markets in the small villages and towns of southern Colombia in 1970 (Symanski, 1971). Some brief comments on the regional context are followed by a discussion of a five-level hierarchy of periodic markets. Validation of this hierarchy is then sought through an analysis of consumer travel patterns, the availability of goods and services, and product flows.

The Regional Context

The region under examination is northern Nariño, a small Andean area astride the Pan American Highway and north of Pasto (Fig. 11.1). The western and eastern boundaries are defined by areas with only sparse population and few markets, but those to the north and south are less clearly defined. In these directions, primarily along the axis of the Pan American Highway, there is reason to argue that other market towns could be included in the region, or that northern Nariño is a subsystem within a larger marketing system. However, there

---

* I gratefully acknowledge the financial support of the H. L. and Grace Doherty Foundation, Princeton University, which made this study possible.

are political, cultural and economic features which lend northern Nariño a distinct regional identity (Ministerio del Trabajo, 1959).

Northern Nariño is agriculturally rich, yet there are blatant visible signs of poverty, and even by Colombian standards the condition of roads and transport connections is poor (Fig. 11.2). Economically, northern Nariño is a hinterland

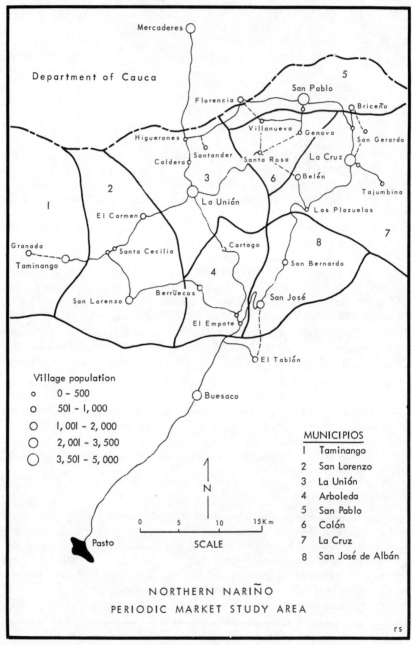

Figure 11.1   Northern Nariño

which feeds both the small metropolis of Pasto and the larger and more powerful national and international urban predators. Like much of Andean Colombia, northern Nariño contributes to the international coffee market. The region also contributes to the internal exchange economy such products as anise for making the popular *aguardiente* (a local alcoholic beverage, of which anise is an

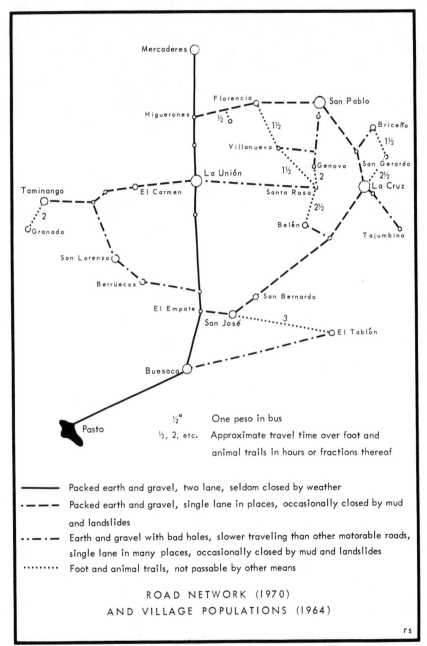

Figure 11.2   Road network in northern Nariño (village population as in Fig. 11.1)

ingredient) saddles and *sombreros* which are sent to the Llanos, and tobacco, beans, peanuts and citrus fruits which are exported to Pasto and the Cauca Valley for bulking to even higher-order centres. Within northern Nariño there is active internal exchange, involving mainly fruits and vegetables which are grown in different but complementary ecological zones. These products also form the basis for some interregional complementary trade with nearby Pasto, from which there is a flow of new and used manufactured goods. In marked similarity to the bulking of agricultural products in the region, this trade is controlled largely by entrepreneurs in Pasto who have capital and information on intra- as well as extra-regional price differences. Finally, in addition to regionally-based traders, there are *ambulantes* (itinerant traders) who circulate among markets and drain wealth from the region; they live in distant rural villages or large cities and come to northern Nariño on an infrequent basis more because of the nature of the products they sell than because of any special knowledge of the region or its inhabitants.

The Hierarchy of Markets

Four interrelated criteria make it possible to identify a hierarchy of periodic markets in northern Nariño. These are: volume of buying and selling on the major market days; the number of additional market days during the market week and the volume of buying and selling on these days; the distance to and the number and importance of places from which buyers and sellers come; and the range and quantity of goods and services available on the major market day (Fig. 11.3).

First-order markets

The two-storey market building in the central commercial district of Pasto is the largest and most important of three or four *mercados* in the city. There is considerable selling activity every day of the market week, but Monday, Tuesday, Thursday and Saturday are the heaviest days of trade. Commercial activity does occur on other days, but frequently these are days of rest, a time for the fulfilment of other obligations, or an opportunity for traders to sell in nearby markets.

Second-order markets

With northern Nariño proper, the size and nature of the markets differ considerably from those found in places the size of Pasto, a city of more than 80,000 people. La Unión, the most important market between Pasto and Mercaderes, has its major market day on Saturday and, while there is some activity every day of the week, it is small compared with the volume of business occurring on Saturday. Tuesday is the principal weekly market day in La Cruz, the other second-order market, although the gathering is not as large as the Saturday market in La Unión. Sunday and Monday are other prominent marketing days in La Cruz, but as with La Unión, these minor market days are relatively unimportant compared with the once weekly major market on Tuesday. La Unión and La Cruz differ in that market activity is less continuous in the latter; thus, vendors in La Cruz do not have permanent selling stands and there are no vendors who sell every day of the week. A further contrast is that La Unión has the only *galería* (two-storey cement market building) in northern Nariño, which promotes full-time selling and attracts customers. To the peasants, the *galería* is a symbol of La Unión's regional importance, and this feature is not insignificant in explaining market attendance habits. The two centres are similar in the relative strength of market days preceding the major market; in both market towns, *negociantes* or middlemen from larger regional centres arrive the day prior to major retailing activity to sell to small, usually local vendors or

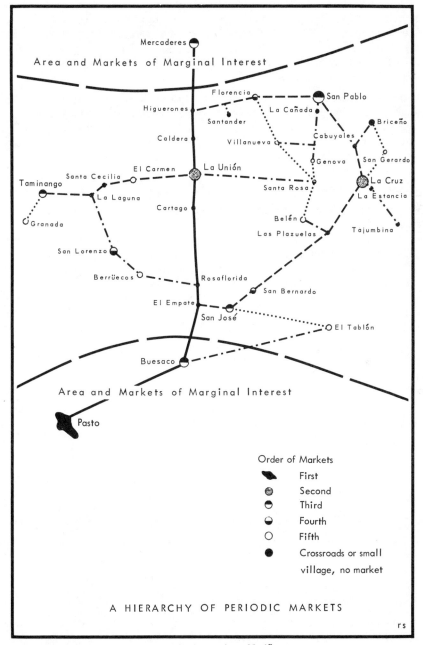

Figure 11.3   Periodic market hierarchy in northern Nariño

revendedores. On the following or major market day, *revendedores* may sell only yards away from non-local *negociantes* who are now competitors.

In the La Unión market, wholesalers arrive by truck and bus from Pasto late Wednesday afternoon or early Thursday morning. They bring gunnysack lots of potatoes, cabbages, carrots, onions, beans and other cold climate products that are not grown in the *tierra templada* hinterland of La Unión. Traders from complementary ecological zones such as the *tierra fría* or cold lands in the La Cruz area find it difficult to compete with the Pasto-based vendors because the latter have easy access to price information and products received from surrounding regions. Pasto is economically (though not geographically) central to the various sub-regions of Nariño.

A similar relationship exists between Pasto and La Cruz, although the linkage is weaker than that between Pasto and La Unión. The La Cruz market is not as large as La Unión's, the transport cost relationship is less favourable, and La Cruz and Pasto are both nodes for ecologically similar hinterlands, yet despite these differences traders from Pasto frequent La Cruz on a regular basis.

Third-order markets

In the typical third-order market, the amount of trade occurring on the major market day is less than in a second-order market and, in most cases, the number of minor market days is fewer. As with higher-order markets, the day preceding the major market has a strong wholesale component. Furthermore, at the mid-point between the occurrence of major market days there is often quite an active market, resulting from local pressures for twice-weekly marketing. These wholesale and mid-week market day patterns are well illustrated by Taminango, San Pablo, and San José. The first has a Sunday major market day while the latter two have Saturday gatherings. In all three, there is actual wholesale trading on the day preceding the major market day (either Friday or Saturday), and all have Wednesday markets.

Fourth-order markets

The fourth-order markets of Santa Rosa, San Lorenzo, and San Bernardo have only one market each week; only Florencia has a weak minor market day and this occurs at mid-week. The volume of trade at this level is considerably less than in third-order markets, and it can be compared to activity in very strong secondary markets in second-order markets. Whereas on the principal market day in most higher-order markets the *plaza de mercado* is filled with buyers and sellers who spill over into adjoining streets, the activity in fourth-order markets is usually not sufficient to cover more than two-thirds of the plaza. At this level there is no difference between the *plaza central* and the *plaza de mercado*. By contrast, the third-order markets of San Pablo, Büesaco, and Mercaderes (though not of Taminango or San José) have either separate market plazas or, as in the case of Mercaderes, a small and partially enclosed cement structure.[1]

Fifth-order markets

All of the fifth-order markets with the exception of Berrüecos lack *parques* and, with the exception of Granada, all have a single market day. Again, there is less commercial activity than is to be found in fourth-order markets; seldom

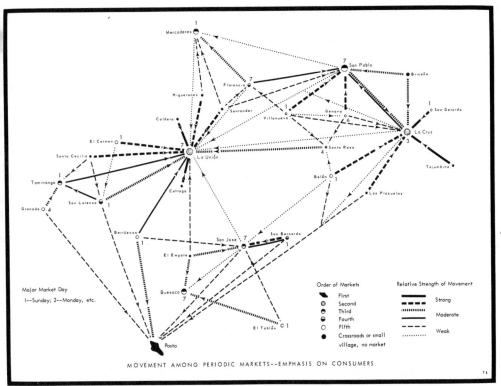

Figure 11.4   Predominant consumer movements amongst northern Nariño periodic markets

is more than half of a market *plaza* occupied by sellers and often there are no more than a few rows or groupings of from six to twenty sellers.

Consumer Travel Patterns

Consumer movements are, of course, related to volume of activity and the number of additional market days (two criteria for defining the market hierarchy). The patterns depicted in Figure 11.4 are based on bus and other modes of travel (foot, horseback and truck) to all markets from any one market on the major market day and the day preceding.[2] It is apparent from a comparison of Figures 11.3 and 11.4 that the amount of traffic, the number of places from which consumers come, the size of market and market town, and the distance travelled are interrelated.

The second-order markets receive heavy traffic from nearby villages and somewhat less from those at a distance. Excluding the first-order market (for which insufficient data are available), these markets have the largest trade areas and they nest most markets lower in the hierarchy. Third-order markets exhibit these qualities to a lesser degree; they resemble those at the next highest level in that they are places to go rather than consumer source areas for other markets. Fifth-order and, to a lesser extent, fourth-order markets differ from higher orders in that the strength of movement to these markets is less than that from these places to other markets. Unlike third- and higher-order markets which nest the lower-order markets and also receive some consumers and vendors from second- and first-order markets, fourth-order markets generally receive customers only from smaller markets or the nearby *campo* or countryside; however, the relationship between San José and San Bernardo is exceptional in this regard. With the single anomaly of very weak movement from Villanueva to Genova, only peasants from the nearby *campo* frequent fifth-order markets, not inhabitants of other villages. Finally, markets at the bottom of the hierarchy are notable for their strong dependence on second- or third-order markets, and for the number of different markets to which consumers from these areas go.

The hierarchy of markets and the complex movement patterns illustrated in Figures 11.3 and 11.4, respectively, may be generalized into a pattern of intensive and extensive trade areas centred on the higher-order markets (Fig. 11.5). The intensive fields define the principal trade areas of the higher-order markets, that spatial set of points from which the great majority of consumers come. The extensive fields, indicated by arrows, are the extended reach of the markets, areas from which some consumers come on an infrequent basis.

Availability of Goods and Services

As with the central place systems of more developed economies, the number of functions in the periodic markets of northern Nariño vary according to market order: the higher the order, the greater the number of different agricultural products and services offered (Fig. 11.6) and, since volume of activity is one of the factors defining the hierarchy, the greater the quantity of any one product or service. These two characteristics vary considerably among markets of the same order as a result of such factors as local specialization, seasonal harvests, varying product preferences, and prosperity of the consumers.

Several important features of periodic markets are suggested by Figure 11.6: fifth-order markets offer a limited range of vegetables and fruits, most of which come from the local area or are brought in from nearby markets. Occasionally, a trader comes with rubber shoes and a few items of clothing, such as *ruanas*, pants, shirts, and hats. Generally, there are few purchases in these markets which can be described as 'extras', superfluous to the peasant way of life.

Livestock almost always are present in fourth-order markets. The demand for clothing, shoes, and kitchenware is sufficiently great that a few itinerant traders find it worth their while to make regular weekly calls at markets of this level. The demand for meals by peasants who come weekly to market from the *campo* induces local residents to prepare and sell soups, cooked meats and sausages, potatoes, beer, soft drinks, sweet and salted bread rolls, and cookies.

In third-order markets, there is a greater range and quantity of the products than in fourth- and fifth-order markets, and speciality products and services are also available. Third-order and higher-level market towns are often small factory and collection-transformation centres. Historically, La Unión was a major centre for the sale and purchase of *sombreros de paja toquilla* (Ortiz, 1945). Today, the major producing area in northern Nariño is the San Pablo-Santa Rosa-Genova-Villanueva set of markets. In San Pablo and Genova, there is a number of small factories that make these hats and buy them in semi-finished form from *campesinos* in the weekly markets, and later distribute them to Colombia's major urban places. The San José-San Bernardo area is similarly noted for its henequen bags.

A further aspect of third-order markets is the availability of uncommon agricultural products. In the San Pablo and San José markets, there is a variety of beans and peppers and condiments, as well as eggplant, cabbages, and carrots

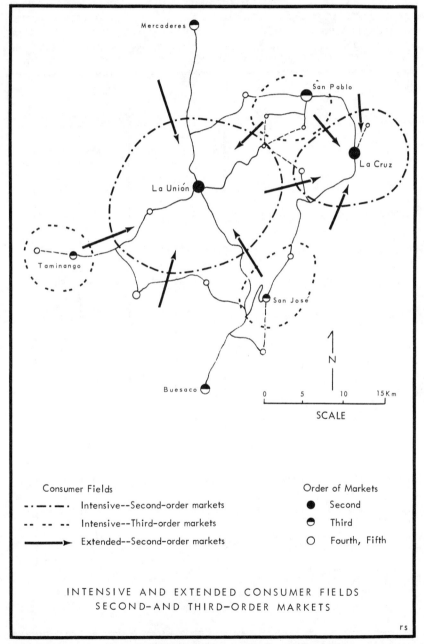

Figure 11.5   Consumer fields for selected northern Nariño periodic markets

that usually will not be found in lower-order markets, unless grown in the immediate area. In northern Nariño many exotic items are brought in from Pasto.

There are exceptions to this pattern. Fresh fish are available in the fourth-order market of Florencia but not in others which are generally larger, such as San Pablo and La Cruz; fish vendors report a lack of demand in many of the larger markets. Even in the major market of La Unión only a single truckload comes once every two weeks. This is to be contrasted with activity in both small and large markets in north central Colombia where fish may be bought weekly and from a number of vendors. Another difference between third- and fourth-order

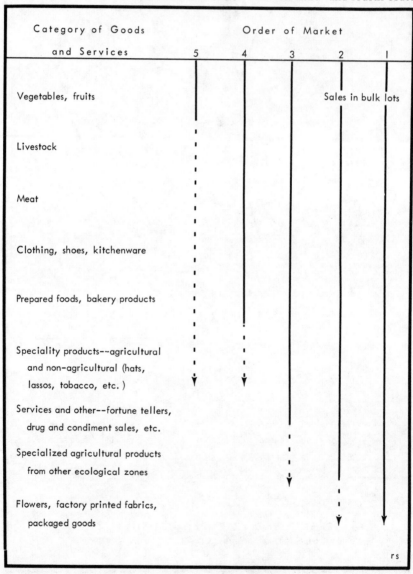

Figure 11.6   Range of goods and services in periodic markets

markets is the obvious presence of *ambulantes* or itinerant traders. Fortune tellers (vendors of commercially printed horoscopes), photographers, student vendors of commercial drugs, condiments, and magazines, and panel trucks with factory-produced cloth or other household goods frequent these markets. In the pre-dawn market hours of third-order markets there are sales in *bulto*[3] lots of corn, potatoes, cabbage, onions, ullocos, and oranges. In higher-order markets sales are made in large lots during most of the market day. In La Unión there are areas where vendors only sell beans in *bulto* lots, while in other sections of the market sellers are offering carrots, ullocos, or potatoes. Areal segregation by product type generally increases with the size of the market.

Production and Product Flows

Certain characteristics of the major flows of goods and services among the periodic markets of northern Nariño are summarised in Figure 11.7. The flow data are based on an analysis of bus and truck shipments of goods and traders, small and large trader estimates of produce exchanges, and local estimates of origin or destination points of produce which does not enter the market-place. These data illustrate additional features of the hierarchy.

With a population in excess of 80,000, Pasto is not only the largest urban place in southern Colombia but it is also the principal centre for the collection of agricultural goods from Nariño, the Putumayo, and parts of the Department of Cauca (north of the Department of Nariño). There are significant exchanges

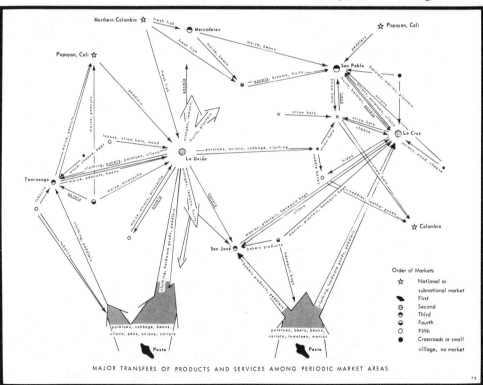

Figure 11.7   Product and service flows between northern Nariño periodic markets

between Pasto and northern Nariño: thus, fruits of the *tierra templada*, some of the grains and tobacco produced in the warmer regions of Taminango and Granada, and various cold climate products cultivated along axes running north, south and west from the La Cruz area move south to Pasto for sale and later redistribution within and beyond the city. Much of the produce received in northern Nariño comes from Pasto, but only indirectly in that most of the goods originate in the rich hinterlands to the west, east and south of the city.

The agricultural goods transported to the western sector of northern Nariño and the area running through Florencia and San Pablo demonstrate the existence of complementarity between these temperate climatic-ecologic regions and the colder hinterland source regions around Pasto and La Cruz. The reason for many of these exchanges is obvious: what is not produced in one area but is in demand may be obtained from a nearby area which has these goods, and *vice versa*. Ecological complementarity, however, is seldom so straightforward. The relatively heavy movement of such products as potatoes, beets, cabbage, and carrots between Pasto and La Cruz (climatically and ecologically similar areas) is partly accounted for by such factors as outright scarcity and seasonal harvests. Cost-distance relationships, market sizes, and local preferences for certain goods are other important factors.

Because of the size of their markets, La Unión and La Cruz receive a large percentage of the goods coming from Pasto (Fig. 11.7), and they redistribute goods to lower-order centres. Thus, while produce moves directly into the third-order markets of Taminango and San Pablo from Pasto, some first passes through the two higher-order markets. La Unión principally redistributes goods to the third- and fourth-order markets of Taminango and Santa Rosa, and to a much lesser extent to lower-order markets. A similar pattern of redistribution occurs between La Cruz and San Pablo and with other markets in the northeast.

These patterns exhibit some cost-distance and accessibility features that deserve attention. San José is not encompassed within either the La Unión or La Cruz fields of redistribution if only because it has a more favourable cost-distance and accessibility relationship to Pasto than to either of these places. Thus, its relationship to Pasto is more direct than is the case for either Taminango or San Pablo, markets of the same order. Taminango has poor road and service connections over the southern route which bypasses La Unión (Fig. 11.2); its best linkage with Pasto is through La Unión and it is even more parasitic on the latter in terms of redistribution than is true of the La Cruz-San Pablo relationship, notwithstanding the fact that the most heavily travelled route to San Pablo from the south is the one which passes through La Cruz. An additional factor in this latter comparison is that La Cruz and San Pablo are more alike in size than are the La Unión and Taminango markets.

Redistribution takes the following general form: bulk loads of produce are brought from Pasto in trucks and buses which usually originate in this northern region. When the produce arrives at the market it is sold both at wholesale and retail, either by those who work for truck owners or large *negociantes* (often one and the same person), or by those who have bought space in the trucks or buses and accompany their purchases. The goods purchased at wholesale in the market-place are in turn either sold directly in the markets in smaller lots or, occasionally, part or all are retained for later sale in the lower-order markets of the area which meet on other days of the week. The spatial pattern of redistribution is of two distinct types: firstly, some vendors who sell directly on the day of purchase are based in the market town where they are selling (they may also go by bus to other lower-order markets during other days of the week to sell their remaining stock); secondly, vendors who live in the lower-order market-places visit higher-order markets to make household purchases, and also backhaul goods for resale in their home or nearby villages.

Pasto is the major manufacturing centre of Nariño, and in northern Nariño there is virtually no industry other than small handicrafts. Most items of clothing, hardware, and kitchenware that enter the periodic markets come from Pasto; a few come from more distant Popayan and Cali.

In the second- and third-order market towns, extra-regional manufactured goods can be purchased in the small local stores (tiendas). However, there is still a significant number of vendors, both from market villages and from Pasto, who enter the plaza with these items. For those from Pasto there are the advantages of low overhead costs and direct contacts with Pasto-based manufacturers. And for all vendors who place their wares in the market-place rather than in a tienda, the factor of relative location is important. In the most general sense, there is the simple locational advantage of being present with goods in or about the market plaza on the major market day. It also appears that relative exposure as a function of location is a consideration. Location along a travelled thoroughfare on a direct route to the market plaza seems to increase sales, but not as much as a site within the plaza, or better, a position at a corner of the market plaza where traffic is heaviest. The same general principle seems to apply to the location of a tienda: one fronting on the market plaza has locational advantages over those situated elsewhere in the village.

Production of the major staple items of the peasant diet at the municipio level is shown in Table 11.1. Only arracachas, beans, maize, manioc and plantains are grown in all eleven municipios. However, all peasants do not cultivate these five, and they are therefore important items in the periodic markets. With a few exceptions (such as those due to delayed harvests), these are among the products that tend to have spatial ranges which are restricted. The large production figures for maize distort its relative importance in the market-place as much of it never leaves the peasant household. Such products as anise, barley, wheat and coffee rarely enter the market-place in the form in which they are harvested or gathered. For example, after being harvested and dried, anise is sent directly to the liquor factories of Pasto or to other major urban centres; it returns to the market-place in the form of the very popular aguardiente.

During the harvest season, small peasant producers sell dried coffee beans, usually in the higher-order market towns or in those which are municipio cabeceras (municipal capitals). Occasionally, these sales occur away from the market-place plaza itself, at the branch office of the Federación de Cafeteros. Peasants in need of cash for the week's market purchases sometimes sell their coffee beans to small bulking merchants located within the market plaza, but this usually occurs only when the beans are of inferior quality and need additional treatment before they will be accepted by the Federación. These bulking merchants pay the peasant less than he would otherwise receive, redry the beans, and then sell them at a profit to the Federación.

Sugar cane does not enter the market-place directly, but only after conversion in trapiches (sugar mills) into the crude brown sugar loaves known as panela. Since the production of *panela* is limited to the *tierra templada* and yet is in considerable demand in the *tierra fría*, market centres such as La Unión may take on local and regional importance. The *panela* loaves command a good price per unit in bulk, and generally have a large spatial range by comparison with many other

Table 11.1 Cultivation of selected products, number of cattle, and exploited agricultural land in northern Nariño.

Municipio / Village / Elevation in Meters / Temperature in Centigrade*	Tamingango 913 24°	Mercaderes 1200 23°	La Unión 1745 20°	San Pablo 1796 19°	San José 1800 19°	Colón 1914 18°	Buesaco 2020 18°	San Lorenzo 2030 17°	Arboleda 2170 17°	La Cruz 2484 15°	Pasto 2504 14°
Arracacha	22	27	27	24	38	64	7	79	37	121ᵃ	53
Beans	219	138	71	45	154	10	642	147	139	43	199
Lima Beans	---	---	---	---	3	---	55	28	5	22	358
Maize	1289	1336	594	1501	1538	639	2962	1493	1389	3122	2426
Manioc	66	388	284	348	258	317	148	417	159	167	101
Onions	1	---	2	---	---	---	3	21	3	166	146
Peas	---	2	---	1	6	---	44	7	2	56	---
Potatoes	---	---	---	32	33	2	78	12	2	170	2177
Sugar Cane	126	564	962	141	124	436	120	321	199	---	39
Anise	---	---	---	12	106	1	86	9	5	191	---
Barley	---	---	3	5	157	9	169	2	39	1463	558
Peanuts	90	84	3	15	40	2	7	90	36	---	2
Tobacco	96	---	---	---	---	---	---	---	---	---	---
Wheat	1	---	4	4	38	3	1261	5	23	187	2745
Bananas ᵇ	2	54	256	3	1	86	2	---	---	---	6
Coffeeᵇ	---	719	1642	163	1152	1053	358	1346	863	72	253
Henequinᵇ	---	---	1	---	---	1	---	---	---	36	164
Plantainᵇ	493	1181	524	389	439	347	270	410	374	40	185
Cattle	1142	8093	3397	4796	4840	2750	9124	6735	4131	12782	16458
Exploited Agricultural Land ᶜ	4750	15305	5356	3776	5181	4001	8884	5307	4531	13002	16444

(Cultivation in Hectares—1960)

Source: Banco de la Republica (1960); Departamento Administrativo Nacional de Estadistica, Republica de Colombia (1964).

ᵃ Underlinning indicates most important municipios listed (excluding Pasto).   ᵇ Compact holdings only. (No data for dispersed plantings.)   ᶜ More than one half of producer's investment in agriculture.

market products. Peanuts and tobacco are rarely found in the markets in their unprocessed form.

If such towns as Mercaderes to the north and Büesaco and Pasto to the south are excluded from consideration, the major beef producing centre in the Department of Nariño is La Cruz. The sale of cattle is an integral part of the major market day at most levels of the hierarchy. In La Cruz (indeed, in other areas of Andean Colombia where cattle are numerous), there are often other market days during the week, the *mercado de feria*. These weekly *ferias* may be for the sale of breeding stock, or as in La Cruz, for the sale of fattened cows which will be slaughtered for the weekly major market. Many of the transactions (and particularly those in third-order or higher markets) are to or among large scale livestock owners who will be trucking their purchases to major urban consuming centres. Finally, in most markets beef as well as lamb and pork are sold as fresh meat in the market *plaza* by large scale vendors who have purchased directly from the livestock market, or by smaller sellers who have made purchases from these larger vendors and who sell in less than animal-size quantities.

Conclusion

The hierarchy of periodic markets in southern Colombia has been described and spatial regularities of the system have been identified. There are relationships between size of market, size of trade area, number of market days, and the range and type of goods offered for sale. Although the exact nature of these relationships undoubtedly varies from place to place and over time, there are several broad generalizations about the spatial structure of periodic markets which should hold when examined cross-culturally. The use of central place theory in this paper has been implicit on the assumption that its most fruitful application in a market context (indeed, in the developing world generally) is as a heuristic device, a conceptual schemata which suggests particular kinds of questions to ask and particular ways of organising data. At the present stage of research into periodic markets (especially in developing countries), this seems to be a less contentious use of this body of normative theory than the search for particular geometries and for invariant, calibrated relationships which involve the acceptance of rather rigid and restrictive assumptions.

---

[1] The separation of economic and village social centres does not appear to be a function of the size of market gatherings. The *plazas principales*, which have been converted into *parques*, are sufficiently large to transact most business. It seems that functional conversion of an area and spatial displacement of an activity is at one and the same time the result and a complex measure of a village's nodality. Higher-order market towns have larger populations, are politically more important, have a greater range and number of economic functions available that are not necessarily or directly related to the periodic market and, in general, have an apparent if not real higher level of prosperity. The visual by-product is aesthetic, a transformation of the traditional *plaza central* from a squared enclosure of dirt and mud and perhaps soccer goals into *a parque* of trees, gardens, benches, cemented pathways and, quite often, the statue of an important historical figure. The *plaza central* or *parque* is the village's most obvious focal point and symbol of pride.

[2] The location of market centres rather than the actual location of consumers has been used because of the difficulty of identifying and depicting the location of individual households.

[3] Sixty kilograms, more or less, depending on the type of product.

12 Itinerant salesmen and the periodic market system of Lushoto district, Tanzania
Gary A. Gezann

In Lushoto district of northeastern Tanzania, there are fifty-three periodic markets at which subsistence-level farmers sell surplus produce and buy produce exotic to the district or manufactured goods. The district stretches over about 100 km (60 miles) from north to south and has an area of approximately 3,500 square kilometres (1,350 square miles). The population of 210,000[1] is fairly evenly spread within the southern two-thirds of the district where the major urban centres are Lushoto, Soni, Mialo (Mkongaloni), Mnazi (Kwemkwazu) and Bumbuli (Figs. 12.1 and 12.2). Altitudes vary from just over 400 metres (1,300 feet) on the plateau to between 1,200 and 1,500 metres (4,000 and 5,000 feet) throughout the mountainous area. Nearly one-third of the mountains have been set aside as government forest reserves where settlement and farming is forbidden (Fig. 12.1). The main crops are maize, beans, cassava, sweet potatoes, bananas and sugar cane, with maize and cassava the main staples. Cash crops are growing in importance and include tea, coffee, wattle bark (for tannic acid), garden vegetables, rice, cotton and tobacoo. Tea and coffee are grown primarily as estate crops, but small-holder production is increasing. Coffee is grown occasionally for personal consumption with the surplus sometimes, though rarely, entering the local markets. The government established a tea processing plant near Mponde market to encourage small-holder tea production. The increase in the cash income of local farmers may lead to growth of the periodic markets in this southern portion of the district. A government-organised agricultural cooperative is responsible for commercial crops entering and leaving the district. Subsistence agriculture remains the larger component in this predominantly agricultural district, and most surplus agricultural products are sold at local periodic markets.

The periodic markets have several features in common. Firstly, they conform to the seven-day week; most meet once per week, but the largest markets meet twice a week. Some meet every two weeks, and a few meet monthly. Markets occur on the same day(s) of each week. Sunday markets are generally found in areas where the men work a six-day week on an estate or in a local factory

---

* I acknowledge with gratitude the assistance of my M.A. thesis adviser, Dr. Milton E. Harvey, and I am particularly grateful for his helpful comments on earlier drafts of this essay.

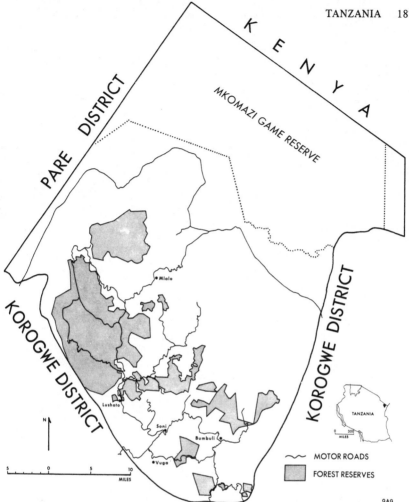

SOURCE : Ministry of Land, Settlements, and Surveys Tanzania

Figure 12.1   Motor roads and forest reserves, Lushoto district, Tanzania

(Allnutt, 1940, 92). Secondly, a fixed site is designated for the market meeting, but this may be moved from time to time. Open fields or uncovered village commons are used as market places. This is true even when the periodic market is situated near a permanent market building with covered stalls. Local residents who bring surplus crops to sell or barter occupy most of the market space and are usually found in the central portion of the market. Around the periphery are the itinerant salesmen with their personal handicrafts or manufactured goods (some domestic but mostly imported).

Thirdly, both sexes are involved in the market transactions. Goods are displayed in piles on either burlap sacks, banana leaves or bright coloured print cloth (kanga). In some markets the sellers are organised into twisted rows. In others they are very haphazard. The drab and sometimes tattered clothing of the males is offset by the brightly coloured prints worn by the women. Occasionally a

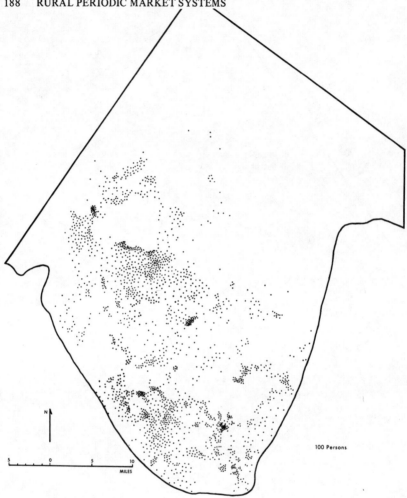

SOURCE : Tanzania 1967 Census of Population
Figure 12.2   Population distribution, Lushoto district, Tanzania

bright silk sari of the wife or daughter of the local Indian businessman may add further colour to the market scene.

Finally, elders of the nearby village exercise local rule of the market. They settle squabbles during the market meeting and sometimes make announcements pertinent to the local residents. Some markets have an overseer; others have an attendant who clears the debris left after each market. The attendant or overseer often charges an entrance 'tax' of one or two corn ears or tomatoes or whatever it is the person has brought to sell, for his services.

An important participant in each periodic market meeting is the itinerant trader. These traders follow regular routes, selling produce and manufactured goods not normally originating within the district. The number of these salesmen present at any one market and the types of goods they sell varies considerably. The main concern of this paper is with these itinerant salesmen, and specifically with the proposition that the number present may indicate the position of a periodic market in a market hierarchy.[2] However, this will be preceded by some comments on the development of periodic markets in Lushoto district, and by a brief discussion of the characteristics of periodic markets.

History of Periodic Markets

Little is known about the origin of the Lushoto market system. Oral tradition relates historical happenings to three major time periods: before the Germans; between the First and Second World Wars; since the Second World War.[3] The Shambala kingdom is relatively young but was fairly well established when the first German missionary visited in 1848 (Krapf, 1860). No mention of a market was made, but an aged resident claims that several markets existed before the First World War. One of the oldest markets was at Vuga for the convenience of visitors in need of a 'tribute' to present to the king at this royal village (Winans, 1962, 138-40). Other researchers claim that the markets of the Usambaras are of indigenous origin and a 'feature of native life throughout what is now Tanga Province' (Allnutt, 1940, 92). Even then the markets were held weekly on a given day at a given place. Exchange was almost exclusively by barter; housewives came from miles around to exchange surplus crops. The market also had a social function and slave exchange was not uncommon.

One of the earliest forms of exchange recorded was between the Washambala and the coastal people, but this took place at Tagata, a village located to the south of the port city of Tanga, outside the present Lushoto district (Poppelwell, 1939, 102-5). In the pre-European era, residents of the Usambaras travelled to the village market at Tagata to barter their maize and bananas for the salt of the coastal Wadigo. Other salt markets found on the plains between the Usambara and Pare Mountains were also patronised by the Washambala and Wapare.

Other early markets were found at the seats of the subchiefs throughout the district. Locations of the early subchief villages were passed by oral tradition and recorded in the *Story of teb Wakilindi*, the legendary parent tribe of the Washambala (Liojjeno, 1936; 1937). Even though the reliability of this legend is questionable, the existence and location of their settlements can be fairly well substantiated.[4] The evidence shows these sub-chiefdoms were located at Vuga, Bumbuli, Mlalo, Mlola and Mrungui (Liojjeno, 1936, 95-7). Except for Mrungui, all the centres had relatively large markets at the time of the field study in 1971. Conclusive evidence on the origins of the Lushoto periodic market system is not available, but oral traditions and several fugitive manuscripts suggest the existence of a small number of periodic markets prior to colonial times.

The Characteristics of Lushoto District Periodic Markets

One of the primary functions of the rural periodic market is to provide a place for the exchange of locally produced agricultural products. People from neighbouring villages arrive early on a market day, while traders from more distant centres appear late. Most markets begin about two hours after sunrise and end by mid or late afternoon, allowing enough daylight for distant participants to return home before nightfall. Attendance at two or three markets per week is common for most families.

There is a distinctive spatial arrangement of traders selling different or the same commodities in the market place. Fruit and vegetables from the mountains are exchanged next to fruit, coconuts, and fish from more tropical areas. In larger markets, the scene is completed with several treadle Singer sewing machines around the perimeter of the area, a barber with his portable chair under a tree, two or three gambling game tables operated by young lads, and perhaps a medicine doctor dispensing his roots and powders and many coloured vials of local medicines. Middlemen buyers from the larger coastal towns haggle for bulk sacks of potatoes, tomatoes or beans. Rice farmers from the plains bring large sacks to be sold by the cup or pile.

Women wear their brightest, newest, and cleanest 'kangas' to market as it is a major weekly social as well as economic activity. Friends and relatives from not-so-near villages meet at the market and exchange news and stories. The low literacy rate among adults makes this function even more important. Young children help their mothers carry the produce and they attend to sales if the mother is buying or gossiping. Announcements concerning either the operation of the market or about a coming social event are sometimes made by the male elders.

Most of the people in the market-place are there to exchange locally produced agricultural products. In addition, agricultural products and manufactured goods exotic to Lushoto district are made available to those peasant farmers who are successful in exchanging their surplus produce for the cash necessary to purchase these 'imported' goods. Circulation of these exotic goods is carried on by itinerant salesmen. The most common items in these two categories of commodities are listed in Table 12.1.

Table 12.1: Itinerant salesmen commodities

Locally produced foodstuffs	Non-local items	
	Indigenous foods	Manufactured goods
Bananas	Fish	Cloth and clothes
Beans	Oyster nuts	Cooking oil
Cabbage	Salt	Kerosene
Cassava		Medicine (local)
Cauliflower		Sundries
Maize		Snuff
Peas		Tobacco
Potatoes		
Rice		
Spinach		
Tomatoes		
Yams		

Source: Author's surveys, 1971

Locally produced foodstuffs are exchanged horizontally within the same economic system, moving from producer to consumer at the same market. Non-locally produced foodstuffs and manufactured goods are exchanged vertically within the system, moving downward by means of a middleman from larger to smaller centres within the economic system. The middleman in this economic hierarchy is the itinerant salesman.

Most of the market participants are involved in the exchange of locally produced foodstuffs. Such an exchange system creates opportunities for varying the staple food and vegetable diet of the peasant. Furthermore, it is a source of food supply to those employed in non-agricultural, cash income jobs such as government workers, agricultural estate workers, and small industry employees. In a few cases, large surpluses of staple foods such as beans and maize are sold in bulk either to buyers from larger centres or areas of crop failure outside the district. The importance of this level of exchange should not be underrated, since it is often the only source of cash income for the peasant family.

The supply of these foodstuffs in a market varies during any given season; also, the types of produce differ seasonally as each crop is harvested and 'floods the market'. Climatic conditions also affect the quantities of these agricultural products available; thus, the ripening and ensuing harvest of crops is influenced by the latitudinal movement of the rains and the physiographic effect of rain shadow between the ocean-facing east and the drier west of the mountains.

Itinerant traders are responsible for the supply of three important food items not produced within Lushoto district: fish, salt, and oyster nuts. Although oyster nuts, known locally as *kweme*, are grown within the district, most are brought from the northern Kilimanjaro district.[5] The Pangani-Mkomazi River and Lakes Buiko and Manka in the plains to the north and east of the district are traditional sources of local fish. A government hydro-electric dam on the Pangani River about seven km (four miles) north of the district has created the Nyumba ya Mungu Lake, and this has become an additional source of fish for the district. From these and several other lakes and rivers, fire-dried and smoked fish are transported into the mountains. Catfish are most common, but several other smaller fish are also sold. Occasionally, some Indian Ocean fish are offered for sale in the markets. On the whole, however, fish do not constitute a very large part of the local diet and rarely are they sold in large quantities.

Salt is available in village retail shops, but it is also sold at the periodic markets, frequently by a representative of the local shop. The salt comes from two sources: ocean water is evaporated in salt pans at Tangata, south of the regional port of Tanga (Poppelwell, 1939, 102-5). Most of the salt, however, comes from deposits on the plains near Makayo northwest of the Usambara Mountains. A special salt market is held at Makayo from May to November. Travelling salesmen bring the salt in bulk and offer it for sale by the cup at the local market-places.

Items sold both in local shops and in many market-places include kerosene, cooking oil, cloth and clothes, and a variety of small manufactured goods. These, together with 'local' medicines, tobacco and snuff, make up a group of manufactured products brought into the district and sold by travelling salesmen. Kerosene is imported into Tanzania by major petroleum companies. The travelling salesmen purchase it in five gallon drums, and sell it one small dipperful (about 80 ml) at a time. Customers bring their own containers, often a discarded medicine or coca-cola bottle. Kerosene is used to fuel lamps or small imported pressure cooking stoves. Vegetable cooking oil is produced and purchased in Dar es Salaam, the national capital, and sold in much the same way as kerosene in the periodic market-places.

Cloth and clothes are purchased wholesale by the travelling salesmen in Tanga or in Dar es Salaam. Some of this merchandise is imported, but much of the cloth is manufactured at the Friendship Textile Mill in Dar es Salaam. Besides the travelling salesmen, local shop merchants often have a representative selling these items at the nearby periodic markets. Tailors with treadle sewing machines are found at market-places having cloth sellers; they fashion shirts, dresses or pants from the newly purchased yardgoods.

Another type of travelling salesman handles large numbers of imported and domestic manufactured goods, here referred to as sundries. These often include shoes, jewellery, pots, dishes, bras, soap, flatware, belts, combs, and plastic flight bags. Salesmen of tobacco and snuff (processed from tobacco leaves grown on the plains) can be identified easily at the market-place because they sell their goods from beneath a black umbrella tied to a pole to protect their products from sun and rain.

The last of these travelling salesmen is the 'local' medicine seller, who is licensed by the government to dispense traditional medicines prepared from roots, herbs and minerals. These medicines are sold in different kinds of containers such as discarded injection vials from the local hospital, leaves and old newspapers.

Itinerant Trader-Based Market Hierarchy

Because cash is needed to purchase these commodities and because these commodities are considered to be luxury items by the majority of the Lushoto residents, the total number of the itinerant traders who visit a market as well as the number of these commodity types available are valid measures of level of importance of each market. Central place theory argues that a hierarchical class-system of service centres exists (Berry and Garrison, 1958, 145-54). Within this class-system, large centres have more functions than small centres. Berry and Garrison ranked centres in Snohomish County, Washington according to their number of functions and 'threshold populations', and Skinner (1964, 5-10) identified a five-level hierarchy in rural China. Skinner's classification was based on the types of goods handled, their source, and the direction of their movement within the system (up or down the hierarchy). Most of the markets of Lushoto district would be classified as 'minor markets' in Skinner's hierarchical system, making it unsatisfactory for the Lushoto case. McKim (1972, 338-9) follows Skinner's system of classification using general observations of functions and market size, though the exact number of functions and measures of 'market size' were not clearly stated. Scott (1972, 317-19) found that the income of a trader was related to the level of the markets attended by the trader. Scott's classification of markets uses general location, periodicity type, functional type (retail, retail-bulking, retail-transportation, etc.), and exchange orientation (horizontal-vertical) to form a hierarchy. The markets of Lushoto district do not fit clearly into any one level of this scheme. None of these methods is suitable for the market system of Lushoto and another method of classification is necessary.

Two general types of exchange activity occur concurrently at all fifty-three markets in Lushoto district. Most of the people in all markets are concerned with the exchange of surplus agricultural produce from their own farms. In addition, markets had at least one itinerant trader providing goods exotic to the district. The number of these itinerant traders and the types of goods they sold at any given market varied with the size (as measured by number of people present) of the market. A census of itinerant traders by type of goods provides the basis for establishing a market hierarchy.

One of the problems of research in periodic markets in Africa (McKim, 1972, 336) stems from the paucity of published official data, which reflects the very real difficulty of collecting accurate information in these market-places. There is constant movement of people and goods into and out of the unbounded area of the periodic market-place, and data collection in all but the smallest markets is extremely frustrating. A notable exception is the itinerant trader: he arrives at the market fairly early, sets up his display of goods, and remains in one place throughout most of the meeting period. Thus, a count of traders and commodities can be obtained with relative ease.

Such a census was taken in Lushoto district during the first two weeks of January 1971 and the results are recorded in Table 12.2. There were nine different types of itinerant salesmen classified by the number of commodities offered for sale. No single itinerant salesman commodity was found at all fifty-three markets. Sellers of cloth and clothes and sundries sellers were the most numerous at any given market while salt, tobacco and fish sellers appeared at the greatest number of markets.

Both the total number of itinerant salesmen per market and the number of commodities offered for sale by these traders were used to identify the hierarchical classification of markets. This classification produces groups of markets based on these two attributes by minimising the within-group variance while at the same time maximising between-group variance.[6] The grouping was continued until further combination produced a group whose within-group variance was greater than its between-group variance. Groups of markets from successively larger groups until a minimum number of groups with the greatest amount of within-group similarity and between-group dissimilarity are found. The grouping algorithm produced a four-level hierarchy as shown in Figure 12.3.

Highest level markets are found at Kwemkwazu, Malindi, Kwemakame, Mgwashi, Soni, Bumbuli, and Funta. The closer areal spacing of these more important markets in the southern portion of the district can be explained by the greater population density in this area. Large tea estates in this same part of the district provide cash incomes which would be reflected by the greater preponderance of these highest level markets. Lowest level markets provide the least variety of itinerant trader commodities and are found either adjacent to the largest markets or in the drier low-population periphery of the mountains.

Service area population obviously is closely related to a market's position in the hierarchy. This relationship was examined using two different measures of market population: the population living within the immediate service area of the market, and the population potential of each market. The delimitation of market service areas is an essential first step for deriving these measures.

The population served by each market is scattered over a large area in several

Table 12.2: Itinerant salesmen census

Market-place	Total salesmen functions	Salesmen total
Kwemakame	10	96
Soni	10	74
Kwekanga	10	54
Lushoto	10	53
Boheloi	10	45
Lukozi	10	36
Funta	9	69
Moa	9	48
Mponde	9	39
Kwemilalo	9	27
Mbaramo	9	12
Mgwashi	8	74
Malindi	8	63
Kwemkwazu	8	49
Baga	8	45
Sunga	8	43
Lunguza	8	40
Mlola	8	33
Mtae	8	32
Tewe	8	21
Mn'gao	8	19
Kishewa	8	12
Bumbuli	7	56
Manolo	7	41
Mdando	7	33
Mishegheshe	7	25
Mshizii	7	22
Kwemn'gongo	7	20
Mkundi	7	13
Ngwelo	7	13
Mkalile	7	11
Mpwant'wa	7	11
Mkongoloni	7	8
Rangwi	6	21
Nkaloi	6	17
Ziwai	6	16
Mamboleo	6	14
Shume	6	11
Herikulu	6	8
Mambo	5	21
Ngulwi	5	15
Bumbuli Hospital	5	14
Kwevidengelesa	5	14
Kwemashai	4	6
Kungului	4	4
Makose	4	4
Malibwi	4	4
Mayo	4	3
Kivingo	3	7
Kibaoni	3	4
Mkuzi	3	3
Mshwamba	1	2
Gologolo	1	1

Source: Author's surveys, 1971

small villages. Census tracts usually are much larger than individual villages, hence census data are not particularly useful. Since each market serves an area extending beyond the small village in which it is located, a village census would not be useful even if it were available. Christaller (1966, 27-80) used Thiessen polygons to delimit market service areas in southern Germany, and the perpendicular bisectors separating one market service area from another were based essentially on the 'Law of Retail Gravitation' (Reilly, 1929). This states in part that a consumer will visit the retail site nearest to him. By connecting the bisectors throughout the system, a network of polygons is drawn. Each polygon delimits the approximate service area for each market. To determine the approximate service areas and population of the fifty-three Lushoto markets, Thiessen polygons were constructed under the following assumptions: firstly, most individuals walk to market and are likely therefore to attend the market nearest

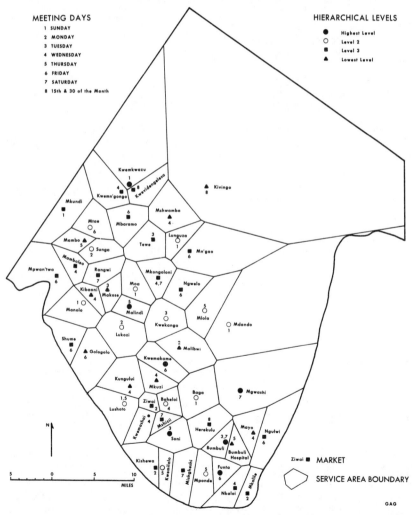

Figure 12.3 Market hierarchy, periodicity and service areas, Lushoto district, Tanzania

to home (a line half-way between markets approximately divides the service areas); and secondly, the delimited service areas are relevant for the lowest-order goods only (Fig. 12.3). The service area map was then superimposed on the population dot map (Fig. 12.2), and the population of each market service area was estimated. Location of each dot within the enumeration area was determined by village locations as shown on topographic maps of Tanzania.

Information compiled by cartographic analysis of the market system in Lushoto district was used to calculate population potentials of the individual market service areas. This is computed by the formula:

$$V_i = \frac{M_i \, M_j}{D_{ij}} + \frac{M_i}{0.5 \, \text{Min.} \, D_{ij}} \text{(for all j)}$$

$$i = 1$$
$$i \neq j$$

where V_i is the population potential at point i
   M_i is the population at n points, and
   D_{ij} is the distance from i to j points.

This potential is a measure of the proximity of each market to the aggregate population of the district. The market with the highest population potential is the market closest to the entire aggregate population (Khos, 1968; Stewart, 1947).

The number of itinerant salesmen for each of the nine types of commodities (Table 12.2) were regressed on service area population and population potential (the latter in both raw and logarithmic form). The transformed values of population potential were used as independent variables in two additional series of regressions. In several cases, the transformed variables yielded more significant relationships. Only those statistics for the most significant relationships for each commodity are shown in Table 12.3.

Two tests were conducted to see if the relationship represented by the scatter of points varied significantly from zero: the student t-test was used to test the hypothesis that the slope, b, differed significantly from zero at the .05 level of confidence (Table 12.3); the F-ratio was used to see if the existing relationship in the sample holds for the population (Hoel, 1971, 256-60). The results of this analysis of variance are also reported in Table 12.3.

The highest correlation and largest b-value emerged from the regression of the number of cooking oil salesmen in each market-place on the population of each market service area ($r = 0.62$, $b = 996.08$), and the lowest was for sellers of local medicines with an r-value of only 0.12 ($b = 143.28$). Only for cloth, salt, fish merchants, and local medicine practitioners did the t-values associated with each r fall below the .05 level. However, the F-ratios from analysis of variance fell below the .05 level of significance in only two cases, local medicine practitioners and cloth merchants.

The only function that had a higher r-value when regressed on population potential instead of service area population was fish sellers: the correlation coefficient rose to 0.50 (significant at the .05 level). The higher correlation indicates that the number of fish salesmen is more closely linked with the broader spectrum of population in and around the market-place than it is with just those people living within the demarcated service area. A possible reason

Table 12.3: Population-Itinerant Commodity Regressions

Independent variable	Dependent variable	r	a	b	Level of Significance t-test	F-ratio
Population	Cooking oil	.6243	2911.2	996.08	99.95	99.99
	Kerosene	.4901	3175.9	756.93	99.95	99.99
	Tobacco and Snuff	.4684	2722.4	408.43	99.95	99.99
	Oyster nuts	.3932	2993.5	615.92	99.95	99.90
	Sundries	.3860	2873.0	187.49	99.95	99.90
	Cloth and Clothes	.2980	3229.3	72.44	95.00	97.50
	Local Medicine	.1158	3629.3	143.28	Below 90.00	25.00
Population Potential	Fish	.5034	161.79	11.36	99.95	99.99
Log Population Potential	Log Salt	.5337	146.94	1.76	99.95	99.99

Source: Author's analysis of field data

might be that as a consumer item, fish are sold in greater volume and the supporting population makes purchases more frequently and comes from a much larger area than the local service area. After logarithmic transformation of population potential (and using this as the independent variable), only salt salesmen had an improved correlation coefficient, from 0.27 to 0.53, which was well within the .05 level of statistical significance. The improved relationship with a logarithmic model suggests that an increase in the population potential results in an exponential increase in the number of salt sellers. Salt may resemble fish in that salesmen are sensitive to the broader population extending beyond the immediate market-place service area.

Neither the use of population potential nor logarithmic transformation improved the *r*-values and significance levels of any of the regressions other than those of fish and salt. Regression of the number of cloth and local medicine traders on population yielded low *r*-values, but as these were the highest found, they were retained. These relatively low *r*-values for cloth and especially local medicine sellers indicate that the number of traders specialising in these items present at a given market is not closely related to the number of people present in the market.

Periodic Markets and Development Planning

The areal distribution and relative importance of rural periodic markets reflects the actions of people in response to their needs; these actions are constrained by the economic alternatives available in the particular market system. Attendance at any given market is the result of both economic and social choices. Knowledge of the relative importance of individual periodic markets should be a valuable indicator of the existing system into which social and economic innovations and services might be inserted. The market infrastructure linked by these itinerant traders provides a means whereby innovations introduced at the highest level markets might be transmitted to the more peripheral centres. New medical, educational, and social facilities will be convenient to a majority of the people if located coincidentally with the highest level market-places. Areas lacking in certain commodities essential for a proper diet can be identified for the planning of an improved system of circulation. At the very least, any reorganisation of the economic and distributive infrastructure of developing regions should begin with an empirical study of the existing periodic market-place system.

[1] This is the 1967 census figure (Tanzania, 1971). Most of the people belong to the Washambala tribe. The local language is a Bantu language with class prefixes. The 'wa' prefix designates a tribal name, the 'u' a place and 'ki' precedes the language of the people. Pronounciation of 'l' and 'r' is not significantly different in many Bantu dialects. Thus, the *Wa*shamba*l*a live in the *U*samba*r*as and speak *K*ishamba*l*a.

[2] The data for the study are based on three pilot surveys and one detailed survey of the fifty-three periodic markets of Lushoto district in January, 1971.

[3] Interviews with several village elders (including Pastor Hyobu of Mialo, Tanzania, whose age has been established at over 100 years) translated from Kishambala by Mrs Borghild Bøe of Størdal, Norway, revealed persistent reference to these time periods.

[4] Much of the story is considered only legend. Feierman (1968, 4-8) gives several reasons for doubting the reliability of this Shambala history.

[5] Local custom has made this seed an important market item; visitors to the household of a new-born infant bring a gift of oyster nuts. Traditionally, the 'meats' are ground and boiled to produce a milky liquid which aids the new mother with her own milk production. It is a cheap source of protein.

[6] The clustering technique employed here used Ward's (1963) H-grouping whereby groups are successively combined whose fusion would minimise the increase in λ. Two groups are merged when

$$\lambda = \text{Min.} \frac{W_i \ W_j}{W_i + W_j} \cdot D_{ij}^2$$

where W_i and W_j are the sizes of groups i and j, and D_{ij} is the distance between the group centroids. The two attributes were standardised prior to grouping. *A priori*, a meaningful hierarchy was one in which there are five or fewer groups.

13 Viability, location and timing of Liberian periodic markets
W. Penn Handwerker

This essay is concerned with the intertwining of the viability, location and timing of Liberian periodic markets, and explores the contrasts between the Liberian system and other West African periodic market systems.[1] Specifically, an attempt is made to determine whether the viability of Liberian periodic markets is contingent upon their location and/or timing and, if so, to isolate the extent to which and the ways in which spatial and temporal competition for buyers and sellers explains the locational and temporal properties of these markets.

The classic (and many modern derivative) geometries of central place theory fit few if any West African market systems, but the absence of fit is perhaps most apparent in Liberia, for virtually all of the assumptions necessary to construct these geometries are empirically invalid. Rather than consumers with equal movement options in all directions being distributed at uniform densities over an unbounded plain, superficial examination of the situation in Liberia reveals that consumer-producers are distributed unevenly over a landscape in which head-loading costs are much greater than the costs of road transport and where a linear road system effectively constrains movement except in certain directions. Although Hill (1966) questioned the applicability of central place theory to West African periodic markets, they have been interpreted in terms of the theory's central premise: people tend to minimise the costs (in time, money, and/or effort) involved in marketing activities (Berry, 1967).[2] The literature on West African periodic markets consistently emphasises the fact that markets are *economic* phenomena whose viability implies a locational and temporal

* This is a revised version of a paper delivered to the Annual Meetings of the African Studies Association, Syracuse, N.Y., in October, 1973. The study is based on fifteen months of field research in Liberia between 1968 and 1970, supported initially by funds from the Ford Foundation, and later by a Pre-Doctoral Fellowship (FOI-MH44672-01) and Research Grant (MH-12095-01) from the National Institute of Medical Health, Washington, D.C. Further analysis has been supported by a grant from the Humboldt Foundation. The critical comments and encouragement of numerous people is greatly appreciated. The author records special thanks to Ruth and Verlon Stone, Indiana University, for their companionship and assistance in the field.

spacing efficiently attracting buyers and sellers (Smith, 1971). Recently, several researchers have developed tests for this proposition (Fagerlund and Smith, 1970; Hill and Smith, 1972; R.H.T. Smith, 1970, 1971, 1974), the results of which are largely consistent with the view that spatial and temporal competition explains the locational and temporal properties of these markets, and that market viability is a function of the synchronization of market location and timing. These properties of Liberian markets are in general accord with this finding.

However, the ways in which market location and timing is synchronized in Liberia and the operation of the competitive processes from which synchronization is derived differ considerably, and this will be the central theme of this paper. The data on Liberian periodic markets illustrate the importance of examining the interrelationship of sales and purchasing strategies used by the rural population served by periodic markets.

The essay also fills an empirical gap in the literature on periodic markets in West Africa; until recently, the main papers on markets in this region were those of Schwab (1947) and Brown (1936, 1941). The essay commences with a discussion of the historical and economic context of Liberian periodic markets. The operation of these markets is then illustrated, and the questions of market viability, location, and timing are discussed in the context of village periodic markets (Table 13.1). Finally, some of the implications of the findings on Liberian periodic markets are considered.

The Institutional Context

In 1970 Liberian periodic markets constituted one part of a system of market-places (one of the three principal marketing channels in Liberia) whose principal function was to channel foodstuffs from producers to urban consumers. Imported goods moved to Liberian consumers through a three-tiered system in which Euro-American firms dominated import and national wholesale functions, Lebanese firms dominated middle-level wholesale and retail functions as store merchants, and African firms clustered primarily in low-level retail functions as shop merchants, hawkers, and travelling market intermediaries. Such commodities as iron, rubber, cocoa, coffee, and palm kernels moved to world markets through a series of specialized channels.

Imports were sold in some market-places (central daily, and village periodic markets (Table 13.1)) by market sellers, and in others (town and neighbourhood daily markets) by hawkers wandering through the markets as they walked around town. Foodstuffs were retailed independently of the market-place system by individual sellers operating from their door-steps (vending in neighbouring villages, labour camps at adjacent plantations, at the houses of resident teachers and missionaries (and anthropologists!), or from stands along the roads) and by clusters of traders in front of supermarkets, stores, shops, and schools, and at road intersections. In some locations, foodstuffs were sold in bulk both by individual sellers and clusters of traders at stands along the roads. Although stores throughout the country functioned principally as channels for a wide range of imported farm equipment, cloth, household wares, food, and sundries (and secondarily as first stage bulkers of cocoa, coffee and palm kernels bound for world markets), a number of stores in rural towns and the larger villages on the road also purchased rice and palm oil. About a half the total sales of country

Table 13.1: Liberian market site classification, 1970

Level	Designation	Number of sellers	Number of commodities	Size of trade area (population served)
1	Central daily market[a]	600–1,000	200–300	10–20,000
2A	Neighbourhood daily market[a]	50–200	30–100	800–2,500
2B	Town daily market	15–150	25–100	500–5,000
2C	Village periodic market	50–250	50–150	500–2,000
3	Cluster of sellers	5–10	10–20	50–150
4	House seller	1–2	1–10	10–25

Source: Handwerker, 1971, 222.

[a] The Central and Neighbourhood daily markets form a unit, the Central markets serving a metropolitan community, the Neighbourhood markets serving neighbourhood areas within that metropolitan community. The only such markets investigated systematically were in Monrovia. However, the Harbel Market of the Firestone Plantations Company appeared to serve similar functions as the Central Monrovia markets, each outlying labour camp having clusters of sellers functioning in much the same way (if not strictly market places) as the Neighbourhood markets in Monrovia.

rice, all the sales of imported rice, and perhaps a quarter to a third of the total sales of palm oil were handled by store merchants at some point from producer to consumer. Further, a number of store merchants operated outlets of the Mesurado Fish and Cold Stores Company (the firm supplying Liberia with most of its fresh fish). Shops complemented stores both spatially and functionally; thus, they are located in neighbourhood rather than central areas in cities, towns and villages on the roads and, in the absence of stores, in a number of villages off the roads. Shops catered to a restricted demand for imported foodstuffs and locally produced gin and rum; customers normally travelled only a short distance, perhaps at short notice, and at times (Sunday, notably) when stores were closed. Off the roads, shop merchants also purchased rice, palm oil and other foodstuffs for delivery principally to the capital, Monrovia.

The vast majority of sales of foodstuffs (both imports such as tomato paste, onions, rice and bouillon cubes, and locally produced rice, palm oil, greens and peppers) occurred in market-places. Seven-day village periodic markets functioned as places where farmers could purchase a variety of imported wares and foodstuffs less expensively or on better terms than at stores or shops with money received from produce brought to the markets for sale. Produce collected at such markets was channelled to daily markets serving people in towns, concessions, and cities. In towns and smaller concessions, a single town daily market functioned as the only bulk-breaking and retailing centre catering to the daily food wants of the local population. The larger and more dispersed populations in Monrovia and such large concession sites as the Firestone rubber plantation at Harbel were served by a more complex system of markets. In these urban areas, one or two central daily markets functioned as bulk-breaking and retailing locations, and also as sites at which produce brought from rural areas was redistributed to a series of neighbourhood markets serving the population in outlying districts.

Unlike the situation elsewhere in West Africa,[3] trade in Liberian market-places has become commonplace and important only within the last two decades. Market-places were not characteristic of Liberian trade from the foundation of the country until the end of the nineteenth century; indeed, market-place transactions were exceptional. At the turn of the century, there were fewer than a dozen documented market-places and, with the exception of two daily markets in coastal towns, were restricted to the northeastern interior. Liberian trade was characterized by two largely distinct trading systems; in the *interior system,* Mandingo merchants travelled out of Sudanic trade centres with merchandise to exchange for produce (principally kola) and craft items collected from the homes of resident traders and individual farmers and craftsmen. Chiefs controlled the supply of the major trade goods in the *coastal system;* small supplies of these goods were accumulated by isolated trade depots and/or periodically collected by merchantmen sailing the western coast of Africa. Although about two dozen government-sponsored markets were added to the interior trading system during the early part of the twentieth century, most of

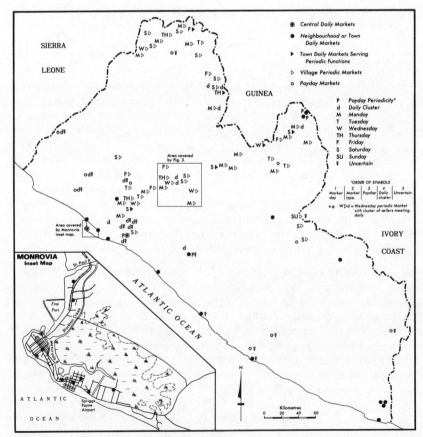

Figure 13.1   Principal marketing sites in Liberia

these markets were sustained only by assigning to villages quotas of sellers. They appear to serve a more administrative than economic function.

Within the last two decades, the number of Liberian market-places has almost quadrupled and, consistent with transport and demand considerations, markets have become dispersed throughout the country (see Fig. 13.1).[4] What had been a dichotomous trading system for nearly 500 years was realigned radically with the introduction of industrial technologies, migration to places of employment and education, the provision of roads, and a changing household organization. As the interior trading system atrophied and the coastal trading system special-ized and bifurcated into separate channels for imports and exports, a new trading system emerged that integrated almost the entire country, utilizing market-places as its sites of exchange. A new set of market-places originated largely from political recognition and legitimization of the activities of *de facto* market sellers. Market sellers themselves originated from three sources: a pool of underskilled and illiterate men who had difficulty finding stable and well paid employment; women in urban areas assuming responsibility for household maintenance inadequately handled by underskilled and illiterate men; and women in rural areas supplementing insufficient cash income, meeting household expenses not provided for by men, or meeting their independent wants

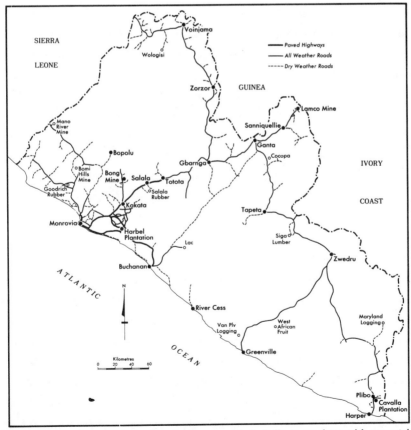

Figure 13.2   Road network in Liberia (open symbols indicate markets with uncertain periodicity)

(Handwerker, 1974). Although a number of market-places established before 1950 (including some which may trace their origins to the seventeenth century) retain many of their functions and characteristics in the contemporary Liberian market system, as often as not such markets either have disappeared or have changed their functions as they adjusted to trade in foodstuffs along a new transport system toward a new set of central places (Stanley, 1970; see Fig. 13.2).

Liberian periodic markets meet once every seven days (excluding Sunday),[5] between fifty and 250 sellers offer between fifty and 150 commodities for sale, and the markets serve between 500 and 2,000 people. In functions provided, these markets are equivalent to but differ systematically from central and neighbourhood daily markets in large urban areas, town daily markets in smaller urban areas, and from clusters and single sellers wherever located (Table 13.1).

The Operation of Liberian Periodic Markets

The operation of Liberian periodic markets involves several classes of buyers and sellers; the business of the markets is organized in terms of the movement of farm produce to urban areas and the movement of imported food, cloth, and household wares to village areas. On the one hand, producer-sellers carry small amounts of farm produce to these markets for sale. A small proportion of this produce is sold within markets to local consumers (farmer-consumers, and professional traders and other specialists),[6] and an even smaller proportion to part-time village retailers and settled professional retailers collecting small quantities of the more durable items (e.g. peppers and palm oil) for re-sale in the market village (and in adjacent villages) during the week preceding the next market day. Most such produce, however, is sold to bulking intermediaries whose accumulated stocks are carried to an urban area for sale principally to market retailers. On the other hand professional intermediaries (men dealing in cloth and household items; women dealing in soap and foodstuffs (notably bread, rice, fish, bouillon cubes and salt)) bring imports (principally) to the markets for sale. Although a small proportion of the items handled by women intermediaries finds its way into the hands of part-time village intermediaries and settled professionals, most sales are made to farmer-consumers. Analysis of the periodic markets around Totota, in central Liberia, illustrates the operation of these markets (Fig. 13.3).

Central Liberia is a high market density region of the country. The markets in this region send food principally to Monrovia, supplying about 12 per cent of the Liberian produced food sold in that city's markets, and secondarily to Firestone's rubber plantation at Harbel. Although patterns of production and sales are relatively undifferentiated in Liberia, a few areas are notable for the volume of certain commodities sent to urban areas. Central Liberia produces considerable quantities of palm oil, and supplies a large proportion of the total consumed in both Monrovia and Harbel. Rice from this area finds its way to Monrovia but, except for that sent directly to kinsmen, only through stores.

Markets in this region begin between 7.30 and 8.30 in the morning, and finish business slightly before or just after noon. Foodstuffs are retailed from ground-covers spread in an open central area of the market. Imported cloth and household items are retailed from thatch or zinc-roofed shelters constructed around this central area. Produce is bulked on the outskirts of the market, adjacent to the road and the parked taxis and trucks.

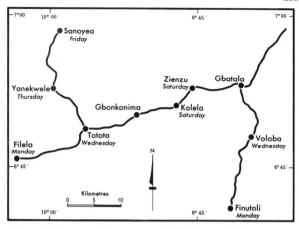

Figure 13.3   Periodic markets in central Liberia, 1970

Between Monrovia and Gbarnga, 201 km (125 miles) upcountry, only three towns served important central functions: Kakata (71 km (44 miles) from Monrovia), Salala (about 109 km (68 miles) from Monrovia), and Totota (134 km (83 miles) from Monrovia). The latter features half a dozen tailors, a mechanic, a carpenter, a gasoline station, four stores (one of which operated an outlet of the Mesurado Fish and Cold Stores Company), several shops, a mission literacy centre and school, a public school, and several bread bakers. Totota also supported several petty traders and a daily cluster of from four to seven foodstuff sellers. Although the traditional resident population was Kpelle, the town included a large proportion of migrants. From the perspective of profes- sional travelling intermediaries, the bulk of whom were migrants, Totota was the centre of a 'circuit' of markets. It was here that all but a few of the professionals regularly visiting these markets made their homes, and it is from the perspective of these merchants that the markets are referred to as a circuit.

In each market of the Totota circuit, there were from fifteen to twenty-five professional intermediaries dealing in cloth, clothing, and household wares; forty different such traders were encountered in these markets. Twenty sellers visited these markets on a regular basis, and fifteen of these sellers lived in or just outside of Totota. Small quantities of African tie-dyed and Batiked cloth from the Koindu (Sunday) international market in southeastern Sierra Leone, and country cloth (six cm (four inch) strips of woven indigenous cotton) from the Bolohun (Saturday) market in northeastern Liberia occasionally appear in these markets. However, the bulk of the merchandise sold by these traders is brought from Monrovia. Depending on the level of sales, these·traders re-stock weekly, purchasing either from middle-level wholesalers or from outlets of the importing firms. Stocks are stored in their homes.

These traders radiate out from Totota regularly visiting a series of five adjacent markets: Filela on Monday, Totota on Wednesday, Yanekwele on Thursday, Sanoyea on Friday, and either Zeinzu or Kolela on Saturday. There is some overlap with market circuits travelled by merchants based in Salala who visit Filela and Totota fairly regularly, and merchants based in and around Gbarnga who visit the Kolela and Zeinzu markets. Traders based in Totota frequently visited the Jennita (Tuesday) market about 37 km (23 miles) toward Monrovia, the Kpakolakweata (Monday) market about 29 km (18 miles) toward Monrovia, the Salala (Friday) market about 21 km (13 miles) toward Monrovia, as well as the Voloba (Wednesday) and Finutoli (Monday) markets on the feeder road from Gbatala into the southern portion of Bong County. In the wet season when aggregate demand is low, Totota merchants occasionally visit the Gbarnga market (a daily market also providing periodic functions), and the 'pay-day' market at Nimba (the LAMCO iron mine on the Liberian-Guinea border). When near-by markets occurred on the same day and an assistant (wife or 'brother') was available, the assistant attended one market while the managing entrepreneur visited the other. In this way, the firms of a few merchants were represented at as many as seven different markets in one week.

Each market in the Totota circuit also attracts a series of women professional intermediaries, dealing in fish or bread, or in a combination of rice, salt, bouillon cubes, and soap. Like the men, most of these women lived in or around Totota; unlike the men, however, women lived in a greater diversity of towns, including villages off the road (see Table 13.2). Characteristically, these women were widowed or divorced, or were married to a trader or other specialist. Between fifteen and thirty such sellers attended these markets, and most travelled a circuit much like their male counterparts. Although a few of these traders visited four or five markets each week, the circuits of women usually consisted of only two or three markets, and women tended to visit particular markets less consistently than men. Whereas professionals dealing in imported cloth and household wares commonly travelled to markets $US.75 to $US1.00 by taxi fare from their homes, women tended to travel to closer markets (Table 13.3). Some of these traders attended to household duties during part of the week, while others visited a market on behalf of their husband when he was in Monrovia purchasing supplies, or when two nearby markets met on the same day. Most frequently, however, these intermediaries did not have a sufficiently large volume of sales to permit them to visit markets farther away than a $US.25 taxi fare and still make an adequate profit. Some fish sellers, for instance, purchased fresh stocks

Table 13.2:   Market visitation patterns of women travelling intermediaries in central Liberian periodic markets, 1970.

| Number of markets visited | Home | | | |
	Totota	Other market towns	Other towns & villages	Total
1		7	4	11
2	6	7	4	17
3	25	5	2	32
4	4			4
5	1	1		2
Total	36	20	10	66

Source: author's surveys and analysis.

Gamma = —.7277; Chi-square = 18.85, df = 4, P less than .001. (Chi-square calculated from a 3 x 3 table with rows 4 and 5 collapsed into row 3; the associated gamma = —.7704).

on a market day, smoked the unsold portions in the afternoon, and attempted to dispose of the smoked fish in their home town and adjacent villages and farm villages before visiting another market where competition from sellers of fresh frozen fish was keen. A Totota woman selling home baked bread visited only Monday, Wednesday and Friday markets; she did not attend the Totota market because bread sellers there were so numerous. She baked bread on Sunday for sale at Filela or Finutoli on Monday; bread baked on Tuesday was sold at Voloba on Wednesday; Thursday she baked bread for sale on Friday at Sanoyea; on Saturday she rested.

Like the professional travelling intermediaries discussed above, bulking intermediaries working out of Monrovia and (less frequently) Salala travelled a circuit of markets collecting as much produce as their capital allowed, and carried the produce to urban areas for resale. Essentially the same group of bulkers visited these markets weekly throughout the year. In contrast to the professional travelling intermediaries, however, these traders visited markets throughout the road system and not infrequently bulkers visited such towns as Gbatala and Gbonkonima featuring large quantities of produce for sale in the town and in adjacent areas but having no official market or market day. Bulkers visited anywhere from three to five markets a week, of which only two or three were part of the Totota circuit.

Although sales in the Totota market circuit were made to part-time village intermediaries, professional settled intermediaries working daily in other market towns who had run short of merchandise, and local specialist populations, seller-producers/farmer-consumers were the central personnel of these periodic markets. Their sales to bulkers initiated the movement of foodstuffs to urban consumers, and their receipts formed the basis for attracting and supporting professionals dealing in imports.

The rural population in Central Liberia consists principally of farm households growing many crops and, except for the staples of rice and cassava, in small amounts. The population density of the region is about 100 people per square kilometre (250 people per square mile), and the population distribution appears to be reasonably uniform. Despite an expansion of cash wants for household

Table 13.3: Supply areas of central Liberian periodic markets, 1970: producer-sellers and women market intermediaries.

Supply area	Producer-sellers	Women intermediaries	Total
Market town	36	18	54
Under one hour walk	47	8	55
One to two hour walk	72	5	77
Three hour walk or further	10 (165)	1 (32)	11
Taxi: US$.25	4	21	25
US$.50	———	3	3
US$.75	——— (4)	10 (34)	10
Total	169	66	235

Source: Handwerker, 1971, 257

subsistence and an associated increase in the volume of food flowing into market channels from particular households over the past few years, food production has not become commercialized (Handwerker, 1973b, 1973c). Surplus food for sale comes from crops grown in the first instance for household subsistence, and decisions to sell food are made by the women as one aspect of their general responsibility for day-to-day household maintenance. Because the productivity of Liberian swidden technologies is notoriously low and food sales occur only in the context of household subsistence, care is taken to balance household cash requirements with household food requirements. Sales strategies dictate infrequent sales of many different foods in small quantities; thus, most farm households make sales only about once a week or so (Liberia, 1968, Table 17) and bulkers necessarily purchase a variety of foodstuffs. Only palm oil dealers tend to specialize in the commodities sought, but even these traders purchase generalized stocks when supplies of palm oil dwindle in the wet season.

As indicated in Table 13.3, about 92 per cent of the 169 producer-sellers interviewed in the five markets of the Totota circuit travelled no more than about two hours (about eleven km (seven miles)) to reach a market. As the radius of the area from which producer-sellers are drawn to market is enlarged from a walk of under one hour to a walk of three hours or longer, an increasingly large number of potential market participants is encompassed. Travel costs become prohibitive beyond a travel time of one and a half hours and despite the increasingly large number of potential market participants at greater distances, the number of people actually drawn to market declines drastically. In the busiest season, a few people may travel up to five hours from north central Liberia (about thirty-two km (twenty miles)) to reach the Sanoyea market. However, the movement of farmers to market generally is constrained; the linearity of the road system, the costs involved in taxi transport, and the length of time and amount of effort it takes to headload goods even eleven km (seven miles) has resulted in market visitation patterns such that most of the farm population (even in this area of high market density) live within convenient reach of only one or, at best, two markets (Table 13.4).

All the principal market personnel appear to make choices with a view to maximizing their profits, and it seems that there are five factors which producer-sellers/farmer-consumers, bulking intermediaries, and travelling intermediaries

Table 13.4:   Market visitation patterns of producer-sellers in central Liberian periodic markets, 1970.

Number of Markets visited	Home			Total
	Totota	Other market towns	Other towns & villages	
1		37	106	143
2	2	8	9	19
3	4	3		7
Total	6	48	115	169

Source: author's surveys and analysis.

Gamma = .7322, Chi-square = 72.79, df = 4, P less than .001

consider when deciding which markets to attend. Producer-sellers/farmer-consumers are most concerned with the prices received for produce brought to the market and the specific range of goods available for purchase at a market. Bulkers are most concerned with the aggregate supply of produce. Travelling intermediaries are most concerned with the aggregate demand of farmer-consumers. Of course, all market personnel are concerned with the costs (in money, time, and effort) of attending a given market. The first four variables tend to exhibit only insignificant variation; prices tend to be uniform and adjustments in price tend to be made rapidly (Handwerker, 1971, 296-319). The data for the Totota circuit recorded in Table 13.5 suggest that markets tend to offer a comparable range of commodities for sale. Because of largely undifferentiated and evenly distributed farm units, the aggregate supply of produce varies principally by season, not by market. As market purchases are contingent largely upon market sales, aggregate demand also varies principally by season and not by market. Only transport costs significantly vary between markets, and then mainly for the farm population. Thus, bulkers doing a moderate business could afford to travel into the central Liberian markets, and professional retailers minimized their transport costs by establishing their homes in Totota, the town central to this series of markets. For the relatively immobile farm population, however, transport constraints severely limited the alternatives from which they could choose (Table 13.4). Only about 15 per cent of the producer-sellers interviewed reported ever visiting more than one market. Most of these people (those living in market towns bounded at least on one side by another market town) live within reach of only two markets. The few people regularly (albeit infrequently) visiting three markets live in Totota where a feeder road breaks up an otherwise linear channel of movement. In Table 13.4, the homes of producer-sellers are arranged in order of the increasing travel costs involved in visiting markets in the Totota circuit. Of course, it is possible to predict with some accuracy that one individual will visit more markets than another, merely by guessing. However, knowledge of the relative travelling costs involved facilitates improvement in the prediction of the relative number of markets visited by more than 70 per cent. A more accurate measure of travel costs than is recorded in Table 13.4 would permit a still greater increase in the accuracy of predictions.

The constraints on the mobility of the farm population inherent in travel costs are bolstered further by the presence of alternative purchasing sites: albeit at slightly higher prices, one can obtain a wide variety of imported goods from stores in the market towns six days a week, and from shops both in market towns and in towns off the roads seven days a week. Further, with considerably less choice and at slightly higher prices, one can obtain foodstuffs daily from clusters of sellers in a number of market towns, and from house sellers in nearly all towns and villages.

The markets of the Totota circuit and, by implication, periodic markets through-out Liberia, cater principally to small, dispersed populations selling local produce and purchasing imports. The purchasing power of these households largely rests upon their produce sales. They produce small amounts of a large variety of crops and have to balance household cash wants against household food requirements; thus, sales are made infrequently, in small quantities, and without specialization. Further, headloading costs (bolstered by the availability of alternative purchasing sites) effectively constrain the distance producer-sellers/ farmer-consumers can travel to market. These people do not sell and buy

Table 13.5:   Commodities in the five markets of the Totota circuit, July—August, 1970

Commodity group	Commodities offered in				
	All five	Four	Three	Two	One
Staples	Rice — country	Eggplant	Cassava	Maize — fresh	Eddos
	Rice — imported	Greens — collard	Plantain	Greens — cassava	Beans
	Palm oil	Greens — other	Maize — roast		Sweet potato
	Peppers	Palm nuts	Onions		Okra
	Bitterballs				Greens — potato
	Fish — fresh				Meat — fresh
	Fish — smoked				Meat — smoked
	Bouillon cubes				
	Salt				
Other food	Peanuts	Candles	Uncooked *fufu*	Ginger root	Sugar
	Kola nuts		Chewing gum	Tomatoes	Cookies
	Fruit — various		Bread — country	Benniseed	Soda
			Bread — wheat	Snails — land	Palm wine
			Chickens		Cane juice
Clothing	Trousers		Shoes		Lappas — country cloth
	Shirts		Sandals		Country cloth strips
	Underwear — men's		Women's headties		Belts
	Underwear — women's		Socks		
	Lappas — African				
	Lappas — European				

sufficiently often to support a daily market and, to judge by comments of professional intermediaries, in certain seasons markets meeting only once a week do not have sufficient aggregate demand to support many professionals.

Market Viability, Location, and Timing

Market viability implies the ability to attract buyers and sellers in sufficient numbers to justify keeping the market open. Although people attended these markets for many ostensibly non-economic reasons, these motivations presuppose the existence of the market as a site of exchange. The question at issue is how sufficient numbers of buyers and sellers are first attracted to a market-place, and how their loyalty to that market is retained over time.

Of course, a sufficient number of buyers and sellers may be attracted either

Table 13.5 (cont.)

Commodity group	Commodities offered in				
	All five	Four	Three	Two	One
	Snuff	Cigarettes	Pipes	Flashlights	Gourds
	Blankets	Tobacco	Cups	Batteries	Morters
	Towels	Matches	Glasses	Toys	Rice fanners
	Soap – Liberian	Enamel basins	Dishes	Shotgun shells	Sheets
	Soap – country	Utensils	Fish traps		Pillows
	Soap – imported	Needles	Perfume		Fish hooks
Other	Sundries	Thread			Game traps
		Jewellery – brass			Hoes – country
					Pots – country
					Woven mats
					Books, magazines
					Radios
					Crop seed
					Medicine – patent
Total	25	13	19	10	29

Source: Handwerker, 1971, Table 61, 248-50.

involuntarily or voluntarily. But the 'viability' induced in the early twentieth century by government levies of market sellers on rural towns (and fines if the requisite number did not attend) had long since been discontinued by 1970. Buyers and sellers were attracted to markets in 1970 because they could make money (Handwerker, 1973c, 1974). Specifically, the existence of a periodic market in Liberia implied that firstly, producer-sellers were sufficiently numerous for the aggregate supply of produce to enable bulking intermediaries to pay transport costs, restock, and pay living costs; and secondly, that farmer-consumers were sufficiently numerous for their aggregate purchases to enable retailing intermediaries to pay transport costs, restock, and pay living costs. The more interesting questions at issue are whether markets compete for farmer-consumers/producer-sellers and whether this competition explains the spatial and temporal properties of these markets. Although experience elsewhere leads one to expect that a market's viability will be explained by spatial and temporal properties emerging in a competitive situation, the historical and contemporary differences between Liberia and other parts of West Africa are significant. These questions can be evaluated by exploring contrasts with propositions advanced about other West African periodic market systems (Hodder and Ukwu, 1969; Fagerlund and Smith, 1970; R.H.T. Smith, 1970, 1971, 1974; Hill and Smith, 1972).

Where the viability of markets is contingent on competition for the business of a rural population, the markets in question should display clearly defined spatial and temporal patterns. In a competitive situation, markets meeting on the same day located close together would be competing in the same service area for the same people at the same time. Initiators of new markets would attempt to find a market site some distance from existing markets, or to select a market day avoiding or minimizing competition from adjacent markets. Through mistaken decisions or changing circumstances markets may be situated at inconvenient locations relative to other markets meeting on the same day. These markets would be eliminated as the rural population attended the more conveniently located market. Such processes 'push' markets apart and result in a uniform spatial pattern of markets meeting on the same day.

Although markets meeting on the same day compete only spatially, sets of periodic markets simultaneously compete spatially and temporally. In a competitive situation, the spatial and temporal features of a set of markets merge together as market initiators select locations and times from alternatives limited by the presence of other markets, and as poorly situated or poorly timed markets disappear. The effect of these selective processes is a synchronization of market locations and times minimizing the marketing costs for the group over which markets compete.

There are two principal groups of buyers and sellers frequenting periodic markets: *travelling traders* (in Liberia, bulkers of produce and retailers of imports) who move from one market to another within a region buying and/or selling goods and services; and *farmers* (in Liberia, farmer-consumers/seller-producers) who attend one or several markets in the region selling produce and purchasing imports and local food items they do not produce themselves. Because of differences in perspective, the synchronization of market locations and times minimizing the costs for one group will not minimize the costs for the other. Distinct patterns of synchronization can be expected from a knowledge of the group over which markets compete. Where the markets are equivalent, the principal constraint on traders is the cost of moving around the existing circuit; for full-time travelling traders returning home only once a 'week', travel costs would be minimized by a circumferential route in which markets which were adjoined in space were also adjoined in time. Although markets meeting on the same days would be forced apart by spatial competition alone, markets meeting on adjacent days (e.g. Tuesday and Wednesday markets) would be separated by relatively short distances. Markets meeting on days separated by one complete day (e.g. Monday and Wednesday markets), or by two days (e.g. Monday and Thursday markets) would be separated by increasingly longer distances. In sum, markets competing over travelling traders would exhibit a direct relationship between the spatial and temporal sequencing of market meetings.

In contrast, farmers would consider waiting costs as well as travel costs (Hodder and Ukwu, 1969, 157-60). Rather than solely considering the distance costs of visiting a given market on a given day, farmers would consider the *time since* the last periodic market visit, the *distance to* the market meeting today, and the *next time* an accessible periodic market would meet. Markets competing over farmers would adjust to the preference for a balance of waiting and travel costs. Again, markets meeting on the same day would be forced apart by spatial competition alone. But markets meeting on adjacent days would be separated by considerable distances. Markets meeting on days separated by one or by two days would be separated by increasingly shorter distances. In sum, markets competing over farmers would exhibit an indirect relationship between the spatial and temporal sequencing of market meetings. Thus, a strong correlation (negative or positive) should be expected between spatial and temporal separation; in both cases, initiators of new markets should select sites and market days on the basis of careful estimates of the competitive potential of adjacent markets.

In Liberia, the viability, location, and timing of periodic markets are interwoven in a number of ways. Periodicity itself is implied by the conditions of sale and purchase. Constraints on the supply of produce relative to imports means that markets meeting only once every seven days can support few professional traders. There are seasons when the aggregate demand and supply at these markets is so small that few professional intermediaries visit daily or pay-day markets because 'the people are too few'; if one is to maintain a viable enterprise, one must go where 'the people are plenty'. Imports are available on a daily basis in stores, shops, and from settled professional intermediaries. Travelling market sellers could establish themselves readily in markets on a daily basis if they felt they could make money.[7]

The seven-day schedule followed by Liberian periodic markets appears to have existed for as long as markets have been found in this region of West Africa. The earliest documented markets met once every seven days, and elders in these markets questioned in 1970 indicated that the market day had not changed since the market was established. Such markets arose in the context of trade between the savanna and the fringe of the coastal rainforest, possibly as early as the seventeenth century. The timing of these markets appears to have initially represented an extension of the Muslim calendar to coordinate the meetings of these markets with those in the savanna regions. The early Liberian settlers brought with them a seven-day week, and all markets created since the establishment of the Liberian state have not surprisingly followed a seven-day week. Although the aggregate supply and demand on which these markets are based increases markedly at some times (notably Christmas, and Independence Day in July), at no time does the rise justify lessening the existing periodicity schedule.

Further, there are discernible regions in which viable markets cannot be maintained. The absence of periodic markets in the eastern interior regions of Liberia can be explained by population densities of about five people per square kilometre (thirteen per square mile). Within 48 km (30 miles) or about a $US1.00 to $US1.50 fare to and from the major coastal urban centres periodic markets are not found, and this is explained by the relative profitability of carrying produce directly to the urban market. Only beyond this point do producer-sellers find it profitable to sell consistently to bulking intermediaries.[8]

Finally, the existence of these markets facilitates the movement of large quantities of produce rapidly and with little deterioration to urban centres. The location of Liberian periodic markets has been affected considerably by the development of the road system. Irrespective of their quality, roads permit the movement of large quantities of goods less expensively, far more quickly and with less deterioration than does headloading. Although bags of rice occasionally were headloaded from central Liberia to merchants on the coast in the early twentieth century, vehicular transport was used in the movement of most foodstuffs shipped to Monrovia and other urban centres in 1970. No independently viable markets existed in central Liberia until a jeep road was constructed, and most of the markets in this region appear to have emerged only after improvements in the road in the late 1950s and early 1960s permitted reliable travel to Monrovia within one day. The changing fortunes of Bopolu, the pre-eminent trading town in northwestern Liberia during the nineteenth century, illustrate the importance of road access. During its heyday, Bopolu had a large specialist population and a daily market, but by 1926, alternative trade routes existed, coastal merchants established posts inland from Monrovia, and the Harbel plantation began to draw workers to its site on the Farmington River. Population and trade shifted to the southeast. Bopolu lost its strategic position, and as Schwab (1947,12) noted, the town 'was a sad relic of its former state. Only nine huts remained, and some of these were scarcely habitable.' By 1970, however, a road into the interior from Monrovia terminated at Bopolu, and once again the site assumed a location of importance and supported a periodic market.

Although market viability, location and timing clearly are interwoven, the importance of competition specifically for producer-sellers/farmer-consumers and of synchronizing market days and locations in particular regions is not clear. The overall spatial dispersion does not conform to the uniform pattern expected in a competitive situation. Nearest-neighbour tests (Clark and Evans, 1954) suggest that, at best, most same-day periodic markets in Liberia are distributed randomly in space (Table 13.6). Allowing for the recent origins of the market system and the paucity of markets for most market days, these results are not wholly unexpected. But the operation of processes of contagion is suggested by the unexpected and consistent tendency toward the clustering of these markets. The overall dispersion of Liberian periodic markets possibly is best explained not by competition, but by constraints on market location implied by the existing transport system.

Table 13.6:   Nearest neighbour analysis of the spatial dispersion of same-day Liberian periodic markets, 1970[a]

Market day	N	R	One-tail probability	Distribution
Monday	17	.60	.0009	aggregated
Tuesday	5	.64	.0618	random
Wednesday	5	.98	.4721	random
Thursday	4	.90	.3409	random
Friday	6	.75	.1314	random
Saturday	16	.75	.0268	aggregated

Source: author's analysis.

[a] The statistic R (Clark & Evans, 1954) is a ratio between the mean observed distance between nearest-neighbouring points and the average distance between nearest points expected by chance in an area of specified dimensions. R varies between 0 and 2.1491, defining dispersions of perfect agglomeration (0.0), perfect randomness (1.0) and perfect uniformity (2.1491).

Perhaps more important is the fact that the initiation of these markets does not seem to have involved the careful decision-making processes one would expect in a competitive situation. The history of the Totota market circuit is a case in point. From the middle of the nineteenth century (and almost certainly from a much earlier time), the trade in central Liberia was carried on primarily by travelling and resident Mandingo traders whose main wares were cloth and other commodities available in the savanna markets; their prime objective was the acquisition of kola for seasonal shipment into the Sudan. At least since the early 1920s, some resident traders travelled circumferential routes within the region selling for cash. During this period, markets serving largely administrative functions were created in this region on orders from the District Commissioner. Although the Zeinzu (then a Clan Chief's town) and Sanoyea (a Paramount Chief's town) markets date from this time, the system of which they were a part in 1970 was a product of the last two decades, and particularly the last ten years. The Zeinzu market was one of many which broke down in the 1920s and 1930s when, as one man put it, 'Government business was tight'. The Sanoyea market declined because the road constructed inland in the early 1950s ran through Totota instead. The Kolela and Totota markets were the first created to send foodstuffs into Monrovia, both commencing in the mid 1950s. Kolela market was opened after the townspeople asked the Town Chief to provide a place where purchases and sales could be made. Not even the Town Chief could recall much serious discussion about the day on which the market should be held, and Saturday was eventually selected because this was the day 'people spend here before they leave for Monrovia.' The Zeinzu market was re-established about 1968 when enough sellers from the town decided to discontinue travelling to Kolela to sell, and Saturday was retained as the meeting day. Totota was opened by the resident Clan Chief as a place where the rural population could earn money with which to pay taxes and purchase their small wants. Wednesday appears to have been selected as the meeting day because the earlier Sanoyea market met on that day. The remaining markets in this region commenced during the 1960s after improvements in the road permitted travel to Monrovia within a single day. A feeder road reached Yanekwele about 1963 and its market was opened by the resident Clan Chief; there seems to be no particular reason for the choice of Thursday as a meeting day. The Sanoyea market was re-opened as a Friday market, in part because Totota had a Wednesday market, in part because the Yanekwele market was held on Thursday, and in part because Friday was the day 'government workers leave for the weekend'. The Filela market opened about 1967. Prior to this time farmers within the Clan whose village was Filela had to travel to either Salala or Totota if they wished to visit a market. Under pressure from his constituents, the Clan Chief opened the market to enable people to sell and buy more conveniently, especially in the 'hungry' season. Monday was chosen as the market day, in part because no other nearby market met that day, and in part because 'people need to buy after the weekend'.

Finally, within the regions where viable periodic markets can be maintained, the precise location of a market often is determined by variables other than space and time; the presence or absence of a Clan or Paramount Chief, and the organization and energy of local producer-sellers/farmer-consumers can be quite decisive. Further, the considerations for selecting a particular market day often are not solely tied to the competitive potential of adjacent markets. This

Table 13.7:   Nearest neighbour analysis of the spatial dispersion of same-day periodic markets in central Liberia, 1970[a]

Market day	N	R	One-tail probability	Distribution
Monday	5	1.56	.0078	uniform
Tuesday	2	0.76	.2578	random
Wednesday	3	1.92	.0011	uniform
Thursday	2	2.14	.0009	uniform
Friday	3	1.69	.0113	uniform
Saturday	4	1.78	.0012	uniform

Source: author's analysis.

[a] The area within which these markets are distributed was determined by encompassing all the markets and the trade areas of the most extreme markets within a circle. The area of the region so delimited was calculated to be 4,060 square kilometres (1,567 square miles).

Table 13.8: Spatial and temporal dispersion of Liberian periodic markets, 1970[d]

Category	Temporal separation	Mean distance apart (kilometres)	
		farmers	traders
1	Same day	50.7	50.7
2	Pre- or post-adjacent	20.2	
3	Post adjacent		34.9
4	Pre- or post-adjacent +1	25.4	
5	Post adjacent +1		38.2
6	Post adjacent +2		40.2
7	Post adjacent +3		37.7
8	Post adjacent +4		33.0

Source: author's analysis.

[a] The variance exhibited by these scores suggests the existence of more than a single underlying population. To avoid untenable assumptions about the distribution of the data, nonparametric tests were used to explore this possibility. The Kruskal-Wallis one way analysis of variance was used in preference to the F-test when the number of 'samples' (i.e., categories of temporal separation) numbered more than two; the Mann-Whitney U-test was used in preference to the t-test when there were only two samples. The data calculated from the perspective of traders and farmers were analysed separately. In the first instance, the probability that only one underlying distribution existed was between .20 and .30. In the second instance, the probability that only one underlying distribution existed was less than .001. The data pertaining to traders appears to exhibit chance variation; the data pertaining to farmers suggests at least two separate populations. To isolate population differences the categories of temporal separation were compared two at a time. The probability of finding the observed scores by chance is as follows: same-day by pre- or post-adjacent day markets, P less than .0002; same-day by pre- or post-adjacent + 1 day markets, P = .0102; pre- or post-adjacent by pre- or post-adjacent + 1 day markets, P greater than .05.

phenomenon is strikingly apparent in the predominance of Monday and Saturday market days. All major businesses in Liberia, including firms working in markets, are closed on Sundays. Markets in the major urban centres tend to be busiest on Saturdays and Mondays as people stock up for Sunday and replenish depleted stocks on Monday, respectively. The popularity of these days for periodic market meetings reflects common knowledge of the fluctuations of demand in urban centres accompanying the Liberian business weekend.

Despite the impression to the contrary that one might gain from these comments, markets *do* compete over buyers and sellers, and the viability of a market *is* contingent upon its spatial and temporal properties being synchronized with those of adjacent markets. The effect of competitive processes is apparent in Table 13.7; where the effect of road linearity is reduced by defining a region of high market density, same-day markets exhibit the expected tendency toward a uniform pattern of dispersion. The effect of competition for farmers is apparent from analysis of spatial and temporal sequencing (Tables 13.8 and 13.9). Circumferential travel routes have disappeared as traders have minimized travel costs by relocating their firms in towns central to markets created for and by farmers. Since there is no optimal synchronization of spatial and temporal sequencing for traders returning home each night, distances calculated from the perspective of travelling traders should exhibit chance variation. Distances calculated from the perspective of farmers should exhibit an inverse relation between temporal and spatial separation. In general agreement with other West African data, both expectations are confirmed.

The conspicuous feature of these Liberian situations is not that they indicate the lack of competition and the unimportance of synchronizing the spatial and

Table 13.9: Spatial and temporal dispersion of central Liberian periodic markets, 1970[a]

Category	Temporal separation	Mean distance apart farmers (kilometres)	traders
1	Same day	29.8	29.8
2	Pre- or post-adjacent	17.4	
3	Post adjacent		24.5
4	Pre- or post-adjacent +1	18.5	
5	Post adjacent +1		26.1
6	Post adjacent +2		21.6
7	Post adjacent +3		25.1
8	Post adjacent +4		25.5

Source: author's analysis.

[a] The variance of these scores was analysed in the ways reported in Table 13.8. The following probability values were obtained: trader sample, $P = .30 - .50$; farmer sample, $P = .02 - .01$; same-day by pre- or post-adjacent markets, $P = .002 - .02$; same-day by pre- or post-adjacent + 1 day markets, $P = .002 - .02$; pre- or post-adjacent by pre- or post-adjacent + 1 day markets, P greater than .10.

temporal features of a set of markets, but that these phenomena are conceptualized as being important only in restricted contexts and in limited ways. The nature of competitive processes is linked to the context in which competition occurs. And a singular context for the operation of competitive processes is established in Liberia by constraints on access to markets implied by travel costs, constraints on sales and purchasing implied by the interdependency of sales and purchasing strategies, and the availability of alternative purchasing sites. In Liberia, competition is felt or anticipated only when markets whose trade areas overlap may meet on the same day.

The mean distance between a market and its nearest neighbouring same-day market is about 50 km (31 miles) for the country as a whole, and about 31 km (19 miles) for the central Liberian markets. With the existing transport constraints on farmers, the trading areas of such markets are wholly non-competitive. There are some instances in which same-day markets are adjacent; thus the Kolela and Zeinzu Saturday markets are separated by only six km (four miles). However, in all such instances trading areas are non-competitive. In the case at hand, Kolela drew people to market from regions to its northwest and south, whereas Zeinzu had access to an extensive region to the northeast with no competing market for about 48 km (30 miles). The existence of these situations appears to be contingent upon the development of the market system. Where market density increases and trading areas begin to overlap, an adjustment of market day or the disappearance of a market is likely; however, the absence of markets over extensive regions permits the continued operation of a number of adjacent same-day markets.[9]

The issues recognized by market initiators elsewhere in West Africa are not very relevant to market initiators in Liberia. Constraints on the movement of farmers severely limit the number of accessible markets, and the effect of their decisions to visit one rather than another market is lessened. Competition among markets is lessened further by low population density, interdependent sales and purchasing strategies dictating infrequent market visits, and the existence of alternative purchasing (non-market) sites. The careful decision-making processes made necessary where population density and productivity is high, where much produce is grown for sale, where selling and buying occurs frequently and is not interdependent, where markets are closely packed and where there exist few or no alternative purchasing sites are unnecessary in Liberia. Competitive pressures among Liberian periodic markets may be alleviated merely by selecting a market day differing from those chosen by neighbouring markets. Except for a preference for Monday and Saturday market meetings to coincide with urban purchasing patterns, the particular day selected has no bearing on market viability and is immaterial to market initiators so long as nearest neighbours differ in the days on which they meet. A rationale for the day eventually selected nearly always can be formulated if someone (such as a visiting anthropologist) asks!

Spatial competition alone will push markets meeting on the same day apart, and proximity in time will imply separation in space. However, a strong correlation between spatial and temporal separation should not be expected. On the contrary, so long as markets meet on distinct days, it may be predicted that the distances separating them would be explicable by chance. This situation in Liberia (Tables 13.8 and 13.9) contrasts sharply with other parts of West Africa.

Conclusion

This essay sought to determine if and in what ways competition over buyers and sellers explained the locational and temporal properties of Liberian periodic markets. The very existence of a periodic market was taken to imply that sufficient numbers of farmers (farmer-consumers/producer-sellers) were attracted to the site. The results of analysis of the locational and temporal properties of these markets are consistent with the view that periodic markets in Liberia compete for this group of buyers and sellers (but not for travelling traders), and that this competition largely accounts for their locational and temporal properties. The dispersion of markets in space and their synchronization of locational and temporal spacing are predictable from hypotheses developed from central place theory in terms of other West African data.

Over the last decade there has been a decided shift in the formal interpretation of West African periodic marketing systems. Although the explanatory power of central place theory at one time was denied, recent studies explicitly place their analyses in the context of the theory. This shift is traceable to Stine's (1962) demonstration that periodic marketing systems represent a special case of central place theory, and Smith's (1971) analyses of West African periodic market systems.

However, it is premature to take the explanatory power of the theory for granted, and a thorough re-evaluation of the theory is in order. The variability of West African and other periodic marketing systems is only beginning to be delineated. Assessment of periodicity and of periodic marketing systems has not been facilitated appreciably by attention to the derived geometries of the theory (Webber and Symanski, 1973, 215). On the contrary, current problems of analysis demand attention to the underlying premises and problems of meshing logical structures with particular sets of data (Webber and Symanski, 1973; R.H.T. Smith, 1974).

From this perspective, the data on Liberian periodic markets are instructive. Just as Stine's (1962) original formulation contained implicit assumptions about the structure of trade modelled after unique features of the Korean situation (Bromley, 1971), the present formulation concerning spatial and temporal sequencing contains implicit assumptions about the nature of competitive processes modelled after features appearing only in limited areas of West Africa. The Liberian data illustrate the interdependence of competitive processes and the context in which competition takes place. Contrasting with other areas of West Africa, competition in Liberia is conceptualized hazily if at all, and only where trade areas of adjoined markets may overlap; it is alleviated merely by selecting different market days.

The statement that the spatial and temporal properties of periodic marketing systems may be explained largely by competitive-selective processes might be accepted as a working proposition, but it is necessary to identify how such processes operate in particular contexts. Empirical and theoretical analyses will be illuminating to the extent that they clarify the intertwining of the activities of market initiators and different kinds of buyers and sellers, and disentangle the web of variables constituting the context in which market participants decide to establish a market at a given site, meeting on specific days, and to visit one market or another, on what days, and how frequently (population density, the transport network, modes of transport, density of markets, the existence and service functions of alternative purchasing activities, the frequency with which people buy and sell different commodities, and the possible interdependency of sales and purchasing strategies). It could well be that market initiators give little thought to the long run viability of a market, and that its persistence or dissolution ultimately is contingent upon the attendance decisions of various kinds of buyers and sellers. But can market initiators determine the group on whose patronage a market's existence depends? and if it is not market initiators, then who? under what circumstances? On the other hand, what are the conditions making particular dispersions of markets viable, and others not? What are the conditions making a particular synchronization of spatial and temporal properties viable, and others not? How strictly do buyers and sellers seek out optimal travel routes and minimum marketing costs, and does this vary in predictable ways? Answers to these questions will not only add substantially to the conceptual understanding of periodic markets, but they will also place the planner-policy maker in a much better position to make informed decisions about modifications to the spatial system.

[1] The data presented in this essay were gathered during a study of Liberia's food marketing system which focussed particularly on the flow of foodstuffs to the capital, Monrovia. The data derive from participant-observation, informal and intensive interviews, and surveys of various kinds of farms, intermediaries and consumers in the three principal settlement locations in Liberia: urban (Monrovia), concession (the Firestone Plantations Company site at Harbel), and rural (seven village locations and associated markets distributed over the coastal, central and interior regions). The data for the case-study of the Totota markets consists of interviews in Monrovia (in the markets and at their homes) with bulking intermediaries, travelling intermediaries and producer-sellers/farmer-consumers. The author gathered data by observation, participation, conversation and detailed, lengthy interviews with selected informants. Where survey data on business operation and market trade areas were sought, an attempt was made to interview everyone. The surveys of travelling intermediaries tended to be exhaustive, and two-thirds or more of the bulkers and producer-sellers were interviewed. The general methodology and scope of the research undertaken in Liberia is reported in Handwerker (1971). Further data on the Liberian market system are available in Handwerker (1971, 1973a); the analysis in Handwerker (1971) consists of a preliminary overview of the market system, and all of the topics discussed there eventually will be dealt with in greater detail. This essay supersedes the partial analysis of Liberian periodic markets presented in Handwerker (1971, 245-59).

[2] Central place theory is a theory of choice in which preferences are defined, and alternative modes of action chosen, on the basis of least 'cost' as measured in units of time, money and/or 'effort' (see Stine, 1962, and Webber and Symanski, 1973).

[3] The single and notable exception is Sierra Leone. The cultural similarities among the peoples of contemporary Liberia and Sierra Leone have long been recognized, and the two countries themselves exhibit many parallels, consistently in contrast to the rest of West Africa. As in other areas of life, the organization and operation of Sierra Leone's contemporary market system appears quite similar to Liberia's market system, and the market history of the two countries appears to have been interrelated. The early system of markets existing in northeastern Liberia appears to have been part of a more extensive series of markets, one part of which existed in the southeastern region of Sierra Leone, around Koindu. These markets, in turn, appear to have been the only markets in Sierra Leone until recently (Riddell, 1974).

[4] With the exception of the roads from Monrovia into northwestern Liberia, the road from Zwedru to Greenville, and the road past Gaye Peter Town connecting Buchanan with the Ganta-Tapita highway, the author travelled all the main roads and many of the feeder roads in Liberia, and located all but fifteen of the markets in Figure 13.1. The principal exceptions are the markets in northwestern Liberia and the Sunday periodic market at B'hai on the Liberia-Ivory Coast border in western Grand Gedeh County. Information on the former

area was collected from people bringing produce from the region into Monrovia; details of the latter market were gathered together with data on the production and sales of farm produce in a village located in western Grand Gedeh County. Further, these data were cross-checked with those of anthropologists working in the interior regions of Liberia. A standardized interview guide was used to gather data on the organizational features of the fifty-three functioning periodic markets which were located. Detailed data were collected on fourteen periodic markets, and notes varying considerably in scope (concerned principally with noting the major variations) were collected on about twice this number.

[5] The Government of Liberia restricts trading to Monday through Saturday inclusive. Only two markets in 1970 operated on Sunday, one a daily market in Monrovia catering principally to traders retailing food from their households during Sunday afternoon and evening, the other a periodic market situated off the road on the border of Liberia and the Ivory Coast in western Grand Gedeh County.

[6] A number of markets serve both periodic and daily functions; in the larger towns (e.g. Gbarnga, Saniquellie), much of the produce offered for sale on the periodic market day appears to be sold to local consumers rather than bulking intermediaries.

[7] This is what appears to have happened in the transition from periodic to daily markets in the larger upcountry towns. In six of these markets, the transition appears to have been smooth; the most explicit statements from respondents indicated only that 'people began to sell daily', no doubt as a result of the increasing number of non-food producers moving to these towns.

[8] The periodic market at Nyaaka thrived when the road from Harper terminated there, but after the road linking Harper with Zwedru was completed in the late 1960s leaving Nyaaka on a short feeder road, the market deteriorated drastically. Producer-sellers bypassed the market to carry their produce directly to Plibo, the Firestone Cavalla plantation, and to Harper. Producer-sellers from all areas of the country occasionally bring produce directly to Monrovia, but this represents a very small proportion of Monrovia's total food supply, and such trips tend to be mainly for social visitation, not trade. Where this produce is not intended for kinsmen, its sale simply reduces the costs of transport.

[9] Indeed, one could predict that adjacent rather than separated same-day markets would exist in these circumstances (Berry, 1967, 86-8). Same-day markets are pushed apart as they attempt to dominate a hinterland exclusively, but such domination is achieved by spatial separation only when more than two markets are competing. Where only two markets compete, a maximum service area is achieved by spatial propinquity.

14 Rural markets in Kenya
L.J. Wood

A wide range of anthropological, economic, geographical, historical and
sociological aspects of markets and marketing have been examined in a number
of developing areas during the last twenty years. Two issues recur in this
literature: firstly, there is the question of the relevance of contemporary geographical theory to the understanding of period market systems; and secondly,
there is the issue of the persistence of periodic market systems. Most attempts
to place periodic market systems within a theoretical context rest on the work
of Stine (1962) in which periodic markets are seen as developing area counterparts of low order central places. Several scholars (Hodder, 1961, 158; Hill,
1966, 298) have contended that central place theory is irrelevant to a study of
periodic market systems; however, there seems to be general agreement that,
with some modifications to accommodate the conditions prevailing in
developing areas, the rationale of central place theory provides a framework
within which the structure and functioning of a rural periodic market system
can be understood (Skinner, 1964 and 1965; Eighmy, 1972). A key feature of
Stine's argument is that it is the itinerancy of traders (an adaptation made
necessary by the limited purchasing power and the low travel capability of
residents in most rural areas of developing countries) that is responsible for the
existence and periodic nature of market meetings and the integration of a
periodic market system. There is little doubt that in some parts of the world
there are professional itinerant traders who follow regular circuits of market
visits, but it is possible that in some areas the role of the itinerant trader has
been overemphasized.[1] Concerning the future of rural periodic markets, it is
often asserted that periodic markets are temporary features and that with
increasing population density, a steady rise in rural incomes, broadened norms
of consumption, and improved transport, markets lose their periodic character
and become daily. This implies that eventually, the focus of rural trade will
shift from the daily rural market to the permanent retail shop; the market-place
will expire (Skinner, 1965, 211-21; Hodder and Ukwu, 1969, xii; Fagerlund
and Smith, 1970, 336; Eighmy, 1972, 313). The aim of this essay is to describe
various aspects of the rural market-place system[2] of Kenya and to comment on
the applicability of these propositions to the Kenyan system. The essay
commences with a discussion of market development and administration which
is followed by a consideration of market distribution and meeting frequency,
market personnel and functions, and regularities in the market system.

Market Development, Organization and Control

Markets of various types existed in Kenya in precolonial times (Wood, 1974a). Daily urban markets existed in the coastal towns of Mombasa, Malindi and Lamu and rural 'markets operated in several inland areas. An extensive, well-attended network of intratribal, four-day markets existed in the Kikuyu areas (Dundas, 1909; Routledge and Routledge, 1910, 105-106; Cagnolo, 1933, 41-44). In the most densely settled areas these markets were often about eleven km (seven miles) apart and were arranged so that no two markets in the same neighbourhood were held on the same day. Women were the major market users although trade in some items was confined to men. The markets displayed considerable order in their internal layout with all sellers of the same goods grouped together, as is characteristic of most markets in Kenya today. Intratribal markets operating on a daily basis existed in the lakeshore Luo areas (Anon., 1882, 744; Pringle, 1893, 123) but little is known about their organization. In both the Kikuyu and Luo areas, the major function of the markets seems to have been to facilitate local exchange: in the former, exchange was largely between the different altitudinal and crop-producing zones, while in the Luo areas the predominantly fishing communities of the lakeshore traded with the inland, largely agricultural peoples. Some scholars have argued that markets in sub-Saharan Africa developed only with the stimulus of external trading contacts (Hodder, 1965), but in both the Kikuyu and Luo areas the distinctly local origins of the trade items and the almost total absence of contact with long distance trade routes suggest that the markets could well have developed as a result of local initiative. In both areas the marked local variations in the availability of products may have been the major factor stimulating market development. There is some evidence of regular intertribal markets on the borders of Luo and Luyia territory and by the turn of the century it is thought that embryonic regular markets were operating within Luyia areas (Wagner, 1956, 161-5). Linguistic evidence suggests that this may represent a diffusion of the market idea outwards from a Luo core (Wood, 1973a, 15). In the Digo areas of the coast there existed intratribal markets (Prins, 1952, 57) which probably operated every fourth day. Less regular and less well organized markets, also with a local function, operated infrequently within and between many other tribal groups, often under the stimulus of famine conditions (Wood, 1973a, 25-6). Alien-stimulated markets, mostly originating in the latter part of the nineteenth century, occurred at several points (e.g. at Taveta, Ngong, Mumias), on the main caravan route from the coast to inland areas. Initially, these markets operated only when a caravan was present, supplying them with basic food items in exchange for non-local items such as cloth and beads; some eventually became of local importance and began to operate regularly.[3]

The contemporary market system in Kenya evolved largely in the twentieth century, and an awareness of the conditions under which the system developed is necessary for an understanding of both the spatial and temporal attributes of the system and its functioning. In the first few decades of the twentieth century, British colonial government policy was directed primarily towards the establishment and stabilization of a white settler population; concern for the development of African areas was subordinate and remained so until about 1950. Zones for European settlement were carved out and reserves were demarcated for the major settled African populations. A series of punitive expeditions was launched against dissident groups, and an administrative system of districts and locations (many of which were essentially tribal units and distinct tribal subgroups, respectively), was created for the maintenance of peaceful conditions and for effective government. Hut taxes (later poll taxes) were instituted to provide revenue for administration. Administrative control was followed in some areas and preceded in others by incursions of Asian and coastal traders who often established *dukas* (small shops). In 1892, the most inland *duka* was only a few miles from Mombasa (Jackson, 1930, 328). At many stations on the railway inland from Mombasa (which was started in 1896), small bazaars of Asian *dukas* were established, and the district administration centres where there were small concentrations of non-agricultural people who needed supplies of basic foodstuffs also attracted traders. The need to pay taxes forced the African population either to sell surplus produce or to engage in paid employment. The contact of the African population with western culture also inculcated among the local population a demand for a new range of products. The new peaceful conditions and the evolving crude road network combined with these factors led to an increase in trade. Initially, most trade was carried out in the district administrative centres where township markets were usually promulgated soon after the post had been established. Rules for the control of township markets, laid down in 1903, prohibited hawking in towns possessing a market, specified opening times, stipulated layout of the market-place, and established procedures for the collection of fees from market sellers (East Africa Protectorate, 1903).

It is unclear what was happening to trade in the rural areas during this period, although it is thought that most of the precolonial markets continued to function and in some districts (e.g. Siaya; see Fig. 14.1), markets were developing independent of colonial influence. In 1924 Local Native Councils were established in most districts to 'make and pass resolutions for the welfare and good government of the native inhabitants in respect of any matters affecting purely local native administration' (Colony and Protectorate of Kenya, 1924). One of their responsibilities was the provision, maintenance and regulation of markets. In Kitui District, three markets were established in 1925 and by 1927 there were twelve markets in the District (Stanner, 1969, 128). In many districts however, it was not until a further ordinance (Colony and Protectorate of Kenya, 1935) prohibited the sale or purchase of any kind of native produce except in a market-place that markets began to proliferate, with one or more markets being established in most locations. Today, most markets are found in conjunction with such facilities as shops, a hide drying shed, and a police post; it is likely that shops and markets developed simultaneously.

The Local Native Councils became African District Councils and later, County Councils; the latter are responsible for market inauguration and control today and legally, trading in rural areas may only be conducted at official market-places or in designated trading centres. Markets are still being established in many parts of the country. The County Councils usually authorize new markets only after requests have reached them from the local population via the local government hierarchy. If the people of an area feel that they have too few market-places or market days, representation is made through the local subchief to the chief and the locational council for an increase in market provision. The request is then passed to the relevant committee of the County Council, which generally operates at the district level. This body normally refuses requests for new market-places in close proximity to existing markets; indeed, some districts

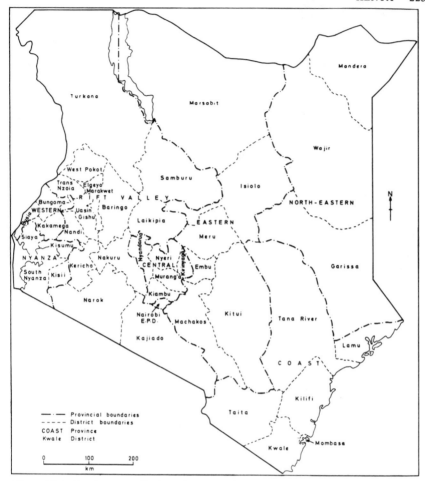

Figure 14.1   Provinces and districts of Kenya, 1970

have by-laws prohibiting the establishment of new markets within five km (three miles) of existing markets, and committees only approve new market days that do not create conflict with existing market days. In a few instances, County Councils have unilaterally decided where markets should be sited and when they should operate. It is not unusual for markets imposed by the County Councils to fail completely, indicating presumably that the markets have been established where there is little demand for market facilities or that inappropriate operating days have been chosen.

The basic physical layout, setting, and organization of rural markets is similar in most parts of Kenya. The market arena usually consists of a small, fenced, rectangular plot of land which is normally lined on three sides by small shops and ancillary service establishments (bars, etc.). A trading centre comprises both the market-place and shops, although not all trading centres have an operative market. Shopowners and some government employees are normally the only residents at a trading centre. The market arena is entered through one or more

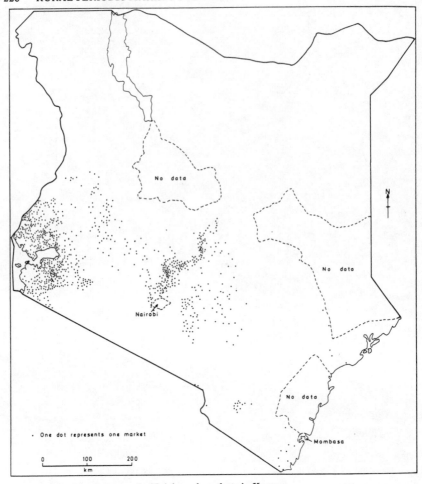

Figure 14.2   Distribution of official rural markets in Kenya

gates where a market clerk collects fees from sellers wishing to use the market. In theory, the money collected in market fees is intended for the payment of market personnel (clerks and sweepers) and for the improvement of market facilities (provision of latrines, water, covered stalls, etc.). However, few markets have any permanent structures other than the market clerk's shed and most sellers display their wares on the bare ground.

Market Distribution and Meeting Frequency

In late 1970, there were 984[4] official rural markets in Kenya of which 930 (94.5 per cent) were located by the author. Most of the markets, when viewed at the national level, are concentrated within an hour-glass-shaped area (Fig. 14.2). The markets of the Lake Victoria area form one bulb and those of the highlands of central Kenya form the other. The only other areas where substantial numbers of markets occur are in the Taita Hills of the south-east and in the coastal zone. A few isolated markets occur along the Tana River and on the Tanzania border west of the Taita Hills. All of the indigenous agricultural areas have markets, but regular markets are absent in the areas where nomadic pastoral activities dominate. This is not unusual since the nature of nomadic life itself is hardly conducive to the regular congregation of people at fixed sites, nor is nomadism convenient for the acquisition of possessions.

Of the 984 rural markets, 85 meet daily, while the remainder have periodic meetings. All the periodic markets operate within the European seven-day week, although some of the daily markets in the Digo area of Kwale District have a major market every fourth day, possibly a vestige of a precolonial market calendar. The periodic markets do not all meet with similar frequency: 477 (53.1 per cent) meet weekly, 367 (40.8 per cent) meet twice weekly, 53 (5.9 per cent) meet three times per week, and two (0.2 per cent) meet on either four or five days per week. In Kwale District, all markets are officially daily. In Nandi District all markets are weekly but in other districts there is a juxtaposition of markets meeting with different frequencies. The dominant frequency type varies from district to district (Fig. 14.3). Explanation of the areal variations in the patterns of frequency types is difficult; in some areas, traditional meeting frequencies might have been influential. For example, in those parts of the immediate shorelands of Lake Victoria where daily markets are particularly common, there were daily fish markets in precolonial times; in Kikuyu areas there was a four-day market week in precolonial times and the closest parallel to this within a seven-day week is the twice-weekly market, the dominant frequency type in the Kikuyu areas of Central Province. The factors that influenced the choice of traditional market calendars remain obscure. The perishability of food may certainly have been important but there is also evidence that cultural factors may have influenced the choice of meeting days (Wood, 1973a, 96). In most of the lightly settled areas, weekly markets are particularly numerous, but at the national level there is no relationship between meeting frequency and population density.

Market Personnel and Functions

There are three components of the rural commerce system in most areas of Kenya: one is involved in the transfer of crops such as tea, coffee, pyrethrum and maize to urban areas for processing and possible export (numerous independent co-operatives and centralized marketing boards are involved). A second consists of permanent retail establishments concerned with supplying the rural population with urban-produced goods. Finally, there is the system of rural daily and periodic markets, the importance and functions of which can be best appreciated by considering the composition of a market population.

As in precolonial times, markets are most extensively and frequently used by females. Relatively few males are involved in exchange in markets in Kenya, although tobacco, snuff, ropes, livestock, clothes, empty bottles and a few other items are often handled by men. The dominance of women in market-place exchange is a feature that has been noted for many parts of sub-Saharan Africa (Herskovits, 1962, xi). This role may well reflect a continuation of the practice, developed to meet earlier prevailing conditions of insecurity, of allowing women to trade whilst warriors remained some distance from the market-place (Pedler, 1955, 139). Though this practice has been noted for some societies in precolonial East Africa (Fearn, 1957, 42), the predominance of women today probably reflects an extension of the woman's traditional concern

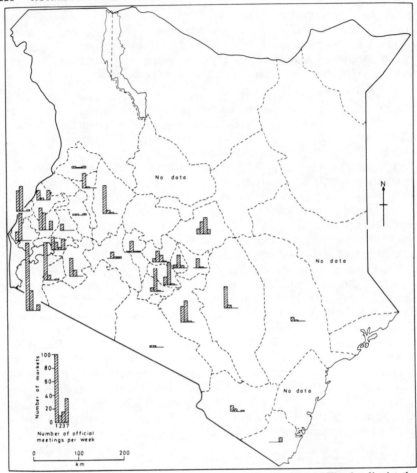

Figure 14.3 Distribution of market frequency types (one market in Kiambu district that meets four times a week and one market in Kalamega district that meets five times a week not shown)

and responsibility for the supply of basic foodstuffs. The high degree of involvement of the adult female population in market activity is reflected in the fact that 356 home interviews of adult females in various parts of the country identified only four women who did not regularly visit at least one market (many regularly visited more than one). In the majority of cases, market visits were used to both sell and buy goods. The number of prospective sellers in a market-place provides a reasonable tally of the total number of people visiting the market for exchange purposes. The dual purpose of most market visits reflects the general scarcity of money in rural areas (many must effect a sale before they can make a purchase) and illustrates the limited value of a strict dichotomy between sellers and buyers (or traders and consumers) in the context of rural Kenya. However, analyses of the market transactions conducted by both home-contacted respondents and people in numerous markets suggest that division into *marketers* and *traders* (Bohannan and Dalton, 1962, 13; Hodder and Ukwu, 1969, 173) is relevant in Kenya.

Most Kenyans who use markets are marketers; they sell goods of home production (crops, cooked food, and craft items) and buy goods for domestic consumption. The motive behind the sale of goods is thought to be an immediate demand either for cash itself (to pay school fees, taxes, etc.), or for some item or service available in the market or nearby shops. The items offered for sale to satisfy this demand may not necessarily be surplus items. The majority of marketers travel only a few kilometres to market, on foot, one or more times per week and many regularly visit more than one market-place.

A relatively small proportion of the local market-using population consists of traders (i.e. individuals who buy goods for resale). Most traders confine their activities to rural markets (i.e. both purchase and sale take place in rural markets) and work on a part-time basis, engaging in market-associated activities on only a few days each week. The majority of these rural, part-time traders (like most rural residents) are primarily farmers, who live in dispersed settlements and travel home after each market visit. Most of their trade involves little capital investment, and they deal in small quantities of local agricultural produce. Some deal in food products (maize, millet, milk, eggs), some in craft items (pots, mats), and some in both. They buy goods in one market for resale in another whilst simultaneously selling goods bought elsewhere; occasionally, traders process bought goods (for example, they grind maize) to increase the resale value. This rural trade is made possible, and to some extent necessary, by variations in physical conditions, local cultural factors and dietary preferences. In some areas, there are distinct zones producing a range of crops, but more subtle variations also provide the opportunity for trade. For example, micro-climatic variations may mean that maize ripens in one area a month earlier than in another area only a few kilometres away, thus stimulating trade in maize within a maize-producing area. In some parts of the country, an emphasis on cash crop production has led to a decline in the amount of land devoted to subsistence crops. This has created a comparatively large market in these areas for basic food items and again has stimulated local trade.

The two roles of marketer and part-time rural trader are complementary. The marketers form part of the clientele of the rural traders and provide a considerable portion of the basic trade goods of the traders: the rural traders form part of the clientele of the marketers and provide the marketer with items that may not be available in the immediate vicinity. However, it is likely that many exchanges in markets are between marketer and marketer.

Only a small proportion of local rural residents are traders whose trading activities extend beyond, or originate outside rural markets (i.e. traders for whom either purchase or sale is away from a rural market-place). Some of these traders have the characteristics of the rural traders in that they deal in small quantities of low value goods and work on a part-time, irregular basis. In this category are *accumulator traders*, who visit a series of local markets buying small quantities of such items as eggs and vegetables for later sale in an urban area. There are also individuals who buy an item in quantity from a rural or urban shop (e.g. a sack of salt or threads for basket making) and resell it in small lots, over a long time period, in one or more rural markets. There are only a few of these types of market trader who, like the rural traders, are both farmers and traders. In comparison with marketers, part-time traders average more market visits per week, visit a greater number of market-places, travel further to market and rely to a greater extent on motor transport.

Other market traders whose activities are not confined to the rural markets are more professional in that their activities often involve considerable capital investment and a higher and more regular involvement in trading. Usually, these traders are not resident in the local area. A few strategically placed markets on the main national road network are frequented by wholesalers who buy large quantities of agricultural produce for bulk transport and sale to urban shops and urban market sellers. These wholesalers may operate outside the market or they may use a separate wholesaling section within the market-place. However, these wholesaling activities are only typical of a small proportion of rural markets and there is generally only a small flow of goods out of the rural market system. Professional traders play a more important role in the flow of goods into the rural market system. In a few places local shopkeepers transfer some of their goods (sugar, soap, matches) to the market-places on market days but this is rare. The most widespread professional traders are the clothing sellers. Clothing sellers, most of whom are men, are probably the only full-time traders found in most rural markets although by no means all clothing sellers are full-time. Some depend on local shops for their supplies, but many bring relatively large stocks of clothing long distances from major urban centres. Some clothing sellers use only one market outlet to sell their wares but others, often operating well outside their home area, regularly visit several markets and are thus itinerant retailers. Such evidence as is available suggests that most clothing sellers return to the same local base after each market visit.

The majority of a market population comprises marketers and the next most important group are those part-time traders who confine their activities to rural markets. There are also a few part-time traders and a few professional traders who are concerned with the urban-rural and rural-urban flow of goods. Both the marketers and the part-time traders are mainly women for whom market activities are only one of many commitments. The professional traders are often men. At any one time, there is a clear distinction between a marketer and a part-time trader but there is not always a clear distinction between a professional trader and a part-time trader involved in the movement of goods between rural and urban areas. There are marked seasonal variations in rural market attendance and it is likely that the proportions of marketers, part-time traders and professional traders in a market vary. Many marketers may become part-time traders at times of the year when there is an acute demand for cash, and it is also likely that clothing sellers may be particularly active in periods following an influx of money into the rural areas (for example, after the seasonal coffee crop payments).

While rural markets in southwestern Nigeria perform three economic functions simultaneously (local exchange, internal trade, and central place functions (Eighmy, 1972, 299-300)), the prime economic function of rural markets in the majority of rural areas in Kenya today is local exchange. The rural market in Kenya facilitates horizontal exchange, defined here as the redistribution of rural products through the rural areas. A similar function was noted for the precolonial markets of Luo and Kikuyu areas. The market plays only a small role in internal trade, this aspect of commerce having been largely pre-empted by the various co-operatives and central marketing boards; it has limited central place functions as such (these functions are largely performed by the permanent establishments found beside markets), although the facilities of the market can be considered an important type of central place service. With the dominance of the local exchange function of markets in Kenya, it is not surprising that the brokers, middlemen, agents, etc., characteristic of many markets in West Africa, are not present in Kenyan rural markets. Similarly, the ritual and political significance that is often attached to markets in West Africa (Hodder and Ukwu, 1969, 126) is also usually absent, although markets in Kenya are undoubtedly of social importance.

Regularities in the Market System

From the point of view of the rural population, the main economic function of a market is to remedy basic food and craft product shortages and/or to facilitate the acquisition of small amounts of cash. A large proportion of rural households want to use market facilities regularly and many market users patronize more than one market-place either for marketing or for trading. If the market requirements of the rural population are efficiently satisfied by existing market facilities (one of the functions of local government authorities is to meet rural demands for market provision), then certain relationships and regularities should characterise the contemporary market system. Specifically, at a variety of scales of analysis, one would expect to find more market-places and market meetings in areas with a high population density than in areas with a low population density, and a spatio-temporal provision of markets which ensures that no individual in a dispersed rural population is inordinately disadvantaged with regard to either spatial or temporal access to market facilities.

Markets and Population

A population distribution map with each dot representing 10,000 people closely resembles the map of the distribution of markets. Detailed national analysis, at both a regional and a local scale, indicated a very strong relationship between population density and rural market provision, whether the latter was measured by the density of market-places or the density of market days (Wood, 1974c). Measured on either a district or a location scale, mean market area (district and location areas divided by the number of market-places) and mean area per market day (district and location areas divided by the number of market days) decrease rapidly (i.e. market provision increases rapidly) up to a population density of about seventy persons per square kilometre (180 per square mile) (Fig. 14.4). Above this level, increases in population density are matched by only slight decreases in the mean area per market or market day (i.e. slight increases in market provision). With the varying meeting frequencies found from district to district, the number of market-places might be considered a biased measure of market provision but, because of the juxtaposition of meeting frequencies, there is an average of two market meetings per market-place per week in most districts. A study of anomalous districts suggested that, except in areas of sparse settlement, the total number of market days in an area is more crucial in relation to population density than the number of market-places.

Although population density is the major factor governing the degree of market provision in most parts of Kenya, there are several areas where factors other than population density appear to have considerable influence. In Uasin Gishu, Nandi and Nakuru Districts there appear to be too few markets for the respective population densities. These districts, and parts of some other districts (for example, Nyandarua, Kericho and Bungoma), were in the past mainly European extensive farming areas where the African population which was housed in labour lines was supplied with some basic foodstuffs and paid a cash wage. The conditions were not conducive to the development of rural markets. Parts of the former 'White Highlands' have now become major resettlement areas (e.g. Nyandarua and parts of Bungoma), intensive African cultivation has replaced extensive land use, and rural markets have developed. However, in Uasin Gishu, Nakuru, and in parts of Nandi — despite Kenyanization — many of the large farms remain and the European-derived characteristics of the areas are perpetuated.

In some of the most developed and predominantly African rural areas, particularly in parts of Murang'a and Machakos Districts, there appear to be too few market facilities. There are indications that the number of markets in these areas has declined in recent years suggesting that the level of modernization may affect the population density-market provision relationship. Thus, it seems that the closure of some market-places occurred with the concentration of trade at a few well located markets, and there has not been an absolute decline in the amount of market trade. Such polarization of trade may be encouraged by certain facets of modernization, particularly increased accessibility.

In several of the locations close to Kisumu Town (population 32,431), there appear to be more market facilities than the local population densities warrant. This may reflect an extra demand for market facilities resulting from the proximity of a large urban population, although this anomaly does not occur elsewhere. In Busia District an apparent overprovision of market facilities is reflected in many very small markets and several that do not function regularly, suggesting that Busia County Council has acceded too readily to requests for more markets. In Kisii District there appear to be too few market days for the population density. In this district market-places are often used unofficially,

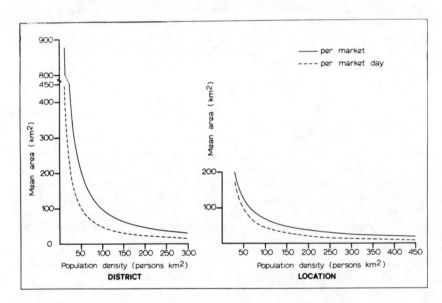

Figure 14.4 Market provision and population density (district figure based on data for 23 of the 27 districts with markets; excluded districts (Taita, West Pokot, Kajiado and Tana River) contain large unsettled areas. Location figure based on data for 87 locations)

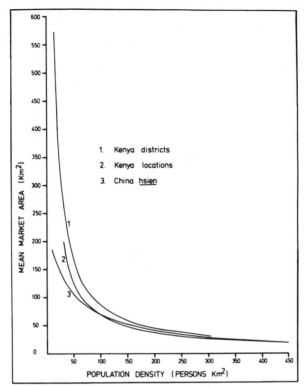

Figure 14.5   Relationship between mean area per market and population density in China (Skinner, 1964, 34) and the areas of intensive agriculture in Kenya (Wood, 1974c)

suggesting that again the weak relationship between population density and market provision may stem from inappropriate County Council control. In Kwale District there are more market days than might be expected from the population density; markets are officially scheduled as daily but at several markets major meetings only occur every fourth day.

Despite these few irregularities, it is readily apparent that there is greater market provision in areas with a high population density than in areas with a low population density. It is interesting to compare the relationship between mean market area and population density in the areas of subsistence and semi-subsistence agriculture in Kenya with that noted for pre-1947 mainland China (Fig. 14.5). There is a striking similarity in the relationships, suggesting that there are basic processes underlying the balance between market provision and population density in culturally contrasted areas of the world with very different histories of market development.

Markets in Space and Time

In an area with a relatively even distribution of population an equitable spatial allocation of market-places would be one that approached a uniform pattern. A nearest neighbour analysis of the distribution patterns of rural markets in Kenya has shown that only eight of the twenty-seven districts with markets have a pattern significantly different from random (Wood, 1972). This included seven districts with a significantly uniform pattern of markets and one district with a significantly clustered pattern. The major reason for the inconclusive results (Wood, 1975a) of this analysis appeared to be the highly uneven distribution of population in many districts. When some allowance was made for uneven population distribution it became apparent that there is a tendency for more uniform market patterns to occur in districts with a relatively even population distribution. In spatial terms therefore, markets in many districts are distributed in at least partial accord with the spatial distribution of population. The major exceptions appear to be Kwale and Uasin Gishu Districts.

Investigation of temporal order in the market system requires consideration of both the number of market meetings in an area on each day of the week and the arrangement of market meetings through the week at individual market sites (Hill and Smith, 1972, 346-9). At the national level, there is little variation in the number of market meetings from day to day (Wood, 1973b). There is some avoidance of Sundays (presumably for religious reasons), but a chi-square test indicated that there is an equal likelihood of a market operating on any one day from Monday to Saturday, inclusive, as on any other day. Chi-square tests at the district level indicated that only three districts (Nakuru, Nyandarua and Kisii) have a significantly inequitable temporal supply of markets (i.e. an excessive concentration of meetings on particular days). Nakuru and Nyandarua, where most markets meet on Wednesdays and Sundays, both formed part of the 'White Highlands', and it is likely that the importance of Sunday as a market day reflects the fact that this was the only free day for workers on the European farms. At most markets in Nakuru, Wednesday market meetings were added to existing market schedules after Independence (1963). In Kisii, there is a concentration of market meetings on Thursdays and Sundays.

A variety of market schedules is possible at market-places where meetings are held two, three, four and five times in the seven-day week. Since a market meeting presumably pre-empts trade from the previous day and temporarily exhausts the potential for trade on the following day, then the most efficient meeting schedules should logically be those that avoid a concentration of market meetings at any one time of the week, i.e. those that maximize the lengths of the marketless periods. For example, at a twice weekly market it may be claimed that a meeting schedule that leaves intervals of two and three marketless days is more efficient than any other schedule. Using this criterion, 87 per cent of the 422 markets which meet on two, three, four or five days per week have the most efficient schedules, suggesting that there appears to be a considerable amount of temporal order in the market system.

Various researchers have attempted to examine simultaneously the spatial and temporal dimensions of market systems in parts of West Africa (Fagerlund and Smith, 1970, 342-7; Smith, 1970, 32-7; Smith, 1971, 325-41; Hill and Smith, 1972, 349-54). It is suggested that the relationship between the locational and temporal spacing of markets should be inverse: markets which are physically proximate should be temporally distant, and *vice versa*. Analyses of this kind in Kenya are complicated by the juxtaposition of markets with different meeting frequencies and by the existence of a variety of schedules for markets meeting with the same frequency. Experiments with a variety of possible adjacencies for a set of markets displaying a mixture of meeting frequencies, demonstrated that one might reasonably expect the nearest same-day market to be further away than the nearest adjacent-day market in the majority of cases; further agreement with the temporal-locational spacing hypothesis could only be expected for a limited number of markets. Measurements were made from the site of each of 1,142 market meetings in twenty-two districts, and 787 (68.9 per cent) of the measurements indicated that the nearest same-day market was further away than the nearest adjacent-day market. When the results were averaged on a district basis, the results for only one district, Kisii, were anomalous.

These analyses demonstrate a considerable amount of spatio-temporal order in the distribution of markets. However, most rural residents do not travel throughout the district on marketing ventures; rather they patronize market-places within a limited distance of their homes. Therefore, if markets are arranged efficiently both in space and time from the point of view of the rural resident, there should be an operating market within easy walking distance of most homes on several days of the week. Tests of this proposition, using randomly selected points as possible home sites, indicated that it is likely that markets meeting on several different days will be found within a reasonable distance of rural homes such that rural residents could, if desired, visit a market on several days of the week.

The rural markets in Kenya appear to be distributed efficiently in both space and time, and members of a dispersed rural population may make regular visits to one or more markets. Of course, the various definitions of efficiency may be unrealistic and perhaps irrelevant for the rural population. However, a detailed analysis of the market-visiting behaviour of local residents in Meru District indicated a deliberate awareness of the spatio-temporal synchronization of market meetings (Wood, 1974b). It seems almost as if residents possess mental maps of market space which change from day to day according to the relative locations of operative markets; market visits are based on these varying partitions of space. Detailed analysis of the aggregate movement patterns of market users in Kisii District suggested that distinct sets of markets (occasionally called market rings or circuits) do not exist and that the most realistic functional unit of market organization is probably the individual's market system (Wood, 1975b). The composite pattern of intermarket links created by members of the rural population appears to be a network in which all markets are directly or indirectly connected.

An Overview of the Kenyan Rural Market System

Although rural markets existed in a few areas of Kenya in precolonial times, the contemporary market system has developed largely during the twentieth century under an amalgam of colonial influences. The set of markets in any area of Kenya today can be viewed as one part of a balance. On one side of the balance there exists the demand for market facilities. In most parts of the country population density acts as a realistic surrogate for demand; extra weights may have to be added in areas close to large urban centres and some weights deducted in areas where there has been substantial European settlement or where modernization is well advanced. The local government authorities, headed by the County Councils, control the balance. In most areas the demand for market facilities is fairly accurately balanced by market provision, as the local authorities are constantly reviewing requests from the local population for adjustment to the existing facilities. In a few areas however, County Council control is inappropriate and the balance is not maintained. This situation results in the use of markets on unofficial market days and/or the development of unofficial markets (the local response to a gross underprovision of facilities), or a large number of officially registered markets that are defunct or that only sporadically function (the result of an overprovision of facilities).

Rural markets in Kenya are found in conjunction with small groups of permanent retail establishments. If trader itinerancy was a key factor in the genesis of periodic markets in Kenya, one would not expect periodic rural markets and permanent retail establishments to co-exist so consistently and harmoniously. Although periodic rural markets and retail establishments are found adjacent they form parts of separate systems. The primary function of the rural market-place system is to facilitate horizontal (rural-rural) trade. In most areas of the country the decision to inaugurate a new market rests initially on requests from the local population for more market facilities. Particular groups (for example, shopkeepers with premises adjacent to a market) may attempt to influence decisions about the frequency of market meetings, but the main concern of the legislative body is to ensure an equitable provision of market facilities for the rural population. This results in a set of markets organized for the benefit of the rural resident who may wish to visit several markets during the week rather than for professional traders wishing to follow a sequential round of market visits. The extensive and individual nature of the marketing activities of both marketers and part-time traders create a dense network of links (flows of people, money, ideas, and goods) between markets.

The periodicity characteristics of rural markets in Kenya can be explained from the point of view of rural residents who may be either marketers or part-time traders. Few rural households are completely self-sufficient and relatively few have a regular cash income. The market is a place where small amounts of cash may be obtained and where basic food and craft product shortages can be remedied. Most rural market users are farmers first and foremost who may not have the time to market every day (nor possibly the goods to sell daily, nor the need to buy daily, nor the urgent desire for cash). They want and/or need and/or have the time to market once or twice or three times per week. The continuous demand for marketing facilities at any one location is limited by the dependence of the local population on foot transport and the subsistence nature of the economy. By concentrating marketing activity on set days, periodicity of market meetings reduces the risk to both marketer and part-time trader of failing to find either a buyer for sale items or a seller of required items in the time available for market activities. This argument requires some extension to account for the spatio-temporal synchronization of market meetings. If rural residents could satisfy their needs at one market-place, then a spatio-temporal synchronization of market meetings would be superfluous. In Kenya, however, the normal marketing needs of marketers appear to necessitate visits to several market-places. It is the recognition of this fact by the bodies responsible for market inauguration that results in the generation of a spatio-temporally synchronized market system.

The system of retail establishments is concerned mainly with the flow of urban-produced goods from urban to rural areas, i.e. downward vertical trade. The physical adjacency of shops and market-places in the rural areas of Kenya is mutually beneficial: shop turnover is greatly increased on market days (money obtained in the market may be spent in the shops), and markets located within large clusters of shops often have a greater attendance than markets in small trading centres. However, there is relatively little overlap at this local level between the system of retail establishments and the rural market system either in terms of the types of goods handled or the flow of goods from one to the other. Shopkeepers occasionally transfer goods to the market-place, and very rarely a marketer may leave some unsold items in a shop for sale. Most of the flows of goods between the two systems occur through the major urban centres: the clothing sellers buy most of their clothes in urban centres and both the accumulator part-time traders and the wholesalers sell their wares in urban centres.

The existence of permanent retail establishments in rural areas implies a comparatively high, continuous density of local purchasing power. In most rural areas there is sufficient demand for low value urban-produced goods (in particular, sugar, salt, soap, matches, maize and flour) to maintain several general stores selling essentially these low value goods but sometimes also stocking a few higher value goods (for example, cooking utensils, clothes, umbrellas, and blankets).[5] In most areas there is insufficient demand to maintain shops specializing in high value goods. In accordance with Stine's thesis, if specialized traders in high value goods are to exist in these areas then they should operate on an itinerant basis. In most rural areas of Kenya the only specialized traders in high value urban-produced goods are the clothing traders who are found in the rural markets. The clothing traders take advantage of the congregations of people provided by the rural markets and many make use of the spatio-temporal synchronization of market meetings to maintain a threshold. However, the clothing trader is essentially an extension of the system of retail establishments into the system of periodic rural markets.

The dominant local exchange function of most rural markets in Kenya, the inapplicability of the thesis that itinerant traders lend cohesion, the periodic nature of market meetings, and the integration of rural markets does not constitute a denial of the relevance of central place theory to an understanding of the rural market system. Rural markets provide a service to the local, dispersed population and neither market-places nor market days in Kenya occur randomly. Whilst some of the elements that normally are considered symptomatic of a central place system have not been examined, the spatial patterns of the rural markets, the spatio-temporal synchronization of operating markets, and the resultant journey-to-market patterns of individual market users all reflect the principle of distance minimization which is a building block of central place theory.

Finally, some comment on the future of the rural periodic market in Kenya is in order. The inability of pedestrian rural residents to travel far in a short period of time, and their limited total demands for exchange are important factors in the argument for the existence of market periodicity. However, personal mobility is increasing gradually as more and better bus and taxi services are established and as rural incomes rise sufficiently to facilitate the use of such transport. Population densities are steadily increasing but in addition, rural attitudes and desires are changing with economic and social progress. In the past, an increase in population density has not necessarily led to an increase in market meeting frequency. It is likely that the effects of modernization on the rural market system will also vary from place to place. Observations in a number of the most modernized areas of Kenya indicate that trade will become concentrated on well-located markets. In one area polarization is reflected in an enlargement of attendance at a few periodic markets, without an intensification of meeting schedules, and in the expiry of some other markets, resulting in an overall decrease in both the number of market days and market-places in the area. However, in another area, there is evidence of a well-located market gradually losing its periodic character by a process of temporal infilling and of neighbouring markets declining in size. Thus, it is impossible to say whether or not most major periodic markets will eventually become daily. Rural markets in Kenya are not on a continuum with permanent retail establishments: they are parts of two separate systems and there is a vast difference between the functions and the facilities offered by a rural market and those provided by a cluster of permanent retail establishments. The rural market (periodic *and* daily) permits horizontal exchange of agricultural produce on a part-time basis; it accommodates the irregular nature (both seasonally and weekly) of individuals' demands for exchange and it allows people to sell as well as buy. The need for these facilities is related to the subsistence character of rural life. The overall amount of rural market trade as it is today will no doubt decrease slowly as the amount of vertical trade through rural shops, co-operatives and marketing boards increases, but the evanescence of the rural market with its current functions awaits the time when agriculture is commercialized and the majority of the population receives a regular, reliable income and can depend on purchased food for sustenance. The rural market (whether periodic or daily) and the rural shop will thus continue to exist side by side in the majority of rural areas of Kenya for many years to come. The largely separate but juxtaposed existence in rural areas of Kenya of a system of permanent retail establishments, concerned primarily with vertical trade, and a system of periodic rural markets, concerned mainly with horizontal trade, is probably a reflection of the recency of any form of institutionalized trade in many parts of the country. Organized rural commerce has developed largely in the past seventy years and the adjacency of the two systems represents, physically and functionally, a compromise between the technology of the colonizers and the requirements of the rural population.

---

[1] One study of markets in northern Nigeria suggests that the periodic markets there may be sequenced spatio-temporally more for the benefit of the consumer than the itinerant trader (Hill and Smith, 1972, 353).

[2] Many of the markets in the major urban centres of Kenya are similar in both function and appearance to the urban markets of Western Europe. Typically, the markets are daily and consist of stalls in a covered building. Usually, the stalls are rented on a monthly basis by professional, full-time traders who acquire much of their produce through wholesalers. Some of the produce sold in the rural markets finds its way to the urban markets, but rarely in the latter is the seller also the producer. At lower levels of the urban hierarchy, however, markets in urban centres are often similar to rural markets; for example, Nyeri Town (population 10,000) possesses both a covered market which operates daily and an open enclosure where markets are held on three days each week. Small town markets which appear to possess the characteristics of rural markets are so considered.

[3] For a fuller account of precolonial markets in Kenya and the development of the contemporary rural market system see Wood (1974d).

[4] This figure refers to thirty-six of the forty-one districts in Kenya in 1970: Mombasa District and Nairobi Extra Provincial District, which are predominantly urban, have been excluded and data are not available for three districts (Kilifi, Garissa and Samburu). Of these three districts, only Kilifi is likely to have any regular markets. It seems, however, that in Kilifi District only the municipal markets are controlled and that in the rural areas markets of the size and type observed elsewhere in Kenya do not occur, although no official information is available to support this suggestion.

[5] It seems that many rural shops in Kenya are only marginally profitable. In Meru District in 1959 a gross turnover of three or four shillings per day was quoted as normal for shops in the general retail category (Meru African District Council, 23.3.1959, Appendix M). In many areas there is a very high ratio of shops to people, and factors such as long-overdue rents and limited stock suggest that some shops may be uneconomic. Very marginal profits may be acceptable since few African shopkeepers in the rural parts of Kenya are totally dependent on retailing for a livelihood: their families actively participate in semi-subsistence farming. Shop profit may therefore be considered similar to a second income and small profits may be compensated for, to some extent, by the prestige gained from being a shop-keeper. For a related discussion of various aspects of rural trade in part of Uganda see Funnell (1973).

15 Weekly markets in the Puebla region of Mexico
E. Gormsen

The periodic markets of ancient Mexico made such an impression upon Cortes and his crew that their characteristics were recorded in some detail in the traveller's accounts (Cortes, 1942, vol. 1, 56 (market of Tlaxcala), and 99-101 (market of Tenochtitlan); Diaz del Castillo, 1939, vol. 1, 328-30 (market of Tlatelolco)). They were impressed by the general bustling activity, the variety of merchandise for sale, the regular arrangements of different items in the market-place and the supervisory authority controlling commercial proceedings. The mechanism of these precolonial markets which was quite similar to the one in Spain, known to the conquerors, has persisted to the present, despite marked changes in the number and the patterns of population. Indeed, some large weekly markets have even been included as picturesque attractions in the itineraries of tours arranged by travel agencies. The exotic market life was described in many publications of the colonial period as well as in most nineteenth century travel accounts (Brocklehurst, 1883; Evans, 1870; Gooch, 1887). However, the authors mostly contented themselves with descriptions confined frequently to the market place of the capital.

In recent years, some more systematic studies of Mexican weekly markets were completed, and they have helped to identify the socio-economic aspects of the market mechanism. Following several investigations of market systems in Guatemala in the 1930s (McBryde, 1933 and 1947; Redfield, 1939; Tax, 1954), Malinowski and de la Fuente (1957) studied the market system in the central area of the state of Oaxaca in 1940. Tlaxiaco and its hinterland in the same state is dealt with by Marroquin (1957), who reported on field research with students carried out in 1953, while Foster (1948) referred to the Patzcuaro area in Michoacán.

This essay is concerned with weekly markets in the Puebla region. After some salient features of the natural and cultural environment of the area have been identified, the paper discusses the importance of modern transport in the functioning of the market system; the internal spatial organisation of market-places; the functions of periodic markets in Puebla and the activities of itinerant traders; and finally, seasonal fluctuations in market activity.

---

* Field research was carried out within the Mexico Project of the German Research Fund (Deutsche Forschungsgemeinschaft) in 1964-65 with some additional observations in 1973.

The Puebla region, surrounded by the highest volcanoes in Mexico, is very suitable for a study of this type because it includes three areas differing substantially in natural environment and social patterns as well as in the spatial distribution and relative importance of periodic markets.[1] The central basin of Puebla-Tlaxcala has a high density of agrarian and industrial population and it also has numerous market-places (Fig. 15.1). The basin slopes with various tectonic faults towards the south from some 2,000 metres (6,500 feet) to about 1,200 metres (4,000 feet) above sea level, to the Mixteca Poblana; this is an arid, sparsely populated area with higher population concentrations occurring only in

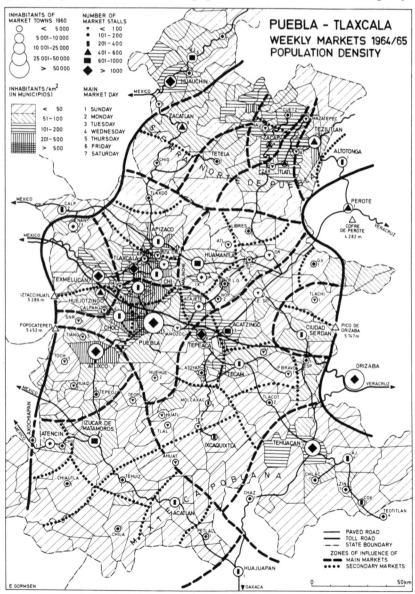

Figure 15.1   Weekly markets in Puebla-Tlaxcala area, 1964-5

the irrigated valleys. There is a series of small market-places irregularly dispersed but in close functional relation with the few very large markets: Atlixco, Matamoros, Tehuacán, and Tepeaca-Acatzingo. Towards the northeast of Puebla and beyond the old volcano of La Malinche, there are wide highland plains of 2,400 metres (8,000 feet) and above where the population density is low and the number of markets is small due mainly to the persistence of relatively large farms, in spite of land reform programmes. In contrast to this situation, the Sierra Norte de Puebla slopes steeply eastward towards the coastal lowlands; this area is densely populated by Indian subsistence farmers and is quite well served by medium size and smaller markets.[2]

Regional differences in the size of weekly markets and in the extension of their orbits of attraction are due to a combination of physio-geographic factors, historical events, and recent modernization. After the Spanish Conquest, the process of miscegenation and acculturation did not create a homogeneous population in the whole country. On the contrary, some areas, such as the Sierra Norte and a few villages on the slopes of La Malinche close to the city of Puebla, were scarcely affected, and this is partly related to the spatial differentiation in business initiative and in the readiness to adopt agricultural and other innovations. In general, even in remote areas, the *mestizos* play a more important role in commerce than the indigenous population. Industrialization, which commenced in 1834 with the establishment of the first mechanised textile factory in all of Latin America, has also influenced central place relations and behavioural patterns in the closer hinterland of the city of Puebla.

The subdivision of large private and ecclesiastical estates which took place as a consequence of the agrarian revolution of 1910 resulted in the emigration of a small well-to-do class as well as in a decline in some trades; the net result was a certain levelling of the social hierarchy, especially in the southern region (Marroquin, 1957, 90; Nickel, 1970, 20). The importance of some market towns declined while others increased considerably in significance. This development was intensified by the simultaneous expansion of motor transport which, owing to climate and landform conditions, was relatively more easy in the arid zone than in the Sierra Norte.

The Impact of Modern Transport

In the central area of Puebla-Tlaxcala, a dense network of privately owned bus lines developed years ago under very difficult conditions (Gormsen, 1971 map d), and this has given the peasants access to the larger market-places in addition to their local market. This is especially convenient when high order goods are sought. Extremely large numbers of buyers and sellers congregate in some markets on market day; thus, in Tepeaca every Friday, approximately 1,450 traders and marketers assemble in the huge cemented *Zócalo*[3] of this small town of a little over 5,000 inhabitants. Only the butchers install themselves under a simple roof of corrugated sheet metal whereas all the other vendors pitch their sun shades in the open. This market is a typical *tianguis,*[4] where even sewing machines and bedroom furniture are offered in the open air.

The buses which transport thousands of visitors from up to eighty km (fifty miles) away block the through road from Tehuacan to Puebla which is virtually abandoned on non-market days (especially since the opening of the new toll road in 1966). Between 15,000 and 20,000 people visit the Tepeaca market, and every Tuesday a similar number is to be found at Acatzingo, only twenty km (twelve miles) east of Tepeaca. These markets complement one another in their vast zone of influence which, however, is not very densely populated. Many market visitors come from the areas east of La Malinche and from the arid zone to the south, especially since a paved branch road was opened to Ixcaquixtla in 1962. Prior to this, the daily bus journey from Puebla to Ixcaquixtla took from five to seven hours, and frequently it was delayed by difficult road conditions for twice this period.

The improvement of this road not only has strengthened the position of Tepeaca, but it also reshaped the fundamental pattern of spatial relationships in the entire area. Settlements far from the roads are nowadays within easy reach as truck and bus traffic on the unimproved tracks is possible in the dry climate. The two main *plazas* on the new road, Molcaxac and Ixcaquixtla, are visited by people whose homes are frequently four or five hours distant by foot, while such remote local markets as Huatlatlauca, Tlaltempan, and Ahuatempan (to the west and south-west) are declining in importance and will eventually perish, as has happened in other cases.

Until very recently, pack animals were the main form of transportation in this region. Thus, in a one hour period in the early afternoon of 22 October 1964 no fewer than 113 donkeys left the market of Molcaxac travelling west; about noon on 15 November 1964, approximately 850 donkeys and mules were resting at Ixcaquixtla before their return trip. However, a census taken in the same town on 4 March 1973 recorded only about 280 pack animals, although the number of stalls was considerably larger in 1973 than in 1964 (349 compared with 223 (Table 15.1)). This is another indication of the increasing importance of motor traffic especially since the present government has developed a programme for the improvement of branch and feeder roads.

In the Sierra Norte de Puebla, far more people walk to the *plaza*, carrying their load with help of a tump-line on their back; young pigs for sale are kept on the lead. As a consequence of the mountainous terrain, trails are so steep that motor traffic is confined to a few well formed roads, and bus transport is relatively unimportant.[5] Road transport is quite critical for the traders' business: whole-salers and middlemen are able to transport perishable tropical fruits, and itinerant retailers can visit several markets in weekly rotation. Even in the *plaza* of Cuetzalan (a market where few people arrive by motor transport, but where nearly all the visitors wear their traditional costumes) a puffing textile dealer announcing his wares with a battery operated loudspeaker is in regular attendance.[6] However, isolated village markets in this roadless area are hardly ever visited by *mestizo* itinerant traders (Bromley, 1969, 68).

The Internal Spatial Organisation of Market-Places

The internal organisation of the market-place in San Martín Texmelucan (north-west of Puebla and in the centre of a fertile farming area in the upper basin of the Atoyac River) is typical of many large markets. The town is favourably located on the main traffic route from Mexico City to Puebla; its population has increased from 3,400 at the turn of the century to 13,800 in 1960, thus outstripping by far the old district town of Huejotzingo (3,900 to 7,400 in the same period (Gormsen, 1966)). Apart from the busy through traffic, the character of Texmelucan has altered little, and the *Zócalo* is quite modest in appearance. However, on Tuesdays, the market-place of nearly 1.5 hectares (3.8 acres) and adjacent streets are filled with people coming from places up to thirty km (nineteen miles) distant and especially from the densely populated lower slopes of the mountains to the west, where almost every village can be reached by bus (Gormsen, 1971, map d). The settlements that depend entirely on the Texmelucan market had about 80,000 inhabitants in 1960, and also many people come regularly from the areas of neighbouring markets (e.g. Nativitas, Nanacamilpa, and even Huejotzingo although its Saturday market is quite large, frequently having more than 500 traders).

The arrangement of goods within this huge market is shown schematically in Figure 15.2. Only the northern part of the market-place proper is covered by a solid metal roof, and some booths and small shops are housed in a special building along the western and northern walls. Most of the *fondas* (a small cooking place with one or two tables where spicy local dishes are served) are here, as are fruit and vegetable stalls and *abarrotes* (which sell every kind of foodstuffs except bread, meat, and greengroceries). However, a great deal of basic Mexican food (especially corn (maize) and a variety of beans) is sold by special *semilla* dealers. Most of the traditional hand-made products like *sarapes* (woollen blankets), *sombreros* (palm-fibre hats), pottery, sandals, and fibre goods are offered in the southern part of the *mercado*, while the biggest vendors of industrial goods are installed along the street leading to the *Zócalo*. Some of the traders here are shopkeepers in the same street who on market days display their merchandise in the open air.

The 1,860 market stalls counted in October 1964 vary enormously in size and economic importance. Only about half are regular booths with at least a small table and two or more vendors, the rest being individual dealers, mostly women, who crouch or sit on the ground. Some 25 per cent of the latter are marketers (Bohannan and Dalton, 1962, 13), selling very small quantities of their own produce, especially small animals, flowers, or local fruit which are piled up in small heaps.[7] The number of these traders varies seasonally. A few women who walk through the market and barter *tortillas* for vegetables or charcoal belong to this category as well as some artisans selling pottery, wooden spoons, or sandals which they make on the spot. The majority, however, are forestallers (McKim, 1972, 340) who sell fruit and vegetables by the piece which they have bought either from the producers in their home villages or from the trucks of middlemen in the market itself.

There are also several large stalls with solid tables and modern balances offering a wide range of greengroceries; some sellers of manufactured consumer goods such as hats, hardware, and plastic toys set up displays on the ground. At the top of the scale, there are traders who specialise in durable goods who either drive to the market with their own pick-up trucks or run a related shop in town. They may make most of their profit as wholesalers selling mainly to hawkers who in turn sell in the market-place. Some of the traders in each of these groups are itinerant, and visit a more or less fixed circuit of up to six markets a week.

On market day there are at least 3,500 persons directly engaged in selling in the Texmelucan market and, while it is difficult to estimate accurately the number of buyers, a total of about 15,000 market visitors, excluding children, seems likely, which clearly outnumbers the population of the town.[8]

There does not appear to be a direct relationship between the number of

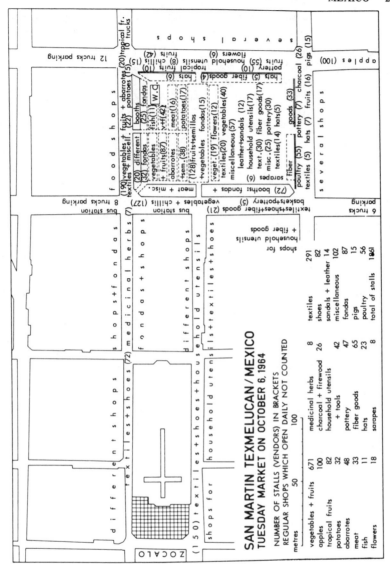

Figure 15.2 Tuesday market at San Martin Texmelucan

inhabitants of market towns and the size of their respective markets. A comparison of Tlaxcala (7,500 inhabitants; 1,093 stalls), Chiautempan (11,300; 340), and Apizaco (15,700; 265) reveals a disproportion which can only be explained historically: the predominantly indigenous population of the small state of Tlaxcala look upon their capital as *the* central place in every respect. The neighbouring towns of Chiautempan and Apizaco have developed only since the end of last century as industrial and railway centres, respectively (Gormsen, 1966). From Sunday to Friday, Tlaxcala with the Governmental Palace on the *Zócalo* shaded by beautiful old trees, has an air of one of the ancient residencies of small European sovereigns; on Saturdays the tranquil scene is enlivened by thousands of *campesinos* (peasants) invading not only the market place and the *Zócalo*, but also the Government offices, the cinemas, and the *cantinas* (taverns).

The main characteristics of Texmelucan and Tlaxcala markets are quite representative of other markets in the area; the proportion of sellers of different goods varies with the size and the hinterland of the market in question as well as with the season of the year. As a general rule, a smaller ratio of durable goods sellers is to be expected in smaller markets (cf. Texmelucan and Tlaxcala with Nativitas and Chignahuapan, Table 15.1), but the relationship is not especially close. At least half of the non-durable goods stalls specialise in the sale of fruit and vegetables but this figure includes most of the forestallers. Textiles and shoes are next in importance. The relative importance of established commerce should also be taken into account, the sales of which may increase considerably on market days. In minor towns, one or two well stocked general stores may provide serious competition for itinerant traders, especially as the rural clientele is often indebted to the storekeepers.

In medium size cities (20,000 to 50,000 inhabitants) such as Atlixco, Izúcar de Matamoros, Tehuacán, and Teziutlán, the population is supplied by local commerce as well as by daily working market halls. Even in these towns, there is a sharp increase in the number of stalls and visitors on the *dia de plaza* (traditional market day), and the life of the city centre is completely dominated by the market. In some cities, additional market-places have been constructed, in order to relieve the congestion.[9] In Puebla, there are several modern market buildings in addition to the main *Mercado de la Victoria*. All these buildings are open daily for the convenience of the city population. On Thursdays, however (the traditional *dia de plaza*) there is a huge influx of rural people, with a somewhat smaller number coming also on Sundays. Formerly, Saturday was the second important market day, as Miguel Ceron Zapata observed in 1714: 'Although there was not anything missing you looked for at the *Plaza Mayor* on all the days, during the *feria* or *mercado* on Thursdays and Saturdays of every week people from the neighbouring villages – and even from twenty *leguas* away – arrived for selling their goods of local textiles, cordage, and fruit in such an abundance that it happened very often they returned home with the same what they had brought' (Leicht, 1934, 471).

The Functions of Markets

Certain changes have occurred in the economic functions of the traditional market since the colonial period (Leicht, 1934). While the daily urban market has always been first and foremost a retail distribution centre providing the urban population with goods, the number and variety of items available as well as the types of traders have changed substantially. Until the seventeenth century, the market virtually was supplied only by Indian marketers who sold their country produce directly to the urban consumers.[10] At that time the main purpose of an Indian's visit to the market was to sell, whereas nowadays the *campesinos* as well as the urban population go to the market primarily to buy goods that are offered by full-time traders. Only small amounts of special produce pass directly from farmers to urban consumers; most agricultural produce is bought in the countryside by middlemen or semi-governmental storehouses without passing through a market-place. Thus, an inversion has taken place in rural-urban relations from centripetal to centrifugal, and Hodder's

Table 15.1: Durable and Non-Durable Goods Stalls in Selected Mexican Market-Places

Market-Place	Enumeration Date	Stalls			Goods Stalls by Type (%)						
		Number	Durable Goods %	Non-Durable Goods %	Fondas	Fruit & Vegetables	Meat & Fish	Clothing & Shoes	Hardware & Household Goods	Pigs & Poultry	Miscellaneous
Texmelucan	6.10.64	1,861	42.8	57.2	4.7	50.1	2.4	21.3	9.4	3.6	8.5
Tlaxcala	21.11.64	1,093	39.2	60.8	3.3	53.1	4.4	16.6	6.7	5.5	10.4
Huamantla	21.10.64	556	40.5	59.5	2.7	53.6	3.2	19.6	11.2	1.1	8.6
Teziutlan	27.11.64	478	36.2	63.8							
Zacapoaxtla	25.11.64	410	31.2	68.8							
Zacatelco	22.11.64	372	21.8	78.2				n.a.			
Zacatelco	23. 9.73	496	27.6	72.4							
Ciudad Serdan	24. 1.65	291	36.8	63.2							
Ixcaquixtla	15.11.64	223	39.5	60.5	4.4	50.7	5.4	24.7	9.4	0.0	5.4
Ixcaquixtla	4. 3.73	349	35.2	64.8	7.5	51.6	5.7	23.2	6.3	0.0	5.7
Guadelupe Victoria	6.12.64	191	34.0	66.0							
Libres	6.12.64	148	43.2	56.8							
Tetela do Ocampo	13.12.64	108	33.7	66.3				n.a.			
Nativitas	7. 2.65	103	16.5	83.5							
Chignahuapan	13.12.64	64	17.2	82.8							

Source: Author's field work

n.a. — not available

distinction (1971, 350) between daily and periodic markets in West Africa as being distribution and bulking centres, respectively, does not seem to be valid in Mexico. Further evidence for this proposition is provided by the fact that most peasants go to the market with empty baskets.

Not all of the markets have abandoned the bulking function, and Tepeaca, besides having a livestock market with some 2,000 cattle and other animals has developed into an important wholesale emporium. Between 6 and 7 a.m., when the first retailers begin to install themselves, there is intense activity at the western part of the *Zócalo*. All kinds of fruit and vegetables are piled up in crates and sacks on the pavement in front of heavy trucks, parked side by side. Depending upon the season, between 150 and 250 trucks bring agricultural products from all over the country. Some of this produce is sold in complete or half truck-loads, but most of it is bought in smaller quantities by retailers for sale in other markets. In many cases the trucks which arrive in the morning with one kind of fruit or vegetable leave in the afternoon with a completely mixed load. The majority of the truck drivers are *fleteros* (i.e. carriers who do not trade), but a few of them act as middlemen and buy goods on their own account in their home town for sale in Tepeaca.

Small bulking points are still to be found in remote areas, but even here not all of the cash crops are collected on market days. In the arid region where the production of corn and beans rarely exceeds the basic annual needs of a family, people may have to sell a small 'surplus' (a sackful or two) in order to obtain a few *pesos* which they need for the immediate purchase of tools or other articles (Bohannan and Dalton, 1962, 13).

Several markets serve as bulking centres for handicraft products manufactured in scattered settlements. During the crop growing season, as many as 2,000 baskets of different sizes are offered for sale at Molcaxac, with an additional 300 at Tepeojuma (both Thursday markets). At Ixcaquixtla, an average of some 6,000 *petates*[11] is delivered weekly. Other fibre goods (for example, more delicate *petates*, small toys and pouches, and table sets) are bought up at the place of manufacture by local traders who sell them in Mexico City, Acapulco, and even in the border cities of the United States.

Since the construction of better roads, non-resident *acaparadores* (middlemen) have played a more important role. On the *día de plaza*, they intercept *campesinos* with their small loads of country produce on the outskirts of the market towns before they reach the market. Thus, the *acaparadores* compete keenly with the established commerce of the village but they do not offer any particular concession (such as favourable prices) to the *campesinos*. They have always been part of this commercial system, but formerly they could not easily avoid having a local establishment because without trucks it was impossible to transport large amounts of merchandise.

In the Sierra Norte, certain aspects of the traditional trading patterns have persisted; in particular, there is considerable exchange within the area itself. This is understandable in the context of the agricultural differentiation of the altitudinal zones, and also of the spatial behavioural patterns of the indigenous population. Thus, former semi-autarkic economic conditions may still be recognised as relict forms. Several handicraft products are traded exclusively within the Sierra proper (traditionally embroidered blouses from Nauzontla and handwoven woollen *ponchos* and waistcoats from Xalacapan near Zacapoaxtla). Pottery from the vicinity of Zacatlan is sold in the markets of the Sierra by women. However, vertical trade connections with the wider economy are developing. Quite a few *acaparadores* buy fowls and eggs from *campesinos* as they approach the market towns, and much of the pottery of San Miguel Tenextatiloyan (on the main road south of Tlatlauqui) is sold by local pedlars in the lowlands of Veracruz and Tabasco. The woollen *rebozos* embroidered with colourful cross-stitch ornaments by the Indian women of Hueyapan fetch such high prices in the Mexico City tourist shops that it is difficult to find them in the *plazas* of Tlatlauqui and Teziutlán. Finally, the Sunday market of Chiautempan has a special function: the hand loom weavers from neighbouring villages deliver the woven *sarapes* to the commercial house, picking up wool in return (Gormsen, 1966, 121).

The activities of the market are not confined to those associated with economic functions, and there is an important social dimension as well. It is perhaps surprising that many *campesinos* spend a considerable proportion of the cash obtained in the market on alcoholic beverages. However, this is not usually solitary drinking for distraction from sorrows, but a very real part of the social life of the market. Often, *pulque* is for sale in the market place, while *aguardiente* (a cheap sugar-cane liquor) is sold in *cantinas* or in some general stores. The market meeting is indisputably the most important social event of the week, and for many rural people it offers the only regular opportunity to meet friends, especially when they all live in small scattered settlements. The significance of this essential market function should not be underrated (especially in comparison with the economic functions), and it may also explain some of the very long journeys to the large markets which seem to have only doubtful economic justification.

Market Hierarchy and Itinerant Traders

There is a reasonably close relationship between the size of a market and the day on which the market meets (Fig. 15.3). Most of the markets with less than 400 vendors meet on Sundays, while all the larger markets and only a few of the lower category are held on the remaining days of the week. A similar phenomenon can be observed in Oaxaca (Malinowski and de la Fuente, 1957; Beals, 1967), being based upon mutual relations between the major and minor markets of the area. In such a situation, buyers have an additional opportunity to shop in a market other than their local market, and itinerant traders can sell on several days of the week, replenishing their stocks at the main market place once a week. Most of the large regional markets are held on Fridays or Saturdays, and this enables retailers to offer such perishable items as fresh fruit at their local Sunday market. The occurrence of most small markets on Sundays can be explained by the *campesino's* wish to combine a market visit with church attendance, especially in areas where the population of large *municipios* lives in small settlements.[12] While every parish or *municipio* would have had its own *día de plaza* in the past, increasing population density has occasioned several divisions of *municipios* so that this simple relationship no longer holds. Also, some municipal centres have lost their former market functions.

As Sunday markets frequently occur in villages which are quite close together, the principle of spatio-temporal synchronization (proximity in space implies separation in time) is less applicable here than elsewhere (Smith, 1971, 328). This situation is even more pronounced in the northern part of the Sierra Norte (Bromley, 1969). The explanation for this situation probably lies in different population densities (Bromley, 1969, 66), in the traditional behaviour patterns of a predominantly indigenous population (almost all of whom have a strong loyalty to their local market), and transport problems. However, the spatio-temporal distribution of the larger markets does lend support to the hypothesis (Figs. 15.1 and 15.3), and it is, therefore, suggested that this question is related to the more or less developed hierarchy within a market system which, in turn, depends to a certain degree upon the socio-economic evolution of a society and may vary from one region to another.

The increased availability of motor transport has resulted in expansion and overlapping of these interrelated systems, which has facilitated the activities of itinerant traders. These are not a homogeneous group, and they differ in their financial capacity, commercial methods, and weekly routes. Forestallers occupy the lower end of the scale; for example, a woman buys several crates of fruit on Friday at Tepeaca, sells part of it in the same market, another part the next day at Tecamachalco, and the rest in a smaller market (perhaps her home town) on Sunday. On Tuesday she may get a supply of vegetables at Acatzingo for sale at Zacapoaxtla on Wednesday and at Tlatlauqui on Thursday. With her goods packed in sacks, she travels by a cheap bus or in an open truck.

The trade in cheap manufactured goods (e.g. textiles or *sombreros*) requires

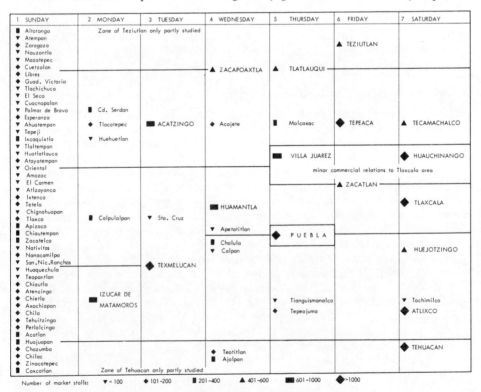

Figure 15.3   Classification of periodic markets in Puebla-Tlaxcala

more invested capital, but it has the fundamental advantage that unsold goods do not spoil. The means of transport and the traders' itineraries, however, are similar to the fruit and vegetable forestaller. Traders appear to follow their circuits in limited areas, e.g. around Tepeaca and Acatzingo in the east, Texmelucan and Atlixco to the west, and Tlaxcala and Texmelucan in the central and northern parts of the region. The southeast is dominated by Tehuacán and very few itinerant traders of this area are to be found elsewhere; occasionally, traders from the Puebla-Tlaxcala area visit Villa Juárez and Huauchinango, but these important central places in the northern Sierra have closer relations with the neighbouring states of Hidalgo and Veracruz.

The spatial extent of their activity was of course restricted as long as the merchants depended upon pack-animals. Nevertheless, the following 1965 report of an 85-year-old vegetable trader from Los Reyes near Acatzingo gives an idea of the enormous distances covered by this means of transportation. In his youth he carried garlic and onions, which were packed at home on Sundays, to the market of Zacapoaxtla. His first stop was Oriental on Monday, his second was Zaragoza on Tuesday, and on Wednesday he arrived at the market of Zacapoaxtla around 10 a.m. He sold his goods and bought tropical fruit (especially oranges) delivered there by peasants from the lowlands. His return trip commenced on Wednesday in order to be in Tepeaca for the Friday market where he would sell the fruit. He remained home on Saturdays, and on Sundays prepared again for his 250 km (150 mile) circuit.[13] Another example is provided by a *sombrero* trader of Tepeaca, who today owns a truck and a store-room at Zacapoaxtla and at Cuetzalan where he has been trading since 1955. In the 1920s, he accompanied his father from his home village, Tepeyahualco (north of Molcaxac) to the markets of Tepeaca, Tecamachalco, Palmar de Bravo, and Ciudad Serdán. They generally started at 5 a.m. and arrived at the next *plaza* about 10 a.m.: Tuesday, Wednesday, and Thursday were spent at home, but if not they went to Tehuacan to buy supplies from *sombrero* factories there.

The Seasonal Rhythm of the Market System

These specific routes were not followed rigidly throughout the year, if only because of the seasonal rhythm of agricultural production. The corn harvest is exceptionally important, especially in the southern arid area, where the produce of the *temporal* (unirrigated) fields of smallholders is very limited. Here, the harvest begins a full month later than on the *temporal* fields of the more humid highland basins. During the last months before the harvest, the numbers of visits to the markets diminishes sharply; they are concerned predominantly with purchasing corn with the proceeds of sales of baskets or *petates*.

The price of corn from the lowlands of Veracruz or from the irrigated fields in the vicinity of Izúcar de Matamoros, rises steadily during the two or three months before the harvest begins in the Mixteca Poblana, and the *campesinos* gather their last centavos in order to keep their families from hunger.[14] As soon as their own crop is harvested, part of it is sold immediately to obtain much-needed cash and prices fall sharply. This results in a double loss for the *campesinos*, because under the prevailing conditions their harvest will never be large enough to enable them to store sufficient quantities for the whole year and to keep a small surplus for sale. The situation for other crops and even the products of rural artisans is not vastly different. For most items there is an elaborate hierarchy of middlemen, and the *campesinos* are subject to a certain amount of exploitation which has replaced, to a certain degree, the former dependence on large landlords (Wolf, 1955; Bonfil, 1962; Stavenhagen, 1963; and Frank, 1968).

The increase in market activity before important feasts is extraordinary, and cannot be explained by rational motives alone, especially when these feasts fall within the time of the shortage before the harvest. Almost all Mexican markets experience a surge of activity at the end of October, when the preparations for the *'día de los muertos'* (All Souls' Day) are taking place. On this day, relatives from far away gather at their home places, and nobody spares on food and drink. There is in the market a special supply of bright yellow 'death-flowers' *(Tagetes erecta L.)*, candles, black-varnished pottery censers, *'pan de muertos'* (body-shaped raised cake), and even small death's heads modelled out of sugar. The national saint, *Nuestra Señora de Guadalupe*, is honoured on 12 December, and this day is accompanied by a sharp increase in market activities as well as local patron *fiestas* which are usually combined with a village fair. If one of these feast days falls within the harvest-time, market sales increase further. For several weeks immediately after the feast, market activity is at a low ebb as the *campesinos* have run short of money. Thus, the seasonal rhythm of the market system is influenced both by the harvesting cycle and by the occurrence of local and national feast days.

Conclusion

Periodic markets in the Puebla region (and, indeed, in Mexico generally) have a long history. The structure and function of the market system have been modified mainly by the increasing availability of motor transport, but elements of the traditional pattern remain and, in combination with other socio-economic and environmental factors, they are responsible for obvious regional differences within the system. Nowadays, in most areas the bulking function seems to be of less importance than elsewhere, but itinerant traders are a key element of the system. Periodic markets have a pronounced social function and there is as well a decided seasonal rhythm to market activities, related to both the agricultural cycle and to the occurrence of feast days.

[1] The region includes most parts of the States of Puebla and Tlaxcala and some adjacent areas. It has an area of approximately 34,000 square kilometres (13,000 square miles), and in 1970 had a population of about three million (two million in 1960).

[2] In addition to the markets shown on Fig. 15.1, there is a number of village markets in the deep valleys of the Sierra, especially within the area north of a line from Zacatlán to Teziutlán (Bromley, 1969). Within a radius of about 25 km (16 miles) around Cuetzalan, Bromley identified sixteen small market-places not included in Fig. 15.1.

[3] In every Mexican town or city the central square (Spanish: Plaza Mayor) is called the *Zócalo*.

[4] *Tianguis* is the Nahuatl (Aztec) word for market and is still used for traditional market-places (see Pyle's essay in this volume).

[5] Among 5,670 persons arriving at the market of Cuetzalan on 8 August 1968, Bromley (1969) counted only 490 who came by vehicle while 225 rode a saddle animal. A count in Zacapoaxtla on 18 September 1968 revealed that about 40 per cent of market participants arrived by vehicle.

[6] The road leading to Mazatepec (built in connection with the construction of a dam) has influenced the market system, and the new market established there is closer to some parts of the *municipio* of Cuetzalan than is the traditional market-place.

[7] Fanny Gooch (1887, 70) noted 'I could buy as many of these piles as I wanted, but each one was counted separately, and payed for in the same way. I offered to buy out the entire outfit of a woman . . . but she only shook her head and wagged her forefinger, saying "No, señora, no puedo".'

[8] Estimates of this kind, are, of course, only approximate, but Marroquin (1957, 196), controlling all the entrances of Tlaxiaco on market day, arrived at a total of some 2,000 visitors with 250 stalls in the market, which is about the same ratio. On the other hand, a census by Bromley (1969) in August 1968 recorded more than 5,000 adults entering Cuetzalan, the market of which had fewer than 200 stalls in September 1964. The number of visitors (which according to Bromley's informants, may double during coffee harvest), looks quite high, considering the fact that there are several competitive Sunday markets within a distance of about ten km (six miles) (see also Foster 1948, 158).

[9] A good example is the recent relocation of the huge Friday market at Toluca (capital of the state of Mexico, 65 km (40 miles) west of Mexico City) visited by many tourists. The old market hall in the city centre is used daily by the urban population while the new market place serves the *campesinos* every Friday.

[10] According to a decree of 1606, issued primarily against Spanish middlemen, only persons who brought vegetables to the Puebla markets with their own mules could sell, i.e. mostly Indians (Lopez de Villaseñor, 1961, 458).

[11] These are palm fibre mats of about a metre square which are used in the lowlands as packing materials for tobacco bundles and the like. Bulking centres for *sombreros* are Tehuacán, Huajuapan and, to a lesser degree, Petlalcingo.

[12] A similar phenomenon occurs with Friday markets in many Islamic West-African regions (Hill and Smith, 1972).

[13] Even longer trader itineraries using pack animals or carrying the goods on their own backs are reported by McBryde(1933, 124-7) from Western Guatemala.

[14] Between 23 October and 2 December 1967, Jaecklein (1970, 125) noted an increase from 3.00 to 4.00 pesos per *cajon* of corn in Ixcaquixtla (cf. Foster, 1948, 160; Malinowski and de la Fuente, 1957, 161; and Marroquin, 1957, 210).

References cited

Abir, M. (1966), 'Salt, trade, and politics in Ethiopia', *Journal of Ethiopian Studies*, IV, 1-10

Adalemo, I.A. (1974), *Spatial and Temporal Configurations of Rural Periodic Markets in Western Nigeria*, Ann Arbor: Unpublished Ph.D. dissertation, University of Michigan

Adler, J.H. (1973), 'Development and income distribution', *Finance and Development*, 12, 2-5

Agrawal, B.C. (1970), *The Religio-Economic Networks in Dhar District, Madhya Pradesh, India*, Madison: Unpublished Ph.D. dissertation, University of Wisconsin

AHN/B (Archivo Histórico Nacional, Bogotá) (1814), Unpublished census for 1814 in Miscelánea de la República

Alao, N.A. (1968), *Periodic Markets in Western Nigeria: Theory and Empirical Evidence*, Evanston: Northwestern University Department of Geography Research Report No. 42

Alexander, J.W. (1958), 'Location of manufacturing: methods of measurement', *Annals, Association of American Geographers*, 48, 20-26

Allix, A. (1922), 'The geography of fairs: illustrated by old-world examples', *Geographical Review*, 12, 532-69

Allnutt, R.B. (1940), 'Gulio', *Tanganyika Notes and Records*, 10, 92-3

Alomia, L.A. (1910), *Boletin de Estadistica*, Quito: Ministerio de Instrucción Pública

A.N.E. (Acàdemía Nacional del Ecuador) (1863), *Almanaque para el Año de 1863*, Quito

ANH/Q (Archivo Nacional de Historia, Quito) (1780), Unpublished census for 1780 in Sección Censos y Padrones

Anon (1882), 'Native routes through the Masai country, from information obtained by the Rev. T. Wakefield', *Proceedings of the Royal Geographical Society*, 4, 742-47

Appell, G.N. (1969), 'The ethnographic classification of the Dusun-speaking peoples of northern Borneo', *Ethnology*, VIII, No. 2

Baker, S.W. (1867), *The Nile Tributaries of Abyssinia*, London: Macmillan

Banco de la Republica, Republica de la Colombia (1960), *Atlas de Economia Colombiana*, Bogotá: Banco de la Republica

Barth, F. (1967), 'Economic spheres in Darfur', 149-73 in R. Firth (ed.) *Themes in Economic Anthropology*, London: Tavistock

Bauer, P.T. and B.S. Yamey (1951), 'Economic progress and occupational distribution', *Economic Journal*, 61, 741-55

Beals, R.L. (1967), 'The structure of the Oaxaca market system', *Revista Mexicana de Estudios Anthropologicos*, 21, 333-42

Benedict, P. (1972), 'Itinerant marketing: an alternative strategy', 81-93 in E.N. Wilmsen (ed.) *Social Exchange and Interaction*, Ann Arbor: Anthropological Papers, Museum of Anthropology No. 46

Benet, F. (1957), 'Explosive markets: the Berber highlands', 188-217 in K. Polanyi, C.M. Arensberg and H.W. Pearson (eds.) *Trade and Markets in the Early Empires*, New York: The Free Press

Benet, F. (1961), 'Weekly suqs and city markets: the transition from rural suq economy to market economy', 86-97 in C.A.O. van Nieuwenhuijze (ed.) *Research for Development in the Mediterranean Basin: A Proposal*, The Hague: Institute for Social Studies

Berg, R.L., Jr. (1968), *The Impact of Modern Economy on the Traditional Economy in Zoogocho, Oaxaca, Mexico and its Surrounding Area,* Los Angeles: Unpublished Ph.D. dissertation, University of California

Berry, B.J.L. (1967), *Geography of Market Centers and Retail Distribution,* Englewood Cliffs: Prentice-Hall, Inc.

Berry, B.J.L., and W.L. Garrison (1958), 'The functional bases of the central-place hierarchy', *Economic Geography,* 34, 145-54

Black, I.D. (1969), 'Dayaks in north Borneo: the Chartered Company and the sea Dayaks of Sarawak', *Sarawak Museum Journal,* XVII, 245-72

Black, I.D. (1970), *Native Administration by the British North Borneo Chartered Company 1878-1915,* Canberra: Unpublished Ph.D. thesis, Australian National University

Blake, G. (1968), *Misurata: A Market Town in Tripolitania,* Durham: University of Durham Department of Geography Research Paper No. 9

Boenisch Burrough, J. (1972), *'Tamus* in Sabah', *Borneo Research Bulletin,* 4, 43-6

Boenisch Burrough, J. (1973), *Sabah Tamus,* Kuching: Borneo Literature Bureau

Boenisch Burrough, J. (1974), 'Two *tamu* surveys in Sabah', *Review of Indonesian and Malaysian Affairs,* 7, 9-24

Bohannan, P. and L. Bohannan (1968), *Tiv Economy,* Evanston: Northwestern University Press

Bohannan, P. and G. Dalton (eds.) (1962), *Markets in Africa,* Evanston: Northwestern University Press

Bonfil Batalla, G. (1962), *Diagnostico Sobre el Hambre en Sudzal,* Mexico

Brocklehurst, T.A. (1883), *Mexico To-day,* London

Bromley, R.J. (1969), *Settlement and Commerce in the Sierra of Puebla, Mexico.* Cambridge: Unpublished B.A. dissertation (Geography), University of Cambridge

Bromley, R.J. (1971) 'Markets in the developing countries: a review', *Geography,* 56, 124-32

Bromley, R.J. (1973), 'The spatial pattern and temporal synchronization of periodic markets', *Swansea Geographer,* 11, 15-25

Bromley, R.J. (1974a), 'Ecuador', forthcoming in B.W. Hodder and A.M. O'Connor (eds.), *Development Planning in the Third World: Geographical Case Studies,* London: Methuen

Bromley, R.J. (1974b), 'The organization of Quito's urban markets: towards a reinterpretation of periodic central places', *Transactions, Institute of British Geographers,* 62, 45-70

Bromley, R.J. (1974c), *Periodic Markets, Daily Markets, and Fairs: A Bibliography,* Melbourne: Monash Publications in Geography No. 10

Bromley, R.J. (1975), *Periodic and Daily Markets in Highland Ecuador,* Cambridge: Unpublished Ph.D. dissertation, Cambridge University

Bromley, R.J. and R. Symanski (1974), 'Marketplace trade in Latin America', *Latin American Research Review,* 9, 3-38

Bromley, R.J., R. Symanski and C.M. Good (1975), 'The rationale of periodic markets', *Annals, Association of American Geographers,* 65, 530-7.

Brookfield, H. (1975), *Interdependent Development,* London: Methuen

Brown, W. (1936), 'The Poro in modern business', *Man,* 37, 8-9

Brown, W. (1941), *Economic History of Liberia,* Washington, D.C.: Associated Publishers

Cagnolo, C. (1933), *The Akikuyu, Their Customs, Traditions and Folklore,* Nyeri: Kenya

Callet, R.P. (1908), *Tantaran'ny Andriana,* Tananarive

Centlivres, P. (1972), *Un bazar d'Asie centrale: forme et organisation du bazar de Tashqurghan (Afghanistan),* Wiesbaden: Dr. Ludwig Reichert Verlag

Central Planning Office (1973), *Papua New Guinea's Improvement Plan 1973-74,* Port Moresby

Chao, Syh kwang (1962), *The Phenomenon of the Travelling Night Market: A Study of its Origin, Growth and Organization,* Singapore: Unpublished Academic Exercise (Social Work), University of Singapore

Chau, J-K (1966), *Chu-fan-chi,* (Translated by F. Hirth and W.W. Rockhill from the 13th century manuscript), New York: Paragon Book Reprint Corporation

Chinese University of Hong Kong Social Research Centre (1971), Unpublished survey of hawkers in Hong Kong

Christaller, W. (1966), *Central Places in Southern Germany* (trans. C.W. Baskin). Englewood Cliffs, N.J.: Prentice-Hall, Inc.

Church, P.E. (1970), *Traditional Agricultural Markets in Guatemala,* Eugene: Unpublished Ph.D. dissertation, University of Oregon

Clark, P.J. and F.C. Evans (1954), 'Distance to nearest neighbor as a measure of spatial relationships in populations', *Ecology*, 35, 445-53

Colony and Protectorate of Kenya (1924), The Native Authority (Amendment) Ordinance, Ordinances, 3, New Series

Colony and Protectorate of Kenya (1935), An Ordinance to control and regulate the marketing of native produce, Ordinances, 14, New Series

Conroy, J. (1974), 'Indigenous small business in urban areas: informal or invisible?', *Yagl-Ambu* (Port Moresby) 1, 310-15

Cook, O. (1924), *Borneo: The Stealer of Hearts*, London: Hurst and Blackett

Coon, C.S. (1951), *Caravan: The Story of the Middle East*, London

Cortes, H. (1942), *Cartas de relación de la conquista de México* (2 vols.), Madrid

Cox, K.R. (1972), *Man, Location and Behavior: an Introduction to Human Geography*, New York: Wiley

Crocombe, R.G. and G.R. Hogbin (1963), 'Land, Work and Productivity at Inonda', *New Guinea Research Bulletin*, 2

Dacey, M.F. (1963), 'Order neighbour statistics for a class of random patterns in multi-dimensional space', *Annals, Association of American Geographers*, 53, 505-15

Déherain, H. (1914), 'Les katamas dans les provinces méridionales de l'Abyssinie', *Comité des Travaux Histoire et Scientifique*, XXIX, 225-41

Departamento Administrativo Nacional De Estadistica, Republica De Colombia (1964), *Directorio Nacional de Explotociones Agropecuarias (Censo Agropecuario), 1960: Departmentos de Nariño y Cauca*, Bogotá: Departamento Administrativo Nacional De Estadistica, Republica De Colombia

Dewey, A.G. (1962), *Peasant Marketing in Java*, Glencoe, Illinois: Free Press

De Young, M. (1967a), 'An African emporium', *Journal of Ethiopian Studies*, V, 103-22

De Young, M. (1967b), 'The internal marketing of agricultural products . . .' *Ethiopian Observer*, XI, 16-35

Diaz del Castillo, B. (1939), *Historia Verdadera de la Conquista de la Nueva España* (2 vols.), Mexico

D.G.E.C. (Dirección General de Estadística y Censos) (1960), *Primer Censo de Población del Ecuador 1950: Resumen de Características*, Quito

D.G.E.C. (1964), *Segundo Censo de Población del Ecuador 1962: Resumen de Características*, Quito

D.G.E.C. (1968a), *Proyección de la Población del Ecuador 1960-1980*, Quito

D.G.E.C. (1968b), *Cartografía Estadística Demográfica a 1962*, Quito

Dickinson, R.E. (1934), 'Markets and market areas of East Anglia', *Economic Geography*, 10, 172-82

Dubois, H-M. (1938), *Monographie de Betsileo*, Paris: Travaux et mémoires de L'institut d'ethnologie No. 34

Dundas, K.R. (1909), 'Kikuyu calendar', *Man*, 9, 37-8

Dutt, A.K. (1966a), 'Daily shopping in Howrah City: a study in social geography and planning', *The National Geographical Journal of India*, 12, 163-77

Dutt, A.K. (1966b), 'Daily shopping in Calcutta', *The Town Planning Review*, 37, 208-16

East Africa Protectorate (1903), East Africa Townships Ordinance, Official Gazette 5

Eighmy, T.H. (1972), 'Rural periodic markets and the extension of an urban system: a Western Nigeria example', *Economic Geography*, 48, 299-315

Ellis, W.H. (1838), *History of Madagascar* (Vol. I), London

Evans, A.S. (1870), *Our Sister Republic, A Gala Trip through Tropical Mexico in 1869-70*, Hartford

Evans, I.H.N. (1923), *Studies in Religion, Folk-Lore and Customs in British North Borneo and the Malay Peninsula*, Cambridge: Cambridge University Press (republished 1970 by Frank Cass & Co., London)

Fagerlund, V.G. and R.H.T. Smith (1970), 'A preliminary map of market periodicities in Ghana', *Journal of Developing Areas*, 4, 333-47

Farruk, M.O. (1970), *The Structure and Performance of the Rice Marketing System in East Pakistan*, Ithaca, N.Y.: Unpublished Ph.D. dissertation, Cornell University

Fearn, H. (1957), *The Economic Development of the Nyanza Province of Kenya Colony, 1903-1953*, London: Unpublished Ph.D. thesis, University of London

Feierman, S. (1968), 'The Shambaa' in A. Roberts (ed.) *Tanzania Before 1900*, Nairobi: East African Publishing House

Fogg, W. (1932), 'The suq: a study in the human geography of Morocco', *Geography*, 17, 257-67

Fogg, W. (1935), 'Villages and suqs in the high Atlas mountains of Morocco', *Scottish Geographical Magazine*, 51, 144-51

Fogg, W. (1938), 'A tribal market in the Spanish zone of Morocco', *Africa*, 12, 428-45

Fogg, W. (1939), 'The importance of tribal markets in the commercial life of the country-side of north-west Morocco', *Africa*, 12, 445-9

Foster, G.M. (1948), 'The folk economy of rural Mexico with special reference to marketing', *Journal of Marketing*, 13, 153-62

Frank, A.G. (1968), *Capitalism and Underdevelopment in Latin America*, London

Fraser, J.B. (1826), *Travels and Adventures in the Persian Provinces on the Southern Banks of the Caspian Sea*, London

Fraser, J.B. (1838), *A Winter's Journey from Constantinople to Tehran*, Vol. 1, London

Friends Foreign Mission (1880), *Review 1867-1880*, Tananarive

Funnell, D.C. (1973), 'Rural business centres in a low income economy: some theoretical problems', *Tijdschrift voor Economische en Sociale Geografie*, 64, 86-92

Galindo y Villa, Jesús (1925), *Historia Sumaria de la Ciudad de México*, México, D.F.: Editorial Cultura

Garst, R.D. (1974), 'Ethnic spatial behavior in Kisii border villages, Kenya', *Proceedings, Association of American Geographers*, 6, 62-5

Geertz, C. (1963), *Peddlers and Princes: Social Change and Economic Modernization in Two Indonesian Towns*, Chicago: University of Chicago Press

Glyn Jones, M. (1953), *The Dusun of the Penampang Plains in North Borneo*, London: Colonial Office (mimeographed)

Goldring, J. (1973), 'Business and the law in Papua New Guinea', Paper presented at Seventh Waigani Seminar, Port Moresby

Gooch, F.C. (1887), *Face to Face with the Mexicans*, London

Good, C.M. (1970), *Rural Markets and Trade in East Africa: a Study of the Functions and Development of Exchange Institutions in Ankole, Uganda*, Chicago: University of Chicago Department of Geography Research Paper No. 128

Good, C.M. (1972), 'Periodic markets: a problem in locational analysis', *Professional Geographer*, XXIV, 210-16

Good, C.M. (1973), 'Markets in Africa: a review of research themes and the question of market origins', *Cahiers d'Études Africaines*, 13, 769-80

Good, C.M. (1975), 'Periodic markets and travelling traders in Uganda', *Geographical Review*, 45, 49-72

Gormsen, E. (1966), 'Tlaxcala-Chiautempan-Apizaco', *Heidelberger Geographische Arbeiten*, 15, 115-32

Gormsen, E. (1971), 'Zur ausbildung zentralörtlicher systeme beim Übergang von der semiautarken zur arbeitsteiligen gesellschaft', *Erdkunde*, 25, 108-18

Grandidier, A. (1894), *Carte Topographique de l'Imerina*, Paris

Hall, D.G.E. (1968), *A History of Southeast Asia*, London: Macmillan and Company

Handwerker, W. Penn (1971), *The Liberian Internal Market System*, Eugene: Unpublished Ph.D. dissertation, University of Oregon

Handwerker, W. Penn (1973a), 'Kinship, friendship and business failure among market sellers in Monrovia, Liberia, 1970', *Africa*, 43, 288-301

Handwerker, W. Penn (1973b), 'Some dimensions of rice production and population in Liberia', paper presented to the 5th Annual Liberian Studies Conference, University of Iowa

Handwerker, W. Penn (1973c), 'Adaptive strategies among Liberian farm households', paper presented to the 72nd Annual Meeting of the American Anthropological Association, New Orleans

Handwerker, W. Penn (1974), 'Changing household organization in the origins of market places in Liberia', *Economic Development and Cultural Change*, 22, 229-48

Harris, W.C. (1844), *The Highlands of Ethiopia*, 3 vols., London: Macmillan

Hartmann, R. (1968), *Märkte im Alten Peru*, Bonn: Unpublished doctoral dissertation, Friedrich-Welhemls-Universität

Harrison, T. and B. Harrison (1971), 'The prehistory of Sabah', *Sabah Society Journal* Monograph IV

Harvey, M.E., R.T. Hocking, and J.R. Brown (1974), 'The chromatic traveling-salesman problem and its application to planning and structuring geographic space', *Geographical Analysis*, 6, 33-52

Hay, A.M. (1971), 'Notes on the economic basis for periodic marketing in developing countries', *Geographical Analysis*, 3, 393-401

Hay, A.M. (1974), 'Some alternatives in the economic analysis of periodic marketing', paper presented to Institute of British Geographers Developing Areas Study Group

Herskovits, M.J. (1962), 'Preface', vii-xvi in P. Bohannan and G. Dalton (eds.) *Markets in Africa*, Evanston: Northwestern University Press

Hill, P. (1966), 'Notes on traditional market authority and market periodicity in west Africa', *Journal of African History*, 7, 295-311

Hill, P. and R.H.T. Smith (1972), 'The spatial and temporal synchronization of periodic markets: evidence from four Emirates in northern Nigeria', *Economic Geography*, 48, 345-55

Ho, S.F. (1972), *Hawkers in Mongkok District: A Study in Retailing Geography*, Hong Kong: Unpublished M.A. thesis, University of Hong Kong

Hodder, B.W. (1961), 'Rural periodic day markets in part of Yorubaland', *Transactions of the Institute of British Geographers*, 29, 149-59

Hodder, B.W. (1965a), 'Distribution of markets in Yorubaland', *Scottish Geographical Magazine*, 81, 48-58

Hodder, B.W. (1965b), 'Some comments on the origins of traditional markets in Africa south of the Sahara', *Transactions of the Institute of British Geographers*, 36, 97-106

Hodder, B.W. (1967), 'The markets of Ibadan', 173-90 in P.C. Lloyd, A.L. Mabogunje, and B. Awe (eds.), *The City of Ibadan*, Cambridge: Cambridge University Press

Hodder, B.W. (1969), 'Markets in Yorubaland', 1-109 in B.W. Hodder and U.I. Ukwu, *Markets in West Africa*, Ibadan: Ibadan University Press

Hodder, B.W. (1971), 'Periodic and daily markets in West Africa', 347-58 in Claude Meillassoux (ed.), *The Development of Indigenous Trade and Markets in West Africa*, London: Oxford University Press for the International African Institute

Hodder, B.W. and U.I. Ukwu, (1969), *Markets in West Africa*, Ibadan:University of Ibadan Press

Hodson, A.W. (1927), *Seven Years in Southern Abyssinia*, London: T. Fisher Unwin

Hoel, P.G. (1971), *Elementary Statistics*, New York: John Wiley & Sons, Inc.

Hopkins, K. (ed.) (1971), *Hong Kong: The Industrial Colony*, London: Oxford University Press

Horvath, R.J. (1968), 'Towns in Ethiopia', *Erdkunde*, XXII, 45-54

Horvath, R.J. (1970), 'The process of urban agglomeration in Ethiopia', *Journal of Ethiopian Studies*, VIII, 81-8

Ilori, C.O. (1968), *Economic Study of Production and Distribution of Staple Foodcrops in Western Nigeria*, Palo Alto: Unpublished Ph.D. dissertation, Stanford University

Iran (1971), *Rural Household Consumption Survey*, Teheran: Iranian Statistical Centre

Jackson, Sir F.J. (1930), *Early Days in East Africa: with a Foreword by Lord Cranworth*, London: Longmans

Jackson, R.T. (1970), 'Land use and settlement in Gemu Gofa, Ethiopia', *Occasional Papers* No. 17, Department of Geography Makerere University, Kampala

Jackson, R.T. (1971), 'Periodic markets in southern Ethiopia', *Transactions of the Institute of British Geographers*, 53, 31-42

Jaecklein, K. (1970), 'San Felipe Otlaltepec', *Göppinger Akademische Beiträge*, 12

Johnson, E.A.J. (1970), *The Organization of Space in Developing Countries*, Cambridge: Harvard University Press

Johnson, M.R.D. (1974), 'Information flows in Nigerian agriculture', abstract of paper presented at Institute of British Geographers Conference, Norwich, U.K.

Johnston, C.H. (1844), *Travels in Southern Abyssinia*, London

Kaplan, D. (1960), *The Mexican Market-place in Historical Perspective*, Ann Arbor: Unpublished Ph.D. dissertation, University of Michigan

Kaplan, D. (1964), 'City and countryside in Mexican history', *América Indígena*, 24, 59-69

King, L.J. (1969), *Statistical Analysis in Geography*, Englewood Cliffs, N.J.: Prentice-Hall, Inc.

Kirk, J.H., P.G. Ellis and J.R. Medland (1972), *Retail Stall Markets in Great Britain*, University of London Wye College Marketing Series No. 8

Kissling, C.C. and H C. Weinand (1975), 'Location – allocation modelling for rural mobile markets in the Papua New Guinea highlands', *Proceedings, I.G.U. Regional Conference 1974* Palmerston North, 133-44.

Knos, D.S. (1968), 'The distribution of land values in Topeka, Kansas', Lawrence: University of Kansas Bureau of Business and Economic Research

Krapf, J.L. (1843), *Journals of the Reverend Messrs. Isenberg and Krapf,* London

Krapf, J.L. (1860), *Travels and Missionary Labours in East Africa,* London: Trubner & Co.

Kuls, W. (1963), *Bevölkerung, Siedlung und Landwirtschaft in Hochland von Godjam,* Frankfurt

Lacaze, H. (1881), *Souvenirs de Madagascar,* Paris

Lefebvre, T., *et al.* (1845-1849), *Voyage en Abyssinie,* Paris

Leicht, H. (1934), *Las calles de Puebla,* Puebla

Liberia (1968), *Agricultural Survey of Bong County,* 1967, Monrovia: Department of Planning and Economic Affairs

Lim, Charlotte (1973), Personal Communication

Liojjeno, Abdalla bin Hamedi bin Ali (1936-37), 'The Story of Mbega', *Tanganyika Notes and Records,* 1, 28-61; 2, 80-91; 3, 87-98 (Translated by Rolland Allen from the Swahili version, *Habari za Wakilindi,* (Msalabani, German East Africa: U.M.C.A. Press, Part I, circa. 1900; Part II, 1904; Part III, 1907))

Logan, M.I. (1972), 'The spatial system and planning strategies in developing countries', *Geographical Review,* 62, 229-44

London Missionary Society (1861-70), *Review,* London

Lopez de Villaseñor (1961), *Cartilla vieja de la Nobilísima Ciudad de Puebla* (1781), Mexico

Lösch, A. (1967), *The Economics of Location,* New York: Wiley Science Editions

Lu, A.L.C. (1972), *Hawkers and Their Relocation in Hong Kong,* Hong Kong: Chinese University of Hong Kong Social Research Centre

Mabogunje, A.L. (1964). 'The evolution and analysis of the retail structure of Lagos, Nigeria', *Economic Geography,* 55, 304-23

Marshall, G.A. (1964), *Women, Trade, and the Yoruba Family,* New York: Unpublished Ph.D. dissertation, Columbia University

McBryde, F.W. (1933), *Solola: A Guatemalan Town and Cakchiquel Market Center,* New Orleans: Tulane University Middle American Research Series Publication No. 5

McBryde, F.W. (1947), *Cultural and Historical Geography of Southwest Guatemala,* Washington, D.C.: Smithsonian Institution, Institute of Social Anthropology Publication No. 4

McGee, T.G. (1970), *Hawkers in Selected Asian Cities,* Hong Kong: University of Hong Kong Centre of Asian Studies

McGee, T.G. (1973), *Hawkers in Hong Kong: A Study of Policy and Planning in a Third World City,* Hong Kong: University of Hong Kong Centre of Asian Studies

McGee, T.G. and Y-m. Yeung (1973), *Hawkers in Selected Southeast Asian Cities: A Preliminary Comparative Analysis,* paper presented at a Conference on Hawkers in Southeast Asian Cities, sponsored by the International Development Research Centre, Canada

McGee, T.G. (1974), 'In praise of tradition: towards a geography of anti-development', *Antipode,* 6 (3), 30-47

McKim, W. (1972), 'The periodic market system in northeastern Ghana', *Economic Geography,* 48, 333-44

Malinowski, B. and J. de la Fuente (1957), 'La economia de un sistema de mercados en Mexico', *Acta Anthropologica Mexico,* Epoca 2, 1, 3-186

Marroquin, A. (1957), *La Ciudad Mercado* (Tlaxiaco), Mexico

Maydon, H.C. (1925), *Simen: Its Heights and Abysses,* London: H.F. and G. Witherby

Meillassoux, C. (ed.) (1971), *The Development of Indigenous Trade and Markets in West Africa,* London: Oxford University Press for the International African Institute

Melgunof, G. (1868), *Das südliche Ufer des Kaspischen Meeres,* Leipzig

Meru African District Council (1959), *Minutes*

M.G.P.S. (Ministerio de Gobierno y Previsión Social) (1933), *Informe a la Nación 1933-1934,* Quito

Mikesell, M.W. (1958), 'The role of tribal markets in Morocco: examples from the northern zone', *Geographical Review,* 48, 494-511

Mille, A. (1969), 'Les anciens villages fortifiés des hautes terres malgaches', *Madagascar: Revue de Geographie,* XII

Ministerio Del Trabajo, Republic De Colombia (1959), *Nariño: Sus kodalidades Geograficas Economicas y Sociales Como Factores de Planeamiento para la Adopción de un Regimen de Seguridad Social Rural,* Bogotá: Division Tecnica de la Seguridad Social Campesino

Mintz, S.W. (1959), 'Internal market systems as mechanisms of social articulation', *American Ethnological Society Annual Spring Meeting Proceedings,* 20-30

M.I.R.E. (Ministerio de lo Interior y Relaciones Exteriores) (1886), *Informe del Ministro de lo Interior y Relaciones Exteriores al Congreso Constitucional de 1886,* Quito

Montieth, E.I.C. (1833), 'Journal of a tour through Azerbaijan and the shores of the Caspian Sea', *Journal of the Royal Geographical Society,* 3, 1-58

Moulik, T.K. (1974), 'Money, motivation and cash cropping', *New Guinea Research Bulletin,* 53

Mukwaya, A.B. (1962), 'The marketing of staple foods in Kampala, Uganda', 643-66 in P. Bohannan and G. Dalton (eds.), *Markets in Africa,* Evanston: Northwestern University Press

Mullens, J. (1875), *Twelve Months in Madagascar,* London: Ward and Co.

Mushtaq, M. (1968), 'The pattern of retail and wholesale trade in Lahore', *Pakistan Geographical Review,* 23, 37-53

Nanyang University Geographical Society (1973), Personal communication

Nickel, H. (1970), 'Zur Problematik der agrarreform in Latinamerika', *Mitteilungen der Geographischen Fachschaft,* 2, Freiburg

Odetoyinbo, F.O. (1970), *The Periodic Markets in Metropolitan Lagos,* Lagos: Original essay for B.A. degree (Geography), University of Lagos

Onakomaiya, S.O. (1970), *The Spatial Structure of Internal Trade in Delicacy Foodstuffs in Nigeria,* Madison: Unpublished Ph.D. dissertation, University of Wisconsin

Ortiz, Sergio Elias (1945), *La Unión, Municipio Modelo del Departamento de Nariño: Mongrafía Historico-Geografica,* Pasto: Tip. 'La Cosmopolita'

Olivieri-Rodriguez, J.A. (1961), *Market Organization Patterns and Related Problems in Latin America,* Madison: Unpublished Ph.D. dissertation, University of Wisconsin

Overseas Development Group (1973), *A Report on Development Strategies for Papua New Guinea,* Port Moresby: Office of Programming and Coordination

Pankhurst, R. (1963), 'The Maria Theresa dollar in pre-war Ethiopia', *Journal of Ethiopian Studies,* I, 8-26

Pankhurst, R. (1964-5), 'The trade of Ethiopia', a series of articles in *Journal of Ethiopian Studies,* II and III

Patel, A.M. (1963), 'The rural markets of Rajshahi District', *Oriental Geographer,* 7, 140-51

Pedler, F.J. (1955), *Economic Geography of West Africa,* London

Penaherrera, P., A. Costales, and E. Jordan (1961), *Tungurahua,* Quito: Instituto Ecuatoriano de Antropologia y Geografia, Llacta No. 13

Plattner, S. (1973a), 'Periodic trade in developing areas without markets', paper presented to Mathematical Social Science Board Conference on Formal Methods in the Analysis of Regional Systems, Sante Fe

Plattner, S. (1973b), 'The economics of peddling', University of Missouri-St. Louis Center for International Studies Occasional Paper No. 734

Poleman, T.T. (1961), 'The food economies of urban middle Africa: the case of Ghana', *Food Research Institute Studies,* 2, 121-74

Poppelwell, G.D. (1939), 'Salt production among the Wasambaa', *Tanganyika Notes and Records,* 8, 102-105

Portal, G.H. (1892), *My Mission to Abyssinia,* London: Edward Arnold

Pringle, J.W. (1893), 'With the railway survey to Victoria Nyanza', *Geographical Journal,* 2, 112-139

Prins, A.H.J. (1952), *The Coastal Tribes of the North-eastern Bantu (Pokomo, Nyiki, Teita),* London: International African Institute, Ethnographic Survey of Africa, East Central Africa, Part III

Pyle, J. (1968), *The Public Markets of Mexico City,* Eugene: Unpublished Ph.D. dissertation, University of Oregon

Pyle, J. (1970), 'Market locations in Mexico City', *Revista Geografica,* 73, 59-69

Rabino, H.L. (1913), 'A journey in Mazanderan (from Rasht to Sari)', *Geographical Journal,* 42, 435-54

Rabino, H.L. (1915-16), 'Les provinces Caspiennes de la Perse – le Guilan', *Revue de Monde Musulman* (Paris), 32, 1-499

Redfield, R. (1939), 'Primitive merchants of Guatemala', *Quarterly Journal of Inter-American Relations,* I, 42-56

Reilly, W.J. (1929), 'Methods for the study of retail relationships', Austin: University of Texas Bulletin 2944

Riddell, J.B. (1974), 'Periodic markets in Sierra Leone', *Annals, Association of American Geographers*, 64, 541-8

Roblet, R.P. (1882), 'Carte d'Antananarive et ses environs', *L'Exploration*

Routledge, W.S. and K. Routledge (1910), *With a Prehistoric People: the Akikuyu of British East Africa*, London: Edward Arnold

Russell, T.J.P. (1969), *Report of the Oxford University Expedition to the Gemu Highlands*, Oxford

Rutter, O. (1929), *The Pagans of North Borneo*, London: Hutchinson and Company

Sada, P.O. (1968), *The Metropolitan Region of Lagos: A Study of the Political Factor in Urban Geography*, Bloomington: Unpublished Ph.D. dissertation, Indiana University

Schmitz, H. (1973a), 'Bildung und wander zentralörtlischer systeme in Nord-Marokko', *Erdkunde*, 27, 120-30

Schmitz, H. (1973b), 'Der Marokkanische Souk', *Die Erde*, 3-4, 320-35

Schwab, G. (1947), *Tribes of the Liberian Hinterland*, Cambridge: Harvard University Peabody Museum of American Archeology and Ethnology Papers

Scott, E.P. (1972), 'The spatial structure of rural northern Nigeria: farmers, periodic markets, and villages', *Economic Geography*, 48, 316-32

Scott, P. (1970), *Geography and Retailing*, London: Hutchinson University Library

Scoullar, B. (1973), 'Pyrethrum and the Highlander', Port Moresby: Department of Agriculture, Stock and Fisheries, Extension Bulletin 3

Seeman, B. (1853), *Narrative of the Voyage of H.M.S. Herald during the Years 1845-51*, London: Reeve and Co.

Sibrée, J. (n.d.; 1870?), *Madagascar and its People*, London: Religious Tract Society

Simoons, F.J. (1960), *Northwest Ethiopia*, Madison: University of Wisconsin Press

Singh, S.M. (1965), 'The stability theory of rural central place development', *National Geographical Journal of India*, 11, 13-21

Skinner, G.W., (1964), 'Marketing and social structure in rural China', *Journal of Asian Studies*, 24, 3-43

Skinner, G.W. (1965), 'Marketing and social structure in rural China', *Journal of Asian Studies*, 24, 195-228, 363-99

Smith, C.A. (1972), *The Domestic Marketing System in Western Guatemala: an Economic, Locational, and Cultural Analysis*, Palo Alto: Unpublished Ph.D. dissertation, Stanford University

Smith, C.A. (1974), 'Economics of marketing systems: models from economic geography', *Annual Review of Anthropology*, 3, 167-201

Smith, R.H.T. (1970), 'A note on periodic markets in West Africa', *African Urban Notes*, 5, 29-37

Smith, R.H.T. (1971a), 'West African market-places: temporal periodicity and locational spacing', 319-46 in Claude Meillassoux (ed.), *The Development of Indigenous Trade and Markets in West Africa*, London: Oxford University Press for the International African Institute

Smith, R.H.T. (1971b), 'The theory of periodic markets: consumer and trader behaviour', 183-9 in *Pre-conference Publication of Papers, Canadian Association of Geographers*, Waterloo

Smith, R.H.T. (1972), 'The synchronization of periodic markets', 591-3 in W.P. Adams and F.M. Helleiner (eds.), *International Geography 1972*, Toronto: University of Toronto Press for 22nd International Geographical Congress

Smith, R.H.T. (1974), 'Periodic markets and travelling traders', paper presented at the 70th Annual Meeting of the Association of American Geographers, Seattle

Smith, R.H.T. and A.M. Hay (1970), 'Central place aspects of periodic markets', paper presented at S.S.R.C. *Conference on Spatial Hierarchies in African Interurban Systems*, Greystone Conference Centre, New York (November)

Spencer, J.E. (1940), 'The Szechwan village fair', *Economic Geography*, 16, 48-58

Stanley, W.R. (1970), 'Transport expansion in Liberia', *Geographical Review*, 60, 529-47

Stanner, W.E.H. (1969), 'The Kitui Kamba market, 1938-9', *Ethnology*, 8, 125-39

Stavenhagen, R. (1963), 'Clases, colonialismo y aculturación', *América Latina*, 6, 4

Stewart, J.Q. (1947), 'Empirical mathematical rules concerning the distribution and equilibrium of population', *Geographical Review*, 37, 461-85

Stigand, C.H. (1910), *To Abyssinia*, London: Seeley and Co.

Stine, J.H. (1962), 'Temporal aspects of tertiary production elements in Korea', 68-88 in F.R. Pitts (ed.), *Urban Systems and Economic Development*, Eugene: University of Oregon School of Business Administration

St. John, S. (1863), *Life in the Forests of the Far East* (2 vols.), London: Smith Elder and Co.

Straube, H. (1963), *Westkuschitische Volker Süd-Äthiopiens*, Stuttgart

Symanski, R. (1971), *Periodic Markets of Andean Colombia*, Syracuse: Unpublished Ph.D. dissertation, Syracuse University

Symanski, R. (1973), 'God, food, and consumers in periodic market systems', *Proceedings of the Association of American Geographers*, 5, 262-6

Symanski, R. and R.J. Bromley (1974), 'Market development and the ecological complex', *Professional Geographer*, 26, 382-8

Symanski, R. and M.J. Webber (1974), 'Complex periodic market cycles', *Annals, Association of American Geographers*, 64, 203-13

Tamaskar, B.G. (1966), 'The weekly markets of the Sagar-Damoh plateau', *National Geographical Journal of India*, 12, 38-50

Tanzania (1971), *1967 Census of Population*, Dar es Salaam: Bureau of Statistics

Tax, S. (1954), 'The Indians in the economy of Guatemala', *Social and Economic Studies*, VI, 413-24

Temple, P.H. (1969), 'The urban markets of greater Kampala', *Tijdschrift Voor Economische en Sociale Geografie*, LX, 346-59

Thompson, C.T. and M.J. Huies (1968), 'Peasant and bazaar marketing systems as distinct types', *Anthropological Quarterly*, XLI, 219-27

Tregonning, K.G. (1965), *A History of Modern Sabah 1881-1963*, Kuala Lumpur: University of Malaya Press

Tse, F.Y. (1974), *Street Trading in Hong Kong* (3 vols.), Hong Kong: Chinese University of Hong Kong Social Research Centre

Ukwu, U.I. (1969), 'Markets in Iboland', 111-250, in B.W. Hodder and U.I. Ukwu, *Markets in West Africa*, Ibadan: Ibadan University Press

Van Apeldoorn, G.J. (1971), *Markets in Ghana: a Census and Some Comments. Volume 1: Northern and Upper Regions*, Legon: University of Ghana Institute of Statistical, Social and Economic Research Technical Publications Series No. 17

Wagner, G. (1956), *The Bantu of north Kavirondo. Vol. 2: Economic life*, London: Oxford University Press

Ward, J.H. Jr. (1963), 'Hierarchical grouping to optimize an objective function', *Journal of the American Statistical Association*, 58, 236-44

Ward, R.G., N. Clark, D. Howlett, C.C. Kissling and H.C. Weinand (1974a), *Growth Centres and Area Improvement in the Eastern Highlands District*, Canberra: Department of Human Geography, Australian National University

Ward, R.G., D. Howlett, C.C. Kissling, and H.C. Weinand (1974b), *Maket Raun Pilot Project — Feasibility Study*, Canberra: Department of Human Geography, Australian National University

Waterbury, R.G. (1968), *The Traditional Market in a Provincial Urban Setting: Oaxaca, Mexico*, Los Angeles: Unpublished Ph.D. dissertation, University of California

Webber, M.J. and R. Symanski (1973), 'Periodic markets: an economic location analysis', *Economic Geography*, 49, 213-27

Weinand, H.C. (1975), 'Introducing a new marketing concept to Papua New Guinea: the *Maket Raun*', *Australian Geographer*, in press

Wellby, M.S. (1901), *'Twixt Sirdar and Menelik*, London: Harper Bros.

Whelan, F.G. (1970), *A History of Sabah*, Singapore: Macmillan & Co.

Whitehead, J. (1893), *The Exploration of Mount Kina Balu*, London, Gurney and Jackson

Whitehouse, W.F. (n.d.), *To Lake Rudolph and Beyond*

Winans, E.V. (1962), *Shambala, The Constitution of a Traditional State*, London: Routledge and Kegan Paul

Wolf, E.R. (1955), 'Types of Latin American peasantry', *American Anthropologist*, 57, 3

Wong, K-y. and K-s. Sum (1971), 'Retail services in Hong Kong: a study of structure and pattern', *United College Journal*, 9, 251-84

Wood, L.J. (1972), 'Rural market patterns in Kenya', *Area*, 4, 267-8

Wood, L.J. (1973a), *The Rural Market System of Kenya*, Kampala: Unpublished Ph.D. thesis, Makerere University

Wood, L.J. (1973b), 'The temporal efficiency of rural markets in Kenya', *East African Geographical Review*, 11, 65-9

Wood, L.J. (1974a), 'Precolonial markets in East Africa', *Nigerian Geographical Journal*, 17

Wood, L.J. (1974b), 'Spatial interaction and partitions of rural market space', *Tijdschrift voor Economische en Sociale Geografie*, 65, 23-34

Wood, L.J. (1974c), 'Population density and rural market provision', *Cahiers d'Étude Africaines,* 14, 56 ff.

Wood, L.J. (1974d), 'Market origins and development in East Africa', *Occasional Papers* No. 57, Department of Geography, Makerere University, Kampala

Wood, L.J. (1975a), 'A spatio-temporal analysis of rural markets in Kenya', *Journal of Tropical Geography,* 40, 63-71.

Wood, L.J. (1975b), 'The functional structure of a rural market system', *Geografiska Annaler,* 57, Series B, forthcoming

Woolley, G.C. (1962), 'The Timoguns, a Murut tribe of interior Borneo', *Colony of North Borneo Native Affairs Bulletin,* (Jesselton) 1

Yang, C-k. (1944), *A North China Local Market Economy,* New York: Institute of Pacific Relations

Yap, S-k. (1972), *The Spatial Analysis of Pasar Malam in Singapore,* Singapore: Graduation Exercise (Geography) Nanyang University (in Chinese)

Yeung, Y-m. (1973), *National Development and Urban Transformation in Singapore: A Study of Public Housing and the Marketing System,* Chicago: University of Chicago Department of Geography Research Paper No. 149

Yeung, Y-m. (1974), 'Periodic markets: comments on spatial-temporal relationships', *Professional Geographer,* 26, 147-51